TROY DUSTER

The Legislation
of MORALITY

Law, Drugs, and Moral Judgment

THE FREE PRESS, NEW YORK
COLLIER-MACMILLAN LIMITED, LONDON

Copyright © 1970 by The Free Press
A DIVISION OF THE MACMILLAN COMPANY

Printed in the United States of America

Collier-Macmillan Canada, Ltd., Toronto, Ontario

LIBRARY OF CONGRESS CATALOG CARD NUMBER: 72-80469

Printing Number

1 2 3 4 5 6 7 8 9 10

To Alfreda Marguerita
and Ellen Marie

Contents

Preface and acknowledgments

SOME THIRTY YEARS AGO, SVEND RANULF BRILLIANTLY developed the thesis that the middle-classes have a near monopoly on moral indignation. Max Weber and Max Scheler had earlier offered similar propositions, but Ranulf was the first to systematically turn full attention to the thesis and develop it both theoretically and empirically. In his work, Ranulf traced the sources of the "disinterested tendency" of the middle-class to share in the punishment of the "immoral." The following passage is excerpted from his analysis of the ideological foundations of the Calvinistic middle-classes. Witness traces and themes in ideas held by members of the contemporary middle-class:

Calvin condemned indiscriminate almsgiving . . . and urged that the ecclesiastical authorities should regularly visit every family to ascertain whether its members were idle, or drunken, or otherwise undesirable. . . . In the plan of the reorganization of the poor of Zurich, which was drafted by Zwingli in 1525, all mendicancy was strictly forbidden; no inhabitant was able to be entitled for relief who wore ornaments or luxurious clothes, who failed to attend church, or who played cards or was otherwise disreputable. . . . The Puritans of the seventeenth century were equally severe: That the greatest of evils is idleness, that the poor are victims, not of circumstances, but of their own "idle, irregular, and wicked courses," that the truest charity is not to ennervate them by relief, but so to reform their characters so that relief is unnecessary.*

Ranulf went on to show how Calvinism has always found the bulk of its adherents among the middle-classes.

While Weber demonstrated that the geographical expansion of Protestantism in the sixteenth century corresponded with the geographic-developmental expansion of capitalism, Ranulf's thesis was about the middle-class and its version of the world, not about Calvinism *per se*. Accordingly, he looked at the Catholic and Jewish

* Svend Ranulf, *Moral Indignation and Middle Class Psychology*, New York: Schocken Books, 1964, p. 14.

bourgeoisie, and found them equally zealous in their attempts to bind other members of the community in a "moral" straight-jacket.

Before the Reformation, there was a small merchant and trade class in Western Europe. It was from this small but increasingly influential stratum that laws and punishments emanated to punish "crimes" that up until that time no one had thought of as criminal. Gambling and the purchase and indulgence in "wasteful luxuries" were among them. Moreover, up until this period, an important element in punishment was whether the aggrieved party would himself pursue the case. Gradually, the middle-classes succeeded in establishing the principle that the general and anonymous community had its own interests in the prosecution of criminals. Obtaining a confession from the accused became crucial, "an endeavor which led to the inquisitorial trial and to the rack," the relevance of which I hope to draw for problems discussed in this book. My purpose is to take the exemplary case of addiction to drugs and show the social conditions under which the accusatory finger is dipped in moralistic indignation, and the dramatic social difference it makes whether that finger is pointed by or at the middle-class.

In this particular work I have benefited from the advice, support, and counsel of many. However, I would like to begin by acknowledging early and long range intellectual debts. W. S. Robinson and Harold Garfinkel, from quite different perspectives, contributed inestimably to my earliest experiences in trying to proceed with the research and analysis of social issues. Each conveyed a picture of the tenuousness of social order and the extraordinary yet sometimes subtle barriers to knowing.

Raymond Mack has always provided me with support and stimulation, as teacher and colleague, and has been the strongest of consciences for lucidity. For many reasons I am grateful to Aaron Cicourel. His criticism, diligent and determined, has been a considerable contribution to this work, even though I have been unable to incorporate some of his critique that I honor.

Among those who helped me to clarify some ideas on broader issues touched upon in the book were Egon Bittner, Gerard Brandmeyer, Thelton Henderson, John Kitsuse, Peter McHugh, Terry Lunsford,

Gerald Platt, Kenneth Polk, and Henry Tschappat. I would also like to thank John Kitsuse for permission to use materials he collected on a project of common-sense interpretations of deviance.

For a critical reading of the manuscript, in total and in parts, I would like to thank Richard Bass, Howard Becker, Allan Blum, John Doyle, Donald Duster, Ernest Landauer, Barry Munitz, Jerome Skolnick, and Arthur Stinchcombe.

The section on the California Rehabilitation Center is a result of my research there while a consultant to the Research Division. I am indebted to the following persons for their cooperation; Roland Wood, Superintendent, Harold Bradley, then Program Director, E. C. Gaulden, then Chief of Research, Robert Cushman, and Virginia Carlson.

Excellent bibliographical and research assistance was provided by Andrea Fare, Alice Moses, Susan Wedow, and Eleanor Lyon.

For permission to quote from published materials, I would like to thank Holt, Rinehart, and Winston, and the Bobbs-Merrill publishing houses.

I would also like to express my appreciation to Leland Medsker, Director of the Center for Research and Development in Higher Education for support during the last stages. Finally, for gracious assistance in the preparation of the manuscript, my thanks to Joan Bajsarowicz, Lydian Clapp, Julie Hurst, Lynn Pokrant and Ann Sherman.

Berkeley
April, 1969

T. D.

PART I

History and context of the problem

CHAPTER I

The legislation of morality

Introduction

THERE WAS ONCE A TIME WHEN ANYONE COULD GO TO his corner druggist and buy grams of morphine or heroin for just a few pennies. There was no need to have a prescription from a physician. The middle and upper classes purchased more than the lower and working classes, and there was no moral stigma attached to such narcotics use. The year was 1900, and the country was the United States.

Suddenly, there came the enlightenment of the twentieth century, full with moral insight and moral indignation, a smattering of knowledge of physiology, and the force of law. By 1920, the purchase of narcotics was not only criminal (that happened overnight in 1914), but some men had become assured that the purchase was immoral.

An important contemporary shibboleth is "You can't legislate morality." Its importance is not determined by the frequency of its use, but by the intensity of belief that Americans seem to invest in it and by the firmness with which they reject legal attempts to resolve certain moral issues. This single phrase is called forth to squelch arguments about issues from civil rights to temperance. The failure of Prohibition is usually cited dramatically as the final demonstration of the point. Its simplicity is matched by its deceptiveness; it is a short and concise statement containing only two elements. The first element is "legislate," whose meaning is quite clear. A bill passes in a legislative body and becomes a statute. The second part is "morality," and that is much less clear. Many things will be said later about the meaning of morality, but here we may sacrifice elaborated precision for quick agreement by asserting that morality refers to the strong feelings which people have about *right* and *wrong*. If we put these two together we can rephrase: "Passing a law can not change the strong feelings that people have about right and wrong."

The rephrasing is instructive because it frees the mind from the thought-channeling properties of the cliché. With the newly formed construction of the old idea, we find glaring problems that reveal inconsistency and confusion. For example, the moral middle classes will assert at one point that the legislation of morality is impossible, then turn around and take a passionate stand against the legalization of prostitution on the grounds that positive state sanction would undermine the moral structure of society. The belief is firm that the statutes greatly affect the way in which people will feel morally about prostitution. However, if one is capable of opposing, say, racial discrimination and extramarital sex on moral grounds, support of laws prohibiting both would be consistent and logical. Yet some will obviously support one kind of "moral" legislation and not another.

The relationship between law and morality is both complicated and subtle. This is true even in a situation where a society is very homogeneous and where one might find a large degree of consensus about moral behavior. Those who argue that law is simply the empirical operation of morality are tempted to use homogeneous situations as examples. In discussing this relationship, Selznick asserts that laws are

4

secondary in nature.[1] They are secondary in the sense that they obtain their legitimacy in terms of some other more primary reference point.

The distinctively legal emerges with the development of secondary rules, that is, rules of authoritative determination. These rules, selectively applied, "raise up" the primary norms and give them a legal status. . . . The appeal from an *asserted* rule, however coercively enforced, to a justified rule is the elementary legal act. This presumes at least a dim awareness that some reason lies behind the impulse to conform, a reason founded not in conscience, habit, or fear alone, but in the decision to uphold an authoritative order. The rule of legal recognition may be quite blunt and crude: the law is what the king or priest says it is. But this initial reference of a primary norm to a ground of obligation breeds the complex elaboration of authoritative rules that marks a developed legal order.[2]

The most primary of reference points is, of course, the moral order. One can explain why he does something for just so long, before he is driven to a position where he simply must assert that it is "right" or "wrong." With narcotics usage and addiction, the issue in contemporary times is typically raised in the form of a moral directive, irrespective of the physiological and physical aspects of addiction. The laws concerning narcotics usage may now be said to be a secondary set held up against the existing primary or moral view of drugs. However, the drug laws have been on the books for half a century, during which time, as we shall see, this country has undergone a remarkable transformation in its moral interpretation of narcotics usage. Clearly, if we want to understand the ongoing relationship between the law and morality, we are misled by assuming one has some fixed relationship to the other. To put it another way, if a set of laws remains unchanged while the moral order undergoes a drastic transformation, it follows that the relationship of law to morality must be a changing thing, and cannot be static. If narcotics law was simply the empirical element of narcotics morality, a change in the moral judgment of narcotics use should be accompanied by its counterpart in the law, and vice versa. As Selznick points out:

In recent years, the great social effects of legal change have been too obvious to ignore. The question is no longer *whether* law is a significant vehicle of social change but rather *how* it so functions and what special problems arise.[3]

Selznick goes on to suggest explorations into substantive problems of "change." The connection of law to change is clearly demonstrable. If a society undergoes rapid technological development, new social relationships will emerge, and so too, will a set of laws to handle them. The gradual disintegration of the old caste relationships in India has been and will be largely attributable to the development of new occupations which contain no traditional forms regulating how one caste should respond to another.

The relationship of law to morality is not quite so clear. It is more specific, but more abstract. The sociological study of the narcotics problem is critical to discussion of this relationship, because it provides a specific empirical case where one can observe historically the interplay between the two essential components. More than any other form of deviance, the history of drug use contains an abundance of material on both questions of legislation and morality, and of the relationship between them.

Background and Setting

Despite the public clamor of the 1960s about LSD and marijuana, the drug that has most dominated and colored the American conception of narcotics is opium. Among the most effective of painkillers, opium has been known and used in some form for thousands of years. Until the middle of the nineteenth century, opium was taken orally, either smoked or ingested. The Far East monopolized both production and consumption until the hypodermic needle was discovered as an extremely effective way of injecting the drug instantly into the bloodstream. It was soon to become a widely used analgesic. The first hypodermic injections of morphine, an opium derivative used to relieve pain, occurred in this country in 1856.[4]

Medical journals were enthusiastic in endorsing the new therapeutic usages that were possible, and morphine was the suggested remedy for an endless variety of physical sufferings. It was during the Civil War, however, that morphine injection really spread extensively. Then wholesale usage and addiction became sufficiently pronounced so that

6

one could speak of an American problem for the first time.[5] Soldiers were given morphine to deaden the pain from all kinds of battle injuries and illnesses. After the war, ex-soldiers by the thousands continued using the drug, and recommending it to friends and relatives.

Within a decade, medical companies began to include morphine in a vast number of medications that were sold directly to consumers as household remedies. This was the period before governmental regulation, and the layman was subjected to a barrage of newspaper and billboard advertisements claiming cures for everything from the common cold to cholera. "Soothing Syrups" with morphine often contained no mention of their contents, and many men moved along the path to the purer morphine through this route.

It is not surprising that many persons became dependent on these preparations and later turned to the active drug itself when accidentally or otherwise they learned of its presence in the "medicine" they had been taking. . . . The peak of the patent medicine industry was reached just prior to the passage of the Pure Food and Drug Act in 1906.[6]

It must be remembered that there were no state or federal laws concerning the sale and distribution of medicinal narcotic drugs during this period under discussion, and pharmacists sold morphine simply when it was requested by a customer. There is no way to accurately assess the extent of addiction at that time, nor is there now, for that matter. However, there are some informed estimates by scholars who have studied many facets of the period. Among the better guesses many will settle for is that from 2 to 4 per cent of the population was addicted in 1895.[7] Studies of pharmaceutical dispensaries, druggists, and physicians' records were carried out in the 1880s and 1890s which relate to this problem. The widespread use of morphine was demonstrated by Hartwell's survey of Massachusetts druggists in 1888,[8] Hull's study of Iowa druggists in 1885,[9] Earle's work in Chicago in 1880,[10] and Grinnell's survey of Vermont in 1900.[11] The methodological techniques of investigation do not meet present-day standards, but even if certain systematic biases are assumed, the 3 per cent figure is an acceptable guess of the extent of addiction.

The large numbers of addicts alarmed a growing number of medical men. The American press, which had been so vocal in its denunciation of the sensational but far less common opium smoking in opium dens in the 1860s and 1870s, was strangely if typically silent on morphine medication and its addicting effects. Just as the present-day press adroitly avoids making news of very newsworthy government proceedings on false advertising (an issue in which there may also be some question of the accomplice), newspapers of that time did not want to alienate the advertisers, because they were a major source of revenue. Nonetheless, the knowledge of the addicting qualities of morphine became more and more common among a sizable minority of physicians.

It was in this setting, in 1898, that a German pharmacological researcher named Dreser produced a new substance from a morphine base, diacetylmorphin, otherwise known as heroin. The medical community was enthusiastic in its reception of the new drug. It had three times the strength of morphine, and it was believed to be free from addicting qualities. The most respectable medical journals of Germany and the United States carried articles and reports lauding heroin as a cure for morphine addiction.[12]

Within five short years, the first definitive serious warnings about the addicting qualities of heroin appeared in an American medical journal.[13] The marvelous success of heroin as a painkiller and sedative, however, made the drug popular with both physician and patient. It should be remembered that one did not need a prescription to buy it. The news of the new warnings traveled slowly, and heroin joined morphine as one of the most frequently used pain remedies for the ailing and suffering.

From 1865 to 1900, then, addiction to narcotics was relatively widespread. This is documented in an early survey of material by Terry and Pellens, a treatise which remains the classic work on late nineteenth- and early twentieth-century problems of addiction.[14] In proportion to the population, addiction was probably eight times more prevalent then than now, despite the large increase in the general population.

It is remarkable, therefore, that addiction is regarded today as a problem of far greater moral, legal, and social significance than it was then. As we shall see directly, the problem at the turn of the century was conceived in very different terms, treated in a vastly different manner, and located in opposite places in the social order.

The first task is to illustrate how dramatic and complete was the shift of addicts from one social category to another during a critical twenty-year period. The second task is to examine the legal activity which affected that shift. Finally, the task will be to examine the changing moral judgments that coincided with these developments.

It is now taken for granted that narcotic addicts come primarily from the working and lower classes. (In Chapter 7, a description of the contemporary addict population corroborates this for the number known and apprehended.) This has not always been true. The evidence clearly indicates that the upper and middle classes predominated among narcotic addicts in the period up to 1914. In 1903, the American Pharmaceutical Association conducted a study of selected communities in the United States and Canada. They sent out mailed questionnaires to physicians and druggists, and from the responses, concluded that

while the increase is most evident with the lower classes, the statistics of institutes devoted to the cure of habitues show that their patients are principally drawn from those in the higher walks of life. . . .[15]

From a report on Massachusetts druggists published in 1889 and cited by Terry and Pellens, the sale of opium derivatives to those of higher incomes exceeded the amount sold to lower-income persons.[16] This is all the more striking if we take into account the fact that the working and lower classes comprised a far greater percentage of the population of the country in 1890 than they do today. (With the 1960 census figures, the population of the United States becomes predominantly white collar for the first time in history.) In view of the fact that the middle-class comprised proportionately less of the population, the incidence of its addiction rate can be seen as even more significant.

It was acknowledged in medical journals that a morphine addict could not be detected as an addict so long as he maintained his supply.[17] Some of the most respectable citizens of the community, pillars of middle-class morality, were addicted. In cases where this was known, the victim was regarded as one afflicted with a physiological problem, in much the same way as we presently regard the need of a diabetic for insulin. Family histories later indicated that many went through their daily tasks, their occupations, completely undetected by friends and relatives.[18]

There are two points of considerable significance that deserve more careful consideration. The first is the fact that some friends and relatives could and did know about an addiction and still did not make a judgment, either moral or psychological, of the person addicted. The second is that the lower classes were not those primarily associated with morphine or heroin usage in 1900.

The moral interpretation of addiction in the twentieth century is especially interesting in view of the larger historical trend. Western man has, on the whole, developed increasing tolerance and compassion for problems that were previously dogmatically treated as moral issues, such as epilepsy, organic and functional mental disorders, polio, diabetes, and so on. There was a time when most were convinced that the afflicted were possessed by devils, were morally evil, and inferior. Both medical opinion and literature of the eighteenth and nineteenth centuries were replete with the moral interpretation of countless physiological problems which have now been reinterpreted in an almost totally nonmoral fashion. The only moral issue now attendant to these questions is whether persons suffering should receive treatment from physicians. Even venereal diseases, which retain a stigma, are unanimously conceived as physiological problems that should be treated physiologically irrespective of the moral conditions under which they were contracted.

The narcotic addict of the 1890s was in a situation almost the reverse of those suffering from the above problems. His acquaintances and his community could know of his addiction, feel somewhat sorry for his dependence upon *medication*, but admit him to a position of respect and authority. If the heroin addict of 1900 was getting a willful thrill out of his injection, no one was talking about either the willful element or the thrill, not even the drug companies. If the thrill was to be had, there was no reason for manufacturers not to take advantage of this in their advertisements. They had no moral compunctions about patently false claims for a cure, or about including an opium derivative without so stating on the label.

Despite the fact that all social classes had their share of addicts, there was a difference in the way lower class addicts were regarded. This difference was exacerbated when legislation drove heroin underground, predominantly to the lower classes. Writing in the *American Journal of*

Clinical Medicine in 1918, G. Swaine made an arbitrary social classification of addicts, about which he offered the following distinction:

In Class one, we can include all of the physical, mental and moral defectives, the tramps, hoboes, idlers, loaders, irresponsibles, criminals, and denizens of the underworld. . . . In these cases, morphine addition is a vice, as well as a disorder resulting from narcotic poisoning. These are the "drug fiends." In Class two, we have many types of good citizens who have become addicted to the use of the drug innocently, and who are in every sense of the word "victims." Morphine is no respecter of persons, and the victims are doctors, lawyers, ministers, artists, actors, judges, congressmen, senators, priests, authors, women, girls, all of who realize their conditions and want to be cured. In these cases, morphine-addiction is not a vice, but, an incubus, and, when they are cured they stay cured.[19]

This may seem to jump ahead of the task of this section, which is simply to portray as accurately as possible the dramatic shift of addicts from one social category to another during this period. However, the shift itself carried with it more than a description. These were the beginnings of moral interpretations for the meaning of that shift. By 1920, a medical journal reported cases treated at Riverside Hospital in New York City in the following manner:

Drug addicts may be divided into two general classes. The first class is composed of people who have become addicted to the use of drugs through illness, associated probably with an underlying neurotic temperament. The second class, which is *overwhelmingly in the majority* [italics mine], is at the present time giving municipal authorities the greatest concern. These persons are largely from the underworld, or channels leading directly to it. They have become addicted to the use of narcotic drugs largely through association with habitues and they find in the drug a panacea for the physical and mental ills that are the result of the lives they are leading. Late hours, dance halls, and unwholesome cabarets do much to bring about this condition of body and mind. . . .[20]

Whereas in 1900 the addict population was spread relatively evenly over the social classes (with the higher classes having slightly more), by 1920, medical journals could speak of the "overwhelming" majority from the "unrespectable" parts of society. The same pattern can be seen with the shift from the predominantly middle-aged to the young, and with the shift from a predominance of women to an overwhelming majority of men.

In a study reported in 1880 and cited by Terry and Pellens, addiction to drugs was said to be "a vice of middle life, the larger number, by far, being from 30 to 40 years of age."[21] By 1920, Hubbard's study of New York's clinic could let him conclude that:

Most, in fact 70 per cent of the addicts in our clinic, are young people ... the one and only conclusion that we can arrive at, is that acquirements of this practice—drug addiction—is incident to propinquity, bad associates, taken together with weak vacillating dispositions, making a successful combination in favor of the acquirement of such a habit.[22]

A report of a study of addiction to the Michigan State Board of Health in 1878 stated that, of 1,313 addicts, 803 were females, 510 males.[23] This is corroborated by Earle's study of Chicago, reported in 1880:

Among the 235 habitual opium-eaters, 169 were found to be females, a proportion of about 3-to-1. Of these 169 females, about one-third belong to that class known as prostitutes. Deducting these, we still have among those taking the different kinds of opiates, 2 females to 1 male.[24]

Similarly, a report by Hull in 1885 on addiction in Iowa lists the distribution by sex as two-thirds female, and Terry's research in Florida in 1913 reported that 60 per cent of the cases were women.[25] Suddenly, as if in magical correspondence to the trend cited above on social class and age, the sex distribution reversed itself, and in 1914, McIver and Price report that 70 per cent of the addicts at Philadelphia General Hospital were males.[26] A governmental report to the Treasury Department in 1918 found addicts about equally divided between both sexes in the country, but a 1920 report for New York conclusively demonstrated that males were by then the predominant sex among drug addicts. Hubbard's report indicated that almost 80 per cent of the New York Clinic's population of addicts were male.[27] The Los Angeles Clinic had a similar distribution for 1920 and 1921. The picture is clear. Taking only the three variables of age, sex, and social class into account, there is a sharp and remarkable transformation to be noticed in the two-decade period at the turn of the century. Let us examine now the legal turn of events of the period.

Prior to 1897, there was no significant legislation in any state concerning the manufacture or distribution of narcotics. As we have seen, the medical profession was becoming increasingly aware of the nature of morphine addiction when heroin was discovered in 1898. The alarm over the common practice of using morphine for a myriad of ills was insufficient to stem the tide of the great enthusiasm with which physicians greeted heroin. Nonetheless, a small band of dedicated doctors who had been disturbed by the widespread ignorance of morphine in the profession (warnings about addiction did not appear in medical texts until about 1900) began to agitate for governmental intervention and regulation.[28]

From 1887 to 1908, many states passed individual laws aimed at curbing some aspect of the distribution of narcotics. Opium smoking was a favorite target of most of these laws, a development occasioned by the more concentrated treatment given this issue in the American press. Nonetheless, many of the state legislatures listened to medical men who insisted on the need for more control on the widespread distribution of the medicinally used opium derivatives. New York's state legislature passed the first comprehensive piece of legislation in the country concerning this problem in 1904, the Boylan Act.

As with many other problems of this kind, the lack of uniform state laws meant that control was virtually impossible. There is great variety in the law-making ability of each state, and sometimes it seems as though each state reviews the others carefully in order not to duplicate the provisions of their laws. If New York wanted registration of pharmacists, Massachusetts would want the registration of the central distributing warehouses, Illinois might want only physicians' prescriptions, and so forth. It soon became clear that only national and even international centralized control would be effective.

At the request of the United States, an international conference on opium was called in early 1909. Among countries accepting the invitation to this convention held in Shanghai were China, Great Britain, France, Germany, Italy, Russia, and Japan. Prior to this time, there had been a few attempts at control by individual nations in treaties, but this was the first concerted action on a truly international level. The major purpose of this first conference, as well as two other international conventions that were called within the next four years, was to insure that opium and related drugs be distributed only for expressly medical purposes, and ultimately distributed to the consumer through medical channels. The conferences called for regulation of the traffic at ports of entry, especially, but also tried to deal with the complicated problem of mail traffic. The handful of nations represented at the first Shanghai conference recognized the need for obtaining agreement and compliance from every nation in the world. The United States found itself in the embarrassing position of being the only major power without any control law covering distribution of medicinal narcotics within its borders. (The 1909 federal law was directed at opium smoking.) It was very much as a direct result of participation in the international conventions, then, that this country found itself being pressed for congressional action on the problem.

In this climate of both internal and international concern for the medicinal uses of the opium derivatives, Congress passed the Harrison Narcotic Act, approved December 17, 1914.

The Harrison Act stipulated that anyone engaged in the production or distribution of narcotics must register with the federal government and keep records of all transactions with drugs. This was the first of the three central provisions of the act. It gave the government precise knowledge of the legal traffic, and for the first time, the various uses and avenues of distribution could be traced.

The second major provision required that all parties handling the drugs through either purchase or sale pay a tax. This was a critical portion, because it meant that enforcement would reside with the tax collector, the Treasury Department, and more specifically, its Bureau of Internal Revenue. The Bureau set up a subsidiary organization to deal with affairs related to surveillance of activities covered by the new law. The immediate task was to insure that drugs were registered and passed through legitimate channels, beginning with importation and ending with the consumer. Since everyone was required to keep a record, the Bureau could demand and survey documentary material at every stage of the market operation.

Finally, the third major provision of the Harrison Act was a subtle "sleeper" that was not to obtain importance until the Supreme Court made a critical interpretation in 1919. This was the provision that unregistered persons could purchase drugs only upon the prescription of a physician, and that such a prescription must be for legitimate medical use. It seemed innocent enough a provision, one that was clearly included so that the physician retained the only control over the dispensation of narcotics to the consumer. As such, the bill was designed by its framers to place the addict completely in the hands of the medical profession.

It is one of those ironic twists that this third provision, intended for one purpose, was to be used in such a way as to thwart that purpose. As a direct consequence of it, the medical profession abandoned the drug addict. The key revolved around the stipulation that doctors could issue a prescription only to addicts for *legitimate* medical purposes. The decision about what is legitimate medical practice rests ultimately outside the medical profession in the moral consensus which members of society achieve about legitimacy. Even if the medical profession were to agree that experimental injections of a new drug on a random sample of babies would do most to advance medical science, the moral response against experimentation would be so strong as to destroy its claim to legitimacy. Thus, it is only in arbitrary and confined hypothetical instances that we can cogently argue that the medical profession determines legitimate practice.

So it was that the germ of a moral conception, the difference between good and evil or right and wrong, was to gain a place in the exercise of the new law.

Since the Harrison Act said nothing explicitly about the basis upon which physicians could prescribe narcotics for addicts, the only theoretical change that was forseeable was the new status of the prescription at the drug counter. All sales were to be registered, and a signed prescription from a physician was required. But when the physician became the only legal source of the drug supply, hundreds of thousands of law-abiding addicts suddenly materialized outside of doctors' offices. It was inconceivable that the relatively small number of doctors in the country could so suddenly handle over half a million new patients in any manner, and certainly it was impossible that they might handle them individually. The doctor's office became little more than a dispensing station for the addict, with only an infinitesimal fraction of addicts receiving personal care. In most cases, this was simply a continuation of the small number who had already been under regular care.

In New York City for example, it was impossible for a doctor with even a small practice to do anything more than sign prescriptions for his suddenly created large clientele. The government agents were alarmed at what they regarded as cavalier treatment of the prescription by the medical profession, and were concerned that the spirit and intent of the new drug law were being violated. They decided to prosecute some physicians who were prescribing to addicts en masse. They succeeded in convicting them, and appeals took the cases up to the Supreme Court. In a remarkable case (Webb vs. U.S., 1919) the Supreme Court made a decision that was to have far-reaching effects on the narcotics traffic, ruling that:

a prescription of drugs for an addict "not in the course of professional treatment in the attempted cure of the habit, but being issued for the purpose of providing the user with morphine sufficient to keep him comfortable by maintaining his customary use" was not a prescription in the meaning of the law and was not included within the exemption for the doctor-patient relationship.[29]

Doctors who continued to prescribe to addicts on anything but the most personal and individual basis found themselves faced with the real, demonstrated possibility of fines and prison sentences. As I have indicated, there were hundreds of thousands of addicts, and only a few thousand physicians to handle them. If there were thirty or forty addicts outside a doctor's office waiting for prescriptions, *or even waiting for a chance to go through withdrawal*, the Supreme Court decision and the Treasury Department's actions made it almost certain that the doctor would turn them away. A minority of doctors, some for humanitarian reasons, some from the profit-motive of a much higher fee, continued to prescribe. Scores of them were arrested, prosecuted, fined, imprisoned, and set forth as an example to others. The addict found himself being cut off gradually but surely from all legal sources, and he began to turn gradually but surely to the welcome arms of the black marketeers.

And so it was that the law and its interpretation by the Supreme Court provided the final condition and context for a moral reassessment of what had previously been regarded as a physiological problem. The country could begin to connect all addicts with their new-found underworld associates, and could now begin to talk about a different class of men who were consorting with criminals. The step was only a small one to the imputation of criminal intent. The bridge between law and morality was drawn.

At this time, there were some men in the Treasury Department who momentarily recognized the impossible situation of the addict, and the government moved to allow temporary clinics in various cities throughout the country. The purpose at the outset, according to a Bureau report, was to provide an interim period where the addict could get his supply under some kind of medical supervision and not fall prey to the exhorbitant prices of the drug peddlers. Thus were born the controversial Narcotics Clinics that would total forty-four in only sixteen months, and spread to almost every major city in the nation. Closed abruptly by government order in 1922, they have remained as the focal point of the most heated disputes in the United States narcotic policy for the last forty years.

The clinics opened in 1918, and very little is known about most of them, a condition extremely conducive to passionate debate. Those who are against clinics usually cite the literature of the Federal Narcotics Bureau (established in 1930), a literature which is sketchy, poorly documented, and full of moralistic condemnation. In a 1920 report, the Treasury Department had this to say about the problem:

Some of the so-called clinics that have since been established throughout the country without the knowledge or sanction of this Bureau apparently were established for mercenary purposes or for the sole purpose of providing applicants with whatever narcotic drugs they required for the satisfaction of their morbid appetites. Little or no attempt was made by some of these private clinics to effect cures, and prominent physicians and scientists who have made a study of drug addiction are practically unanimous in the opinion that such clinics accomplish no good and that the cure of narcotic addiction is an impossibility unless accompanied by institutional treatment.[30]

There is no documentation given for these "studies" by prominent physicians and scientists who all agreed upon the issue in question. The reference to "morbid" appetites of addicts reflects a judgment of addiction from an agency of government, not from medicine.

Those in favor of the clinics have equally little evidence from the history of the period upon which to base their position. But as Linde-smith points out, where there is information available, and where there is conflict between the two camps, those who claim that the clinics were a relative success have the better of it.[31] The best case in point is the Shreveport, Louisiana clinic. Markedly conflicting reports from the Narcotics Bureau and Terry and Pellens give a clear indication that distortion and falsification are common in the former.[32]

Undoubtedly, some of the clinics were bad ones, guilty of the abuses that the Bureau cites. Some physicians were unscrupulous and prescribed drugs for an extra fee, taking advantage of the addict's inability to obtain the drugs at a lower price on the black market. But some of the clinics were good ones in the sense that the abuses were few, and that men were able to continue their normal lives without being drawn into illegal associations with peddlers, and perhaps driven to a life of crime.

Abuses in the New York City clinic and the attendant newspaper sensationalism brought about an atmosphere of panic in the general public. The large number of addicts in New York made it impossible for the clinic to handle each case individually. This was a fault of the available facilities, of course, and not of the clinic system. Hundreds and hundreds of addicts would line up outside the clinic in the early morning for their supply, the queue stretching for several city blocks on some days. The staff physicians simply prescribed as quickly as they could, not being able to afford to take the necessary time to check records thoroughly for complete identification, registration, and the like. So, some addicts would get their supply for the day, then go back and get in line a few more times so that they would not have to come back so often. The New York newspapers of the time, in the heyday of yellow journalism, sent out reporters. They documented some of the abuses of the New York clinic, but gave such sensational accounts that clinics in general were portrayed as sinful places where the addict could go to satisfy his "morbid" desires and pursue the thrills and pleasures of narcotics. The stories were picked up by papers in various parts of the country, and the public responded with *moral* outrage.

Letters severely critical of the clinic system flooded into magazines and newspapers, and few people had enough positive information to defend it. The American Medical Association officially deplored the situation, and took a firm position against ambulatory treatment of addicts. It was opposed to addicts coming to and going from hospitals or clinics while under treatment. The only alternative was complete institutionalization of the addict, since physicians could hardly be expected to treat the patient in his home, and police his actions to make sure he remained there. The government began closing the clinics in 1920, and had closed all but one by the middle of 1921.

Even while the clinics were open, the illicit traffic in narcotics was gaining ground. With the closing date, many more addicts were eligible prey for the black market peddlers.

The Federal Narcotics Bureau claims that the clinics aggravated the problem of drug addiction. Since there is no evidence of addiction spreading during the clinic period, one wonders what kind of criteria are used.

In 1918, the year before any clinics were opened, 888 federal arrests and 392 convictions for narcotics offenses were reported. In 1919, the year in which the New York Clinic operated and others were opened, arrests totaled 1,008 and convictions 582. In 1920, when the clinics, including the one in New York, were being closed, arrests rose to 3,477 and convictions to 908. In 1921, when the Prohibition Commissioner reported in June that all clinics were closed (one exception), arrests had risen further to 4,014 and convictions to 1,583. The yearly rise continued to a peak in 1925, when the clinics had been closed for several years with 10,297 federal arrests and 5,600 convictions.[33]

TABLE 1

FEDERAL ARRESTS AND CONVICTIONS FOR NAR-
COTICS LAW VIOLATION FOR FOUR SELECTED YEARS
DURING THE USE OF CLINICS, AND ONE AFTER THE
CLOSE OF THE CLINICS (1922).

Year	Arrests	Convictions
1918	888	392
1919	1,008	582
1920	3,477	908
1921	4,014	1,583
1925	10,297	5,600

Today, men make an almost complete association of the addict with criminality. When we hear that someone is addicted to drugs, we seldom think of the physiological problem first. Instead, we conceive of an immoral, weak, psychologically inadequate criminal who preys upon an unsuspecting population to supply his "morbid" appetite. There is no exaggeration here. A pamphlet put out by the Public Health Service of the federal government in 1951, entitled "What to Know about Drug Addiction," had this to say of the addicts the society has come to think of as typical:

Usually, they are irresponsible, selfish, immature, thrill-seeking individuals who are constantly in trouble—the type of person who acts first and thinks afterward. The majority of addicts do not fall clearly into either the neurotic or character disorder groups but have characteristics of both classes.[34]

This is the character-disorder addict, and as the pamphlet indicates, the line between this type and the neurotic is very hard to draw, especially when conceived primarily in moral terms.

The maximum penalty under the Harrison Act was ten years imprisonment. The issues had so shifted in four decades, however, that Congress could pass two bills in the 1950s drastically increasing the punishment. Under the old law, the judge could be flexible in sentencing, but the Boggs Amendment in 1951 set mandatory minimums that increased the prison sentence to ten years with repeated offenses. Then in 1956, Congress passed the Narcotic Drug Control Act that allowed the death penalty for sale to minors. This law also made distinctions between the user and the seller, with the latter singled out for harsher treatment. However, since a very large proportion of addicts sell at some time in order to help supply their habit, judges often have the option of invoking whichever provision they regard as appropriate.

Individual states were very busy during this period passing laws of their own on the sale and distribution of heroin. Many states even went so far as to make laws which made *being* an addict a crime. Despite a recent Supreme Court decision in 1962 ruling this unconstitutional, there is some confusion about this, especially when it comes down to the practice of the police. Illegal possession is a crime, and an addict would almost have to be in possession by definition. The police need only observe him for a period of twenty-four hours to make their case.

Certain social categories lend themselves more to moral condemnation than others. Whereas the lower and working classes had the smallest proportion of addicts in 1900, in 1969 they constituted the overwhelming majority of known addicts. Whereas Blacks were less than 10 per cent of the addict population in 1900, they are now more than half of the addicts known to law enforcement agencies. Whereas there were formerly more women than men addicted, the ratio is now at least seven to one for men. Whereas the middle-aged predominated in 1900, youth is now far and away the most likely of known offenders. The list could go on, but the point is simply that middle America's moral hostility comes faster and easier when directed toward a young, lower-class Negro male, than toward a middle-aged, middle-class white female.

The law drastically altered the conditions that produced the shifts in these categories. It is a short trip across the bridge to a moral judgment.

The present morality is so strong that it lets local policy justify apprehending an addict, putting him behind bars for hours upon hours, and forcing him to go through the most excruciating kinds of agony without medical treatment, in order that he inform on his supplier. In a later section, some time will be spent on the physiology of addiction and withdrawal. For the time, it is sufficient to call attention to the fact that for an addict to go through withdrawal from the drug with no treatment is a hell he wants to avoid so badly that he may cheat, steal, prostitute himself, sometimes even kill. The police know this, and take full advantage of it when a local crime has been committed for which some local addicts may have information. The moral judgment is so serious that it allowed a state's attorney of a major city who is a former law professor to say in open hearings:

In view of my background as a law professor, I am very jealous of civil rights, civil rights of individuals. One of the things I determined when I got in here was that I was going to be particularly careful about that. I must say this to you, that where narcotics addicts are concerned, I haven't many complaints, though I do know the police are a little prone to pick up these men. They have protection of an ordinance, and I must say that the problem is so serious that even if we must admit some of their civil laws or civil rights are being violated, you have to go along with a certain amount of fringe violation, if you see what I mean.[35]

The man speaking was John Gutknecht, State's Attorney for Cook County, Illinois, a man who handled the prosecution of addicts for

Chicago. Gutknecht was talking to Senator Price Daniel in the above exchange, and went on to say:

> So I think you will find that a lot of these arrests and subsequent discharges are in the form of a security measure that possibly we should not countenance, but I don't know how else you can function.
>
> SENATOR DANIEL: You completely answered my next question. My next question was going to be this: How do you reconcile the large number of arrests for Chicago for the period 1953 and 1954, 6,643 with convictions 3,350, just barely over fifty per cent of the arrests, and I believe you have answered it already.
>
> MR. GUTKNECHT: I think you will also have to agree that neither Mr. Tieken in his capacity nor I in my capacity—and we both have civil rights laws to enforce—can, with our multiple jobs, get too excited if a known addict has been unlawfully arrested and then discharged, knowing that because he is a known addict the police have to take little extra measures.[36]

Here we see a swing of the full circle. Up until this point, I have attempted to demonstrate the dynamic relationship between legislation and morality. The circle is closed when *agents of law enforcement* take moral positions that influence differential legal treatment of the population. We "can't get too excited," said the State's Attorney, if drug addicts have their civil rights violated.

In view of these later developments, perhaps the most interesting feature of the early federal legislation was that its proponents did not advocate it out of a moral zeal. The medical men who pressed so forcefully for control on narcotics did not do so out of the moral conviction that addicts should be cut off from their supply of narcotics. Rather, their explicit intention was to prevent the widespread distribution of morphine and heroin to a public that was unsuspecting of its addicting qualities. The scholarly, lay, and medical literature of the period contained warnings about the physiological and sometimes psychological problems that were associated with drugs, and only on rare instances did it engage or address the moral issue of addiction.

The legislation brought about the conditions that were conducive to a reinterpretation of narcotics usage into almost purely moral terms. As long as the sale of morphine and heroin was legitimate, it was not in the interest of any man, or any entrepreneurial class of men, to make a large profit by hiking their own price of the drug above that of the going market. The laws, in pushing heroin into the underworld, suddenly made it extremely profitable to raise the price to an exhorbitant level because the addict would pay any price to keep from going through withdrawal from the drug. Consequently, any addict dealing with the black market was automatically placed *in a class* of law-breakers, and he was associated with the underworld and its "immoral" non middle-class elements. Overnight, the *conditions* were ripe for treating the addict in moral terms. As soon as he could be classed with the undesirables, the nature of his problem could be transformed in the minds of men who were not addicts and who could not understand it.

Suggested Relationship Between Effects of Law in "Moral Areas"

This concluding section will present an introductory theoretical statement suggesting the different effects of law in different kinds of "moral" situations in which the law is violated. At the beginning of this chapter, it was pointed out that those who argue that morality can not be legislated are inconsistent in their observation of the moral-legal issues in the three social problem areas of prostitution, drug addiction, and racial discrimination. One may challenge the comparability of these three problems with some justification. With racial prejudice and discrimination, for example, men already have strong feelings by definition, and the issue is whether law would achieve a change in the direction desired by the legislators. Prior to 1900, quite the opposite state of affairs existed as to drug use, in that men did not feel strongly about heroin consumption. The federal law of 1914 was therefore enacted prior to strong moral judgment about heroin use *per se*. However, it did have the effect of pushing heroin into an arena where strong moralistic feelings existed. (Heroin use came to be associated with the "dregs of the cities" and sensual gratification; it came to be thought of in the same moralistic manner as the opium dens.) By the 1930s, narcotics had joined prostitution and alcoholism as major moral problems in the minds of Americans.

Those who take the position that morality can not be legislated usually favor laws that support the existing moral order, such as their support of laws against prostitution and heroin use. The law is thereby conceived to be a kind of dam that is constructed after moral judgments are developed. The dam acts to hold back the floodtides of a contrary morality (its source unaccounted for), and consequently is seen as necessary to preserve the existing moral order.

This position, summarized immediately below, assumes that once moral judgments are firm, law cannot change morality, but that law can contain and prevent existing morality from changing.

1. Laws which supplement the existing moral order may be effective in preventing the spread of behavior that is immoral (prostitution);
2. laws which create the conditions for the development of a new morality may be successful in creating a new set of moral attitudes about behavior (e.g., drug use in 1914); but
3. laws which attempt to change the existing moral order are doomed to failure (e.g., Prohibition and racial discrimination).

Various modifications are required with points one and two preceding, but for the most part there is substantial agreement about their validity and they have some empirical basis. A major issue to be examined theoretically and empirically in the work is whether the third position stated is an accurate assessment of what men believe, or whether it is an empirical regularity itself that may prove to be a generalization about the way law and morality are related. It is a sociological axiom that what men believe is intricately interwoven with the patterns of their behavior. A primary concern of this book is a clarification of the law-morality issues now clouded by this question.

Raymond Mack once proposed that the effectiveness of a new law directed at a change of social behavior was dependent upon how strongly people felt about the object of the change.[37] He used the example of legislation outlawing the use of a certain kind of match compared with legislation outlawing discrimination. People are not likely to rise up in arms if they are prohibited from buying cardboard matches in favor of wooden ones, or vice versa. The strong historical resistance to civil rights legislation was his opposite case in point. Mack's example of people's reaction to match-buying laws was admittedly not a case of a moral area of behavior, since it was chosen to make that point. Emotional investments are insignificant in this case. But what of instances where there is a question of altering the moral order? What other things can be said to influence the effectiveness of legislation?

There are two dimensions that I would like to suggest as critical to these questions. The first concerns *whether or not the violation involves a victim who can act as a plaintiff.* Edwin Schur has examined this dimension in another context.[38] His analysis of many aspects of "victimless" crimes is extensive and thorough. It suits the purpose here to explore further the question of victims of crimes as it relates to the issue of the possibility of effective law. In a case of assault and battery, the reaction of the society can be swift and firm for the simple reason that an individual can come forward, press charges, and demand redress of his grievance. Contrast this with the behavior of consenting adult homosexuals. There is no plaintiff to protest the action, even though it is just as much in violation of the written law as assault. Some of the consequences of this for law enforcement are immediately obvious, but some are not. Lindesmith has made the same point about the transaction between buyer and sellers of black market narcotics.[39] Neither party to the transaction has it in his self-interest to inform legal authorities, and so the action could ordinarily go undetected and thus unpunished. However, where there is no victim who will act as plaintiff, the police feel forced to enter into the transactions by means of subterfuge. Thus, police will play the role of a "trick" in order to trap the prostitute; they will act as though they are addicted in order to trap the drug peddler; they will play the role of a homosexual in the public men's toilets in order to trap the homosexual, and so forth.

The law enforcement agencies have a much easier time when some individual feels wronged, and will present his detailed version of the violation. Many victimless crimes are solved by a partner dissatisfied with the outcome of the illegal behavior. (Police files are full of cases solved by partners in a robbery who were angered by the way in which the money was divided.) The first important dimension then, concerns the possibility of a plaintiff.

The second dimension is almost as critical, and cuts across the first in the manner diagrammed in the accompanying chart. It concerns the *arena in which the behavior occurs,* namely, whether the circumstances are public or private. The ability of the society to react with sanctions is very dependent upon the visibility of the violation. Exhibitionism is far easier to sanction than is petty theft. Even though both involve a

ARENA OF THE OCCURRENCE

		Public	Private
	Victim as Plaintiff	1. Exhibitionism Denial of voting rights Refusal of minorities at public accommodations	2. Assault and battery Theft
NATURE OF THE OFFENSE	*No Victim as Party to Transaction*	3. Sale of alcohol during Prohibition	4. Homosexuality among consenting parties Narcotics use

plaintiff, the former is by definition performed in a public arena.[40] Law enforcement is most easily achieved, therefore, when there is a public violation and a victim to protest the act. Cell 1 of the diagram presents some examples of this combination.

It is in Cell 1 that we can now begin to make a more systematic analysis of the legislation of morality. *Laws which affect both the public arena and concern victimization will be most effective in changing the existing moral order.* Thus, civil rights legislation is placed in a new light. As we shall see momentarily, it is at the exact opposite pole of discussions about moral legislation on prostitution and drug addiction.

Note that in all four areas represented in the cells, people have strong commitments and feelings. These are all four moral areas, and so it is not simply a question of being able to predict the effectiveness of legislation on the basis of degree of emotional commitment, the substance and nature of values, and the like. An assessment of the possible effectiveness of the law is based here entirely upon such clearly visible and measurable properties as public or private, victim or victimless. The ability of the law to control externally the behavior of consenting homosexuals is minimal. The ability of the law to control externally the behavior of the exhibitionist or the discriminator is maximal. Intermediate between these two extremes are the cases represented in the second and third cells of the diagram. Private violations where there are victims are easier to sanction, and thereby enforce, than public violations where there are no victims to act as plaintiff.

It can now be seen that even though the refusal of the right to vote and narcotics use are both in "moral areas," the probable effectiveness of legislation in these moral areas is dramatically different. A black man who is refused the right to register and vote is thus confronted in the public arena. Further, he is victimized and has "recourse" to agencies of law enforcement where he can press his grievances. In this kind of situation, the morality of a social order can be altered by legislation. In more popular terms, there can be and have been instances of this sense of the legislation of morality. In contrast, the heroin user is no more likely to have his morality legislated than the consumer of alcohol would have been during Prohibition. Both engage in violations of the private sector, and neither case involves a party to the transaction who will act as plaintiff.

The history of narcotics use in the United States sketched earlier has illustrated how the law can shift neutral behavior into that which is strongly overladen with moral condemnation. I have now proposed that the effect of present narcotics legislation, directed as it is to a moral area that is private and "victimless," can not be sufficient to alter the behavior of the drug user in the direction desired by the legislators. What kinds of changes in the behavior of the drug user and his society might be expected from various possible changes in narcotics legislation? So far, there has been an implicit suggestion that more stringent repressive measures cannot produce the results intended. What then, are some of the theoretical and practical considerations that might lead one to propose legal changes; changes that can be expected to alter the moral order even in instances of private and victimless violations? Since it is the narcotics problem that will serve as the specific example of this kind of violation, some background information on the nature of drugs themselves is required before turning to a direct consideration of the larger question just raised.

The effects and uses of narcotics and moral judgment

Portions of Chapter 2 in this book are reprinted from my article "Drugs and Drug Control," in J. Douglas, ed., *Crime in American Society*, Indianapolis: Bobbs-Merrill, by permission of the publisher, all rights reserved.

Introduction

A KNOWLEDGE OF THE PHYSIOLOGICAL EFFECTS of drugs is important to an understanding of the principal social and moral issues in the drug problem. For example, if you believe that heroin is a dangerous drug because it turns the individual into an aggressive, hostile, and uninhibited person, your moral stand will be different than if you believe heroin (1) is destructive to health, or (2) is soothing to the nerves, or (3) simply keeps you awake at night. Indeed, a good many of the intensely moralistic arguments about narcotics are based upon conceptions of the physiological consequences of the drugs. Many of these notions are erroneous, especially the widespread current myths about the opiates. Knowledge of the fact that sustained use of alcohol has far more deleterious consequences to cell life in the body than sustained use of heroin alters the strength of the moralistic pronouncements.

If people informed themselves a bit more about the physical aspects of barbiturates and marijuana, they would probably reverse their social and moral concerns on the two drugs. That is not to say that knowledge of the physiological effects is the only determinant for social attitudes. If Junior is *sneaking* around in the garage taking secobarbital or dexedrine or marijuana, one can anticipate concern irrespective of pharmacological knowledge. Acts have social meanings quite apart from their physical ones. Thus, even when it is pointed out that alcohol is more physically debilitating than marijuana, centrifugal social forces are often strong enough to override this *merely* physical fact, and the parent is capable of saying "Ah, but the meaning of his smoking marijuana is defiance, rebellion. . . ."

Because the physiological effects of drugs are different, the moral issues that relate to their use are different. As an extreme illustration of the point, arguments against the marketing of thalidomide (which produced deformed babies) stem from a different moral base than arguments opposed to the marketing of terpin hydrate (which produces less coughing, but contains codein). Although the differences between the physiological effects of marijuana, LSD, and heroin are less dramatic, the point is equally valid when applied to these drugs.

There are many legitimate moral questions, issues, and arguments on the sanctionable uses of drugs. However, only those positions reasonably informed about the physical basis of the narcotics can rest compelling cases on firm ground.

Narcotics

The term "narcotics" is a multicolored blanket that has been used to cover extremely diverse drugs. In contemporary use, it confuses and obscures as much as it clarifies. Although the technical term means to dull, deaden the senses, or put to sleep, many laymen use the term interchangeably with "drug." A drug can be natural (opium poppy) or synthetic (demerol). Its effect on the central nervous system can be that of a stimulant (cocaine) or a depressant (morphine). Further, it may be highly addictive (heroin), or not in the least productive of physical dependence (marijuana).

In the United States, reference to the drug problem usually is reference to opium and its derivatives, especially morphine and heroin. Opiates have two things in common: they are depressants and they are also addicting. Opiates depress the nerve centers which register pain, and are among the most effective analgesics (painkillers) known. Morphine is commonly used for medical purposes in this country and heroin is sometimes used medicinally in other countries.

Barbiturates are also depressants, but are synthetics used as sedatives. There are many forms, including phenobarbital, secobarbital, and pentobarbital. Physicians often use barbiturates in prescriptions of medicines to bring about relaxation and sleep. Effective amounts often make the user drowsy, and the after-effects of sluggishness and heaviness are quite noticeable and annoying to many. Taken in large enough quantities, the barbiturates are highly addicting.

The stimulants to the central nervous system also come in both natural and synthetic form. The most popular are the synthetic amphetamines, popularly called "pep pills" or sometimes "bennies." Drivers sometimes use them to stay awake at night, and students on occasion use these stimulants in order to study for many hours on end. Quite the opposite of the depressants, these drugs can cause heightened alertness, great nervousness, and sometimes distorted perception and hallucinations when taken in large enough quantities. What constitutes "large enough" is as much a matter of the individual physiology of the user as the actual quantity used.

This introductory list should be sufficient to make the point that the term "narcotic" alone means very little, especially when used interchangeably (and imprecisely) with "drug." Passion is a frequent companion of ignorance, and the two are like a settled married couple in the discourse about drugs. Men hold strong views and express fervent opinions about a vast array of drugs. Where opinions run so strong, many expect that there will be at least moderate knowledge of the legal and therapeutic issues involved, but that is an erroneous assumption. Because the narcotics do alter the actual physical condition of the subject in a significant way, a basic knowledge of their effects should be in the background of subsequent discussions of social and cultural issues. For this reason, the present chapter will briefly explore some of the more important narcotic drugs that are discussed and used in this country. Where possible, some statement will be included which touches upon the social and nonmedical uses of the drug.

Morphine

In the United States, morphine is one of the most popular and effective of analgesics used on the operating table. When a moderate dose is given to a patient in pain, instead of producing sleep directly, the drug evokes a kind of euphoria that is an integral part of the *absence* of pain. The same person taking morphine under normal conditions may feel more fear and anxiety from what is happening to his body than euphoria. This fact should be kept in mind when we turn to the social uses of this and related drugs.

In addition to the pain-killing, morphine in moderate dosage often produces drowsiness and the inability to concentrate, apathy, detachment, and lessened physical activity. However, despite the fact that it is primarily a depressant, it has some ability to act simultaneously as a stimulant. The degree to which this is true depends upon the person, though women tend to react more to the stimulating effects than do men.

Normally the drug takes effect in about fifteen minutes, reaches its peak after approximately twenty-five to thirty minutes, and may continue effective for three to six hours. For some, the effects may last for as long as twelve hours. For most people, the body returns to the old equilibrium at about fourteen to sixteen hours, or if addicted, withdrawal sets in at this point.

In moderate dosage, it may produce itching in the nose and a general feeling of heaviness in the arms and legs. The mouth feels dry, the pupils constrict, respiration is depressed to slower breathing, and hunger is muted. After a time, sleep comes, often accompanied by pleasant dreams.

A full dose, however, has quicker and more dramatic effects. Euphoria may be experienced for a very short period, followed by sluggishness and deep dreamless sleep. An overdose of morphine produces a coma, and death results from respiratory failure. Although morphine's pain-killing effectiveness lasts somewhat longer than heroin's, it produces less euphoria, and actually has more undesirable side effects. The most common of these are nausea, vomiting, and constipation. After morphine is injected, the face and neck become flushed and warm, and the subject may start to perspire. However, morphine actually causes the body temperature to fall, especially with larger doses. Three reasons are generally offered for the analgesic action of morphine. First, it induces a groggy state which allows for a greater endurance of pain. Second, and more debatable, morphine is said to alter the cognitive associations men have with pain. It is argued that while pain is perceived, it is experienced in a different manner so that the subject does not feel the usual fear, panic, or discomfort that ordinarily accompanies its perception.[1] Finally, morphine itself is able to raise the pain threshold.

Tolerance for the drug develops typically after fifteen to twenty days of continued use of the same dosage. That is, the body does not respond nearly as much to a similar quantity injection of the drug as it did during the first experiences. The user must take a more powerful dosage in order to achieve the same pain-killing effects after his physiology has become tolerant of morphine.

It is often reported that as tolerance for the drug develops, the subject needs greater and greater quantities to achieve the same effect because the body becomes accustomed to the previous level. This is true to a certain extent, pertains to certain kinds of sustained use, and varies with the individual. However, it is important to note that this conception of morphine usage implies an infinite progression to greater and greater tolerance. This is not true. While some addicts do achieve a remarkable tolerance level and are able to take perhaps as much as thirty times the normal therapeutic amount, there is a leveling off even for addicts with the highest quantitative consumption.

The argument that addiction is primarily psychogenically based has been thoroughly discredited. More than a decade ago, Wikler and his associates clearly demonstrated the physiological basis of addiction by isolating the withdrawal syndrome for study after frontal lobotomy.[2]

The effects of addiction (see Chapter 3) are generally the same for morphine and heroin. An addicted individual may remain in good health and be productive in his work if he is allowed to remain on the drug.[3] However, this is not to indicate that there are no physiological consequences to morphine usage that provide other kinds of problems. For example, the dulling of pain may effectively deny the addicted individual the important danger signals which indicate and inform that something is wrong in the body. Also, there are sufficient reports of decreased sexual appetite in morphine and heroin users to indicate that there is an important relationship in this area. An addict married to a nonaddict may face this kind of problem, which has a clear physiological basis. Once off the drug, sexual desires reportedly return to normal level.

NONMEDICAL USES

The illegal traffic in morphine is restricted largely to the legal channels of its distribution, and it rarely moves into the black market. Physicians and nurses who have legitimate access to the drug may administer it to patients, close relatives, or themselves to diminish difficult pain. A tolerance may develop, and for a number of reasons, the decision may be reached to continue administration. Morphine addicts who are apprehended by the law are very likely to report that their primary reason for continuing was to maintain themselves at a normal level and to prevent withdrawal.[4] (This is in contrast to the heroin addict, who often reports the desire for euphoria as a primary motivation.)[5]

The morphine addict is therefore likely to be an individual who was addicted *in the course of some medical problem*. Among morphine addicts, physicians and nurses are probably the most frequently represented occupational groups. Morphine addiction is primarily a middle-class addiction because medical practitioners and the patients that they treat in this fashion who subsequently continue usage are likely to be from this level in society.

Heroin

A semisynthetic derivative of morphine, heroin is far more potent and causes considerably more euphoria. The basic effects of the two drugs are the same, and the preceding discussion of morphine applies generally to heroin. However, there are some important differences. Heroin has more of a depressant effect upon the respiratory system and its action is considerably faster. After only twenty minutes, the drug reaches its peak as an analgesic. Relief from withdrawal is almost momentary. As has been noted, there are few undesirable side effects, something which heroin addicts who have tried both are quick to point out.

NONMEDICAL USES

Heroin has medical uses as an analgesic in several countries, including Great Britain, but it has been banned in the United States since 1924. As Eldridge notes, the association of the drug with the underworld produced a "heroin scare" in this country that resulted in a medical backlash.[6] After the Harrison Act, heroin leaped into great prominence in the underworld traffic. It seemed particularly adapted for use in this kind of market because it is easily transported and distributed in bulk in a form that requires only minimal preparation. The user simply has to make some minor alterations with highly accessible additives, and it is ready for injection. Morphine is more difficult to deal with, for it requires a more extensive and deliberate preparation to transform it from a transportable state to readiness for use.

Winick finds no evidence that sustained usage of heroin or morphine produces any toxic effects, nor that either results in damage of any kind to the central nervous system.[7] As many others have pointed out, the physiological problems which heroin users face result from withdrawing from the drug once physically dependent upon it.[8] As long as the individual remains on the drug, he can, and often did up until the first few years of this century (as was pointed out in Chapter 1), live a "normal" and productive life.

At this point, it is important to distinguish between two kinds of heroin users, or, at least two stages of heroin usage. First, there is the user who injects heroin in order to achieve euphoria. Either this can happen from the first few times that one takes it, or one can take considerable amounts all at one time later, after tolerance develops. Some addicts will take the cure voluntarily for a time in order to lower their tolerance and thereby achieve a greater kick (euphoric state) with a smaller dosage. This first group of addicts may "take a trip" to another psychic world that is as much psychological as physiological. Nonetheless, their physical abilities are altered a bit, and they are less dexterous than when not under the drug. Their reaction time is slower, and they generally are withdrawn from the world. It is this addict who has the attitude that he would be very happy if the world would leave him alone, and he would be only more than happy to leave the world alone.

This type of heroin user is much more affected by the drug than the second type, who is fully addicted and who takes the drug primarily to stave off withdrawal. The addict in this setting takes heroin primarily in order to achieve the physiological equilibrium that allows him to continue normally from day to day. He has all the appearances of normality, and it takes chemical tests to detect if he is using heroin. He drives a car, plays baseball, and performs many tasks requiring some manual dexterity (some surgeons have been addicted to morphine). This is not to say that he could not have performed more skillfully if he were not addicted and not under the influence. That is an empirical matter, and the evidence is that sheer physical matters like reaction time are slowed. It is to indicate, however, that men can and do live normal physical lives while addicted to the opiates.

Amphetamine

The amphetamine drugs stimulate the central nervous system, but the responses evoked depend largely upon the mental state and personality of the individual. The two most popular forms are generally known to college students as benzedrine and dexedrine. Their popularity stems from their ability to keep one awake for long study periods just before exams. When taken initially or infrequently, amphetamine generally produces the following effects after moderate dosage: alertness, increased initiative for otherwise boring or dreaded tasks, and greater ability to concentrate. The individual also frequently becomes more talkative and physically active, often giving the appearance of nervousness or agitation.

Larger doses or sustained usage result typically in some unpleasant symptoms, ranging from headaches, palpitation, and dizziness all the way to delirium and mental depression. Clinically, amphetamine drugs do have an analgesic action, and when used in combination with morphine, prolong the latter's pain-killing powers.

Addiction can occur, but it is very uncommon. Some heroin addicts use this drug to accelerate the action of heroin and to achieve a stimulated euphoria that is a different kind of kick. One of the more frequently cited precautions to its sustained use is the masking of fatigue, which can delude the user into assuming that his body can take the physical and mental exertion that is being abnormally pursued.

There is considerable literature and considerable controversy on the therapeutic ability of amphetamine in psychogenic disorders. It has been satisfactorily employed to elevate persons out of mental depressions and certain psychoneuroses. Some reports indicate that there are forms of epilepsy that are aided by its administration. It has even been used effectively for some chronically overweight persons in weight-reducing programs because of its ability to decrease the appetite. However, there are many reports of failures to accomplish the desired ends in each of these areas, and the varying effects of the drug with different personalities have been sufficient to elicit strong warnings from medical researchers that the drug should not be self-administered for these kinds of problems.

Methedrine (*Methamphetamine Hydrochloride*)

Methamphetamine is closely related in its chemical construction and some of its physiological effects to amphetamine. It has one important difference which makes it of special interest: While its effect on the cardiovascular system is weaker than that of amphetamine, it is more powerful as a stimulant to the central nervous system. In this fact lie some significant consequences for its nonmedical and illegal use. The drug is marketed under almost a dozen quite different trade names, the best known of which is methedrine. It is used clinically for the same kinds of things as is amphetamine, such as sustaining blood pressure during spinal anesthesia.

Methedrine is used by some people because of its ability to stimulate the mind without greatly affecting other parts of the body. Those who use methedrine illegally tend to have artistic or intellectual leanings, and as a class are much more self-consciously concerned about creativity and individual expression than are, say, heroin users. As has been noted, the opiates depress the nervous system, and the user floats away from this world and its considerations. Quite to the contrary, methedrine heightens the individual's perceptivity and responsiveness to selected aspects of his environment, and apparently stimulates him to relate to the world rather than to withdraw from it.

Methedrine users seem to be a very small group among a large population of narcotics users, and they have some of the trappings of a separate cult. They are disdainful of heroin addicts, and hold many of the same attitudes toward them as does the general society.[9]

The Barbiturates

Barbital, the first of the barbiturates, was first used at the turn of the century. Following it was phenobarbital, introduced in 1912. Since that time, over 2,500 barbiturates have been developed, and more than fifty have been cleared and marketed for clinical use. They are widely prescribed by physicians, and are commonly used to induce sleep for countless different reasons. They are addicting and can be quite dangerous in dosages that exceed a minimum. In combination with alcohol they have proved unpredictably fatal.

The barbiturates are depressants to the central nervous system and are used clinically as sedatives and hypnotics. The inducement of sleep is the most frequent reason for their use. They differ from the opiates in analgesia because they are unable to produce sleep in the presence of even moderate pain. Barbiturates do not raise the threshold of pain significantly to be called true analgesics.

Despite the sensational play given to heroin and morphine addiction, barbiturate addiction is a far more serious physiological matter. A 1950 research report relates how some volunteers at the federal hospital for drug addicts were given the barbiturates for an extended period:

when the drugs were withdrawn after three to five months, four of five subjects developed convulsions and four of five became psychotic. This experimental demonstration of addiction, later amplified with additional cases, did much to inform the American medical profession that primary barbiturate addiction does occur and that the abstinence syndrome is characteristic and dangerous. [Compared to morphine] . . . barbiturate addiction is a more serious public health and medical problem because it produces greater mental, emotional, and neurological impairment and because withdrawal entails real hazards.[10]

The barbiturate addict is more sluggish in physical mobility and thought. His speech is slow, his memory is poor, and his comprehension is narrowed. Typical patterns also reveal exaggeration of selected personality traits, moroseness, and irritability.

Withdrawal from barbiturates for an addict can be quite serious for his psychic equilibrium. This varies by individual, but hallucinations are frequent. In the early stages of withdrawal, these hallucinations are recognized by the subject for what they are, but as they continue over time, he loses his facility to distinguish between his own unique perceptions and those which are consonant with the consensus of reality—a primary characteristic of schizophrenia. The withdrawal psychosis may clear after a few days, but there have been occasions where hallucinations have persisted for more than a month. Barbiturate addiction withdrawal is a difficult problem to treat symptomatically because the various physical symptoms are hard to distinguish from more traditionally known illness symptoms, such as delirium tremens of the alcoholic, epilepsy, and encephalitis, to name but a few. Extensive investigation and cross-checking is required to rule out these other sources of the physical problems manifested.

A standard reference work on therapeutics states that while the incidence of barbiturate addiction cannot be known, it is not only "common, but appears to be on the increase."[11] In combination with the greater physical seriousness of barbiturate addiction, it seems very odd that morphine and heroin addiction should receive so much more attention. The newspapers and magazines and movies make very little of barbiturate addiction because it is not perceived in the same moralistic tones as addiction to the opiates.

NONMEDICAL USES

In recent years, barbiturates have been used increasingly outside of medical and clinical recommendation, particularly so with illegal marketing. When heroin or morphine is not readily available to a person addicted to one of these drugs, he may turn to a short-acting barbiturate. This would be either secobarbital or pentobarbital, known among addicts as "goofballs" in honor of the effects achieved. It is possible to develop a simultaneous addiction, and in order to stave off withdrawal, an addict who practices this too frequently will have to take both heroin and secobarb.

Because of the unpleasant sluggishness that accompanies barbiturate use, most heroin addicts dislike the drug, and will use it only as a last resort. They can achieve either euphoria or normality with heroin, and in either state do not feel burdened by the drug. With secobarb, on the other hand, they feel definitely restrained in their ability to manage the world. In driving a car, the slowing of reaction time from the accelerator to the brake is even subjectively perceived.

To continue a point of the first chapter, it is interesting to note that increasing public alarm over barbiturate use and addiction has paralleled its development into illegal traffic. The present situation is very much like that in 1912 with morphine consumption: Main usage is clearly with persons who take the drug for medical purposes, and there are few taints and charges of sensual gratification or kicks explaining the addiction. To further the analogy a bit, the lower classes, young male adults, and ethnic minorities seldom take barbiturates now. (The reason is only slightly different: Prescriptions are required, but more important, the subjective desire for sedation seems to be more of a middle-class phenomenon.) If a new federal law outlawed barbiturate use in this country, except under very personalized medical care, and if physicians were imprisoned for "simply prescribing without close attention," barbiturate addicts would suddenly be prime candidates for a black-market traffic. The cost of the drug would go up considerably. The middle-class addicts would fade out of the statistics partly because they could get their own personal care from private family physicians, partly because of systematically differential treatment by the agencies of law enforcement.[12] Those in social categories further and further from the center would appear with great frequency in criminal citations, and barbiturate use would be transformed in the minds of the public into a vicious, evil habit in which only the willfully immoral could engage. An important reason why this has not happened has been the lack of an association between barbiturate use and the pursuit of sensual gratification. As was noted in the first chapter, morphine and heroin use did not come in for strong moral censure until the Harrison Act's interpretation and enforcement and sensational yellow journalism combined to give the public the association with sensual pursuits. Until very recently, barbiturate users were almost entirely in those social categories which do not lend themselves to moralistic denigration.[13]

Cocaine

Cocaine is the drug most responsible for the erroneous public image of the narcotic addict as a "dope fiend," one who takes a drug and becomes an aggressive "maniac" dangerous to himself and others. The drug is obtained from the leaves of the *erythroxlyon coca* trees of Peru and Bolivia. Its most important medical use is to block nerve conduction when applied locally. The drug acts first as a powerful stimulant, producing pleasurable hallucinations, great excitement and often an exaggeration of one's own powers. There is generally a feeling of tremendous mental and physical strength, and indeed, there is some evidence that mental powers are increased by the drug. Because cocaine acts to lessen the perception of fatigue, greater physical exertion is possible.

The tendency to feel stronger and more insightful than is actually the case has been known to produce paranoia in the cocaine user, partly because he then attributes his actual ineffectiveness to a conspiracy. Suffering from feelings of persecution, cocaine users may become physically aggressive towards "hostile" individuals in the immediate environment. Visual, auditory, and tactile hallucinations are reported, especially the feeling of something crawling on the skin, a perception that gives further impetus to the paranoia.

Cocaine usage is rare in the United States, and cocaine addiction is rarer. Physical dependence on the drug is not nearly as clear as with the opium narcotics, and withdrawal from cocaine is not nearly so difficult. One can develop a tolerance for the drug, so that increased dosages are required for the same effect over time, but little is known about the physiological mechanisms of cocaine tolerance.

Even though the drug is a powerful stimulant to the central nervous system in the first stages of its effect, it becomes a depressant in later stages. An overdose will depress the medullary centers causing respiratory failure and death.

Although its usage is not a problem of any size or urgency, the sensational play given to cocaine in various newspaper accounts of its use in the 1920s and 1930s has given to it a significance that is strongly felt whenever narcotics are discussed by laymen. As has been noted, the present-day serious issue of production, distribution, and consumption of narcotics is with the opiates. They depress the nerve centers that register pain, and they take the individual away from ordinary anxieties and restlessness. The opium addict is passive. Yet, men commonly think of the aggressive fiend who "goes crazy" under the influence of narcotics. It is the deprivation of the drug which makes the otherwise passive heroin addict aggressive. It is very specific goal-oriented behavior, and has nothing to do with the effect on the body while under the influence of heroin. Under the influence of cocaine, however, the individual may be highly stimulated to aggressive and hostile action that is a direct consequence of being "on" the drug, not "off" it.

Unfortunately, many people associate the effects of cocaine with the opiates, and this common misconception is a considerable stumbling block to a calm discussion of the narcotics problem. If men are convinced that narcotics usage ravages the body and mind, they are not likely even to entertain an argument about the possibilities of clinical treatment with that drug.[14]

Marijuana (Cannabis)

Marijuana is the term used in the United States for any part of the hemp plant, or any of its extracts, which produces psychic changes when chewed, smoked, or ingested. The technical name for the drug is *Cannabis*, and it was known to the Chinese five centuries before Christ. Because of the relative paucity of research with the drug, we do not know whether it is primarily a stimulant, a depressant, or both. It was used as an anesthetic in surgery two thousand years ago, but has long since been replaced by more powerful and dependable analgesics, such as the opiates. Marijuana has almost no medical use in Western societies, and is not used at all clinically in the United States.

Marijuana has both stimulant and depressant effects upon the central nervous system, and it is impossible to say which is the more important, or predominant, action. It varies with the individual, with his psychic condition at the time of exposure, and the kind of social environment in which he first uses. Becker has a lucid analysis of the importance of these kinds of factors in marijuana usage.[15] In this light, it is fascinating to note that in experimentation with animals, there is no strong evidence that marijuana significantly affects or alters the nervous system as either a sedative or hypnotic agent.[16]

Research on the physiological effects of marijuana usage has concluded that many of the side effects of the drug are very likely accounted for by the central excitation associated with the drug's use.[17] Nausea and diarrhea may result, as may urinary frequency, but they are hardly predictable. The primary reason for smoking marijuana seems to be the achievement of the "high," an exhilaration or euphoria that gives one a disconnected feeling from mundane life. Vivid and pleasing hallucinations are often a part of this, as is a loss of time and speed perceptions. A marijuana user once described his experience of driving an automobile while under the influence of the drug:

I kept saying to myself, slow down, slow down, you're going too fast, way too fast. I was sure that I must have been doing about 60–70 in a 25 m.p.h. zone, and while I had this feeling, some guy comes zooming past me on a bicycle.

Some of the noticeable effects that are reported include heightened sensitivity to touch and a feeling of floating in air, suspended by one's own will. The arms and legs feel a bit heavy, and occasionally the opposite of "high" may result: The individual may become withdrawn and depressed, or he may experience fear and feelings of persecution. The imagination is sometimes stimulated to novel directions; broken ideas and broken thoughts seem profound when they are experienced, and one feels the urge to express them.

Very commonly, there is no perceived effect the first time the drug is used. This corroborates Becker's thesis that learning in a social situation is critical to the nature of the effect produced.[18] Even though some reports indicated that there is a sexual quality to some of the more pleasant experiences, marijuana is evidently not an aphrodisiac. The unfounded public scare reports of the Federal Bureau of Narcotics in the late 1930s associated marijuana with rape and murder, and resulted in the passage of the 1937 federal legislation on the sale and purchase of marijuana.[19] The Bureau assailed the results of an empirical study published in 1945 which disputed these dangers of marijuana use. Just ten years later, the Bureau had changed its position remarkably when, in 1955, the main argument against marijuana was that it led to heroin.[20] This has remained the predominant argument against the drug ever since, a subject to be addressed momentarily.

With continued use, there may be some small degree of tolerance developed for the drug, but it is minimal, and disappears when the subject stops for even a short period. There is no physical dependence upon marijuana, and therefore the drug is not addicting. As for the psychological issue of habituation, a primary reference on the pharmacological effects states:

psychic dependence is not as prominent or compelling as in the case of morphine, alcohol, or perhaps even tobacco habituation. Marijuana habitues often voluntarily stop smoking for a time and do not necessarily experience undue disturbance or craving from deprivation. Organic (physiological) dependence, as evidenced by characteristic withdrawal symptoms, apparently does not develop.[21]

Despite the furor and clamor about it, marijuana is far less physically harmful than is alcohol. For an excellent analysis of the marijuana problem, to which this discussion is indebted, the reader should see Alfred Lindesmith's most recent work on addiction.[22] First of all, it is conclusive that sustained use of alcohol is destructive to cell life in the body. Further, alcohol has been known to produce psychosis, and clearly alters the mind with only moderate intake. Some men lose time perceptions, others are slowed in reaction time, and dexterity is drastically reduced.

Just as is alcohol, marijuana is capable of altering time perception, evoking a euphoria, and releasing inhibitions. As with alcohol, there are rare cases of psychotic episodes resulting from its use. It is not addicting, however, and alcohol demonstrably is.

The strongest thing that those who are against marijuana say about it is that it leads to heroin. In order to prove the point, they argue that heroin addicts used marijuana previous to heroin. Any freshman in an introductory course in methodology or logic can see the foolishness of this proof. We know almost nothing about the population of marijuana users who do not go on to heroin. They aren't talking, and the law enforcement agents and the social scientists have few access routes to them. The argument about marijuana leading to heroin has inadequacies ranging from glaring illogic to a complete inability to deal with critical empirical matters that would allow a reasonable statement about the relationship.

A good analogy would be the relationship between cancer and alcohol. Suppose a team of physicians discovered that a large percentage of persons with cancer drink alcohol regularly. They could not make any statement about a relationship until they found out whether others who drink alcohol regularly tend to develop this cancer. That is, they would at least have to look at a larger population of alcohol consumers than simply those in hospitals with cancer, in order to assert some relationship.[23] Yet that is precisely what people are doing when they say that marijuana leads to heroin. They are dealing only with a population of heroin users, not with the critical population of marijuana consumers. A physician would be ridiculed both within his profession and outside of it if he proposed to make some connection between alcohol and cancer on the basis of looking only at cancerous patients. Yet men are constantly making outrageous claims about the relationship of marijuana to heroin by looking only at heroin users.

A more empirical example is available. It has been for some time common to hear assertions that juvenile gangs in urban areas are breeding grounds for narcotics use. However, findings reported by Isador Chein and his associates from an intensive study of this problem in New York suggest that adolescent gangs actually are strong forces against narcotics usage.[24] Among several hundred gangs, a few will have narcotics use as a part of their activities. These gangs come to the attention of the law enforcement authorities, and then of the press. In fact, gangs typically act as a bulwark against drug use. They have their own systems of internal sanctions, even in high-heroin slum areas of New York.

The essential point is that, if all we know about are the narcotics gangs, then our ignorance expands into an unfounded generalization about narcotics and gangs. If all we know about are heroin addicts and their past association with marijuana, then our ignorance expands into an unfounded generalization about marijuana and heroin connections. Obviously, even a tentative exploratory statement of the relationship is dependent upon a great deal of knowledge about the population of marijuana smokers, not simply those whom the police and newspapers know as heroin addicts.

Were the consequences not so grave, it would almost be amusing to observe the illogic and inconsistency of the contemporary position that marijuana leads to heroin. For example, the very same Federal Narcotics Bureau that asserts this position also acknowledges that marijuana is widely used on college campuses without leading to heroin use:

Collegians on practically every major college campus in the country have used marijuana or other drugs—often with the approval of educators—the nation's narcotics chief has warned Congressmen. Commissioner of Narcotics Henry L. Giordano noted with alarm: "We have had a problem in just about every one of the major universities in the country with marijuana. Fortunately, you will not run into heroin. It is amphetamines, hallucinogenic drugs, tranquilizers and drugs of that sort."[25]

A young man or woman attending college in an urban area of the United States can locate and experiment with marijuana simply by repeatedly asserting in various campus circles that he is interested. The precise traffic is unknown, but there is good reason to believe that marijuana consumption in these areas is considerable. There are common estimates that between 15 and 25 per cent of American college students have experienced marijuana. If marijuana leads to heroin with even the most moderate frequency, there should be droves of heroin addicts in the colleges. The fact that there are almost none is facilely and somewhat erroneously explained on the grounds of heroin's unavailability. True enough, there is no heroin market at the colleges. However, the universities where marijuana is most likely a considerable issue are in or around New York City, Chicago, San Francisco, and Los Angeles. It just happens that there is heroin traffic in all these areas, and an enterprising college student (college students who smoke marijuana are likely to be enterprising) could surely make his way into the appropriate area, make "contact," and return with his heroin packet, physically expending himself no more than he would by going, say, to the right jazz night spot.

No firm statement can be made with authority. However, if a choice has to be made, one is on far safer empirical grounds in asserting that most marijuana users do not go on to heroin, based on extrapolation from the best evidence we have on the consumption patterns of both drugs. What sense is to be made, therefore, of continual assertions that marijuana's primary danger is that it is a path to heroin?

Meperidine (Demerol) and Methadone

Meperidine is a synthetic pain-killer used extensively for medical purposes. It is similar to morphine in that the analgesia may result in euphoria, though this is less likely. It is just the opposite to the barbiturates in that it will kill pain but not put the subject to sleep. Although meperidine is addicting, the withdrawal syndrome is less severe than

47

with morphine. The onset of withdrawal is faster, with muscle twitching and restlessness the more common symptoms. On the other hand, the drug is more debilitating than morphine, and the demerol addict can not manage as well as the opiate addict.

Since it can be used to stave off withdrawal for the opiate addict, he will resort to its use in the interim if available, although there is a strong preference for heroin or morphine.

Methadone is also a synthetic analgesic, and its pharmacological actions are almost identical to that of morphine. It is a very recently developed drug, marketed only since the Second World War. Because it effectively cancels out the withdrawal symptoms of heroin and morphine addiction, and because tolerance for (and physical dependence upon) methadone develop slower than with either of the natural opiates, it was originally greeted with enthusiastic claims as a non-addicting cure for the opiate addict. To this extent, its early history paralleled the claims originally made for heroin. The heroin addict begins to experience the beginning discomforts of withdrawal twelve to sixteen hours after the last injection, but the methadone addict may have as long as seventy-two hours of symptom-free time before withdrawal sets in. Further, the actual symptoms are milder and more prolonged than intense. After the third day of abstinence, the subject may complain of sleeplessness and anxiety, weakness, and possibly headaches. However, this is quite preferable to the extreme discomfort experienced from abstinence from the natural opiates. Wikler has suggested that the milder symptoms from the termination of methadone use are a result of the slower rate of excretion of the drug.[26] In any event, it is most effective and probably finds its most frequent use in the gradual withdrawal of the morphine or heroin addict back to drug-free equilibrium. Methadone may be administered in gradually diminishing doses to the opiate addict over a period of a week or more.

Lysergic Acid Diethylamide (LSD)

Quite unlike every other drug that has been mentioned, LSD is rarely if ever mislabelled a narcotic. Depending upon the bias of the persons expressing themselves on the subject, it is either an hallucinogen or a psychedelic drug. If one is skeptical, hostile, or reserved about LSD, the chances are that he will call it an hallucinogen. The drug often provokes remarkable imagery, and audial and touch perceptions that to "nonbelievers" are like hallucinations outside of the working social consensus of what is really out there. If, on the other hand, one is favorable about the effects of the drug, or is sympathetic to the goals of its users, is a cultist or "believer," then the chances are that he will call LSD a psychedelic drug. The reason is that the effects provoked are seen as mind-enriching experiences that expand the horizons of man's sensory perception and offer new dimensions to thought and imagination.

The effects of LSD vary greatly with the temperament of the subject, his attitude toward the impending experience, the social milieu, and the amount of the drug used. Nonetheless, there are some patterns in the effect of the drug which have emerged. At slight to moderate dosages, between 50 and 100 milligrams, LSD tends to produce minor changes in sensory perception. Some users report no effect, others have experiences that parallel the experiences of those with larger doses.

From 100 to 200 milligrams, the following changes are frequent. First, there is a general feeling of heaviness in the extremities. Not only is the ability to concentrate on select items enhanced, but there appears to be a tendency to fixate one's attention for long periods of time on a single object. (On mescaline, Huxley reports that he could look at his trouser leg for half an hour, fascinated by the intricate weave and the interplay of colors that normally escaped his perception.[27]) Others report how they can look at a vase, a painting, or a leaf for extended periods, marveling at certain internal relationships in the object for the first time. (One might speculate that the ability of the catatonic to "stare" for long periods could be a function of just such heightened sensory fixation. There is already disputed evidence concerning the alleged similarity of the blood chemistry of those who habitually hallucinate to changes in the blood of those who have used LSD.)

It is also common for the subject to see new patterns and movement in ceilings and walls. It is not clear whether colors appear brighter and more sensational because of the increased concentration facility, or whether the receptors are actually transformed. The pupils dilate considerably, and the LSD user finds bright lights very annoying. Auditory receptors are not themselves notably affected, but some report that a familiar piece of music takes on completely new meanings. A Brahms symphony may be experienced and understood for the first time in terms of a wholistic dimension, and contrapuntal structure is seen in a new relationship to the newly perceived whole.

One of the more interesting effects concerns the muting or destruction of the "normalizing" ability of the mind.[28] For example, we learn over time that the hands and feet and arms and legs of adult friends remain a constant size, and do not grow or shrink. So, when we look at a friend whose feet are propped on a table, facing us, we know that although it appears that his feet are much larger than his head, it is not really so. As Brunswik and others have demonstrated in experiments in transactional psychology, the precise image that strikes the retina would lead one to conclude that the object is constantly changing.[29] The viewer or observer achieves a conception of the perceived object as a constant object by normalizing. He surmises from a long history with the object, or similar objects, that it remains normal despite incongruities that continually would challenge him if he relied solely upon what strikes his retina.

To put it another way, if one is to believe one's eyes, he will conclude that his fist is larger than the Empire State Building because when he holds his fist up close to his face and measures it against the structure in the distance, that is what really registers on the retina. Obviously, under normal conditions, men do not conclude this. They normalize the incongruity received on the retina by reasoning and recall. Apparently, LSD affects this normalizing process. It has led some to conclude that LSD allows one to see the world as it really is, without the constraining elements of normalizing, which, it is argued, is a consequence partly of man's recall of sensory experience, but is partly a consequence of his learning relationships *a priori* from his culture. Those who argue against this position assert that the drug simply produces unreality perceptions or hallucinations. This, it seems, is the core of the discussion as to whether LSD is an hallucinogen or a psychedelic.

These two orientations to LSD also reflect a difference between an underlying fear and an underlying optimism about explorations into the psychic unknown, since what LSD does to the mind precisely is an unknown.[30] Tolerance for the drug is minimal, and recedes after a few days abstinence, and there is no physical dependence to worry about. Further, psychotic breaks occur with large doses of alcohol or barbiturates and whether they are more common than with LSD is an empirical matter about which we presently have no empirical answers.

Nonetheless, in 1966, LSD took its place alongside marijuana as an officially labeled "dangerous drug." As with marijuana, there is a stormy controversy over its distribution and use. Lindesmith correctly points to the civil and political issues in marijuana consumption, issues which concern the appropriate relationship between autonomy in the private and in the public areas of life, and which should be argued in the open air.[31]

These same issues are relevant to a discussion of LSD. The argument that we don't know enough about the actual physical effects of the drug or about its psychotherapeutic value is an interesting one: There are hundreds of drugs distributed every year that we don't know enough about, and that have serious and unfortunate effects on body tissues, spleens, livers, kidneys, and so on. There are so many thousand variables to deal with in prescribing the appropriate drug that no drug company could hope to control them all. It may be that certain foods combine with certain drugs in an unknown way. Unanticipated side effects that are quite harmful to the body frequently accompany marketed drugs. Some measure of this is unavoidable. A few of these drugs become sensational cases, such as chloromycetin and thalidomide.

Chloromycetin was an antibiotic advertised and marketed for household use for minor cuts and burns, but it turned out to be a cause of aplastic anemia, a fatal disease.[32] Thalidomide resulted in the side effect of deformed babies. These were simply two of the more sensational cases of drugs we don't know enough about. There are many more, but we can not know about all possible variations and combinations. The best that the Food and Drug Administration can do is to require certain tests that insure exhaustive trials before a drug is marketed.

However, with LSD, we are dealing with the mind and its thought process, not simply with bodily matters. Men in society become especially wary when drugs start altering the working consensus of perceptions of reality and truth. We know some things about the effect of LSD upon the mind. To some observers, these things are alarming, while to others, LSD is a remarkable opportunity for exploration.

Summary

At the beginning of the chapter, it was pointed out that the moral arguments concerning the use of drugs are based largely upon beliefs about the physiological effects of the drugs.

In the 1930s, the Federal Narcotics Bureau saw "danger" in the probability that marijuana would produce aggressive sex maniacs and murderers. When empirical research undercut the foundations of that argument, the big danger became the probability that the drug led to heroin consumption. The conditions and circumstances of marijuana use determine whether it will lead to heroin. The Bureau is now caught in an embarrassing contradiction because it publicly admits that marijuana does not lead to heroin on college campuses.

The strongest argument that is now used against marijuana is that it leads to heroin. That argument is full of logical contradictions and is not based upon any research on the population in question, namely, marijuana users. Indeed, the physiological effects of marijuana are such that Lindesmith is correct in asserting that its use can be treated as a morally private matter and regulated by the state in the same manner as other private consumption matters.[33]

The physiological effects of heroin, however, are such that the private consequences may be of significance in the public sphere. If that is the case, one may wish to implement legislation which addresses itself to the specific public concern for its use.

The legalization of heroin or morphine could not mean very much until the advocate of legalization spells out a detailed program of distribution and consumption. This could range all the way from a free and open market in the drug, the way aspirin is now handled, to a very tightly controlled prescription legalization. In the latter form, only men with specific problems or reasons could obtain the drug. In the former, mass consumption would be possible. Both, however, entail legalization, and for these reasons one need say more than a simple statement about being in favor of new laws.

With heroin, keeping the above qualifications in mind, it seems that the primary issues in its legalization and availability to a mass market might well revolve around the question of how the members of the society feel about the artificial, external lessening of suffering, both physical and psychic. (With heroin, the added dimension is the development of a dependence upon the drug, but then many men are dependent upon other drugs without other men raising a cry of moral outrage.) When the question is raised about whether we ought to alleviate suffering through pill and injection, one is driven back to a moral position.

One speaks from the point of view of a laymen in society and not as a social observer when he says that there are some kinds of psychological problems that people should work out on their own without a pill because that is good, productive of creativity, perhaps even a measure of greatness, and may add more insight into the meaning of life. That is my view, but I hasten to add that this is a moral issue in which my expertise can be no greater than that of any other member of the society in that I argue for what ought to be. The same is true for any "expert" in this field, whether he is a law enforcement agent, a pharmacological researcher, or a student of psychology.

We would do well to distinguish between the fear of the known (alcohol) and the fear of the unknown (LSD). We know that alcohol is a mind-transforming substance with systematic and observable consequences to the physical well-being of the individual. LSD may prove to be a drug that is dangerous to the mind and the body, but at this point in our knowledge, it is hardly consistent to label it a "dangerous mind-transforming drug" while the author of such statements composes that phrase over a dangerous mind-transforming cocktail.

LSD may be dangerous to society at another level, however. A social order is capable of being maintained through an operating consensus of reality. The real danger of LSD may prove to be that it destroys that operating consensus by provoking some to conclude that what they "really" perceive is different and unique from the perceptions of all others; or of even greater significance, perhaps ordinary, mundane life is seen as meaningless and total withdrawal and detachment from one's fellow man is the consequence.[34] LSD's advocates minimize this problem and emphasize the enriching experiences of new dimensions of thought and perception. In any event, it should be clear that whatever moral position one takes, *its basis is what is believed to be* the actual physical effects of the drug.

CHAPTER 3

Who Is a Drug Addict?

THERE IS MORE "EXPERT" CONSENSUS IN THE ANSWER TO the question: "Who *is* a drug addict?" than to similar questions concerning any other form of social deviation. It is odd therefore, that the answer is more physiological in nature than sociological. With juvenile delinquency, an argument can go on tediously as to which adolescents qualify to be placed in that category. Regional variation in the United States alone is so great that the delinquency of New York City is foreign to the juvenile authorities of Eugene, Oregon. Agreement about the drug addict is far more universal. There may be social consequences when one commits a delinquent act, but there are no systematic changes in the body. Yet, it is precisely the bodily changes that allow us to be so certain of accuracy in the identification of the addict. When deprived of the drug, his body loses physiological equilibrium. Thus, we physiologically detect the social deviant.

As DeRopp points out, the first step to an understanding of addiction is contained in the notion of physical dependence.[1] Individuals differ markedly in their physiological make-up. Just as a pint of beer may have a powerful effect upon one person and little effect upon another, given quantities of morphine will make some men more dependent than others. However, once any single individual becomes dependent, he needs morphine just like food, water, and salt:

The morphine or heroin addict is physically dependent on a continuous supply of the drug just as a normal man is dependent on a continuous supply of vitamins. If a normal man's vitamins are cut off he becomes sick. If a heroin addict's drug is cut off he also becomes sick. There is nothing mental or imaginary about this sickness. It is a physiochemical sickness. . . . After a certain amount of morphine or heroin has circulated in the body for a certain time it actually changes the chemistry of the body in such a way that normal function becomes impossible unless the drug is present. This is the chemical basis of physical dependence.[2]

More specifically, the opiate addict who can not obtain his necessary supply begins to experience withdrawal from the drug. This typically occurs about twelve to fourteen hours after the last drug injection. Withdrawal begins with a general feeling of queasiness, accompanied by simultaneous shivering and sweating. After a time, a water discharge begins in the eyes and the nose, a discharge which is felt as uncomfortably hot. It is at this point that the addict has the greatest potential of becoming both socially and psychologically dangerous. He knows that unless he can get another supply of drugs, things will get much, much worse. If he decides (or is forced) to undergo complete withdrawal, he will notice excessive yawning during this early period. This can be serious, with muscular and bone abnormalities developing about the jaw. After a few hours of quasi-sleep, he will awaken to find his flesh cold and covered with goose bumps, a condition which has inspired addicts to give to this, and to the whole experience, the name "cold turkey":

to add further to the addict's miseries his bowels begin to act with fantastic violence; great waves of contractions pass over the walls of the stomach, causing explosive vomiting, the vomit being frequently stained with blood. So extreme are the contractions of the intestines that the surface of the abdomen appears corrugated and knotted. . . . Constant symptoms start afresh within eight to twelve hours.[3]

For some addicts, this may continue for three days, tapering off in intensity after forty hours. For others, it may last for six days with a more gradual subsiding of ailments. A month may pass, however, before debilitating weakness, restlessness, and other problems begin to recede. Because of the conditions and developments discussed in the first chapter, the addict knows that his chances of getting help from a physician are very slim. He also knows that very likely he will be turned away from both private and public hospitals with ill-concealed annoyance and bureaucratic efficiency. All addicts don't make it back from the withdrawal sickness. Some die, and that too, is known. The decision to prostitute or steal is made easier.

However, it is *analytically* important to separate the notion of physical dependence from psychological craving and desire. Many things fall into the latter category, from cigarettes to pickled-beets on-a-warm-night. If one badly wants something of this nature, and the want is not satisfied, there is no evidence of a systematic change in the blood chemistry, no muscular constrictions, no retching, and the like. The whole area of psychosomatic illness is a cloudy one, and psychiatry has generated as much nonempirical speculation on the subject as empirical evidence. Even such problems as duodenal ulcers, long a popular example of the physical consequences of psychological stress, have come under closer critical scrutiny as to the nature of the relationship. There is now considerable and increasing confusion and ambiguity about the cause of ulcers.

Countless pastimes are habit-forming in the psychological sense, but if there is no physical dependence, it is simply misleading to talk of addiction. There are cases where specific individuals may develop a physical dependency on an item that is not typically addicting, but these cases are rare. The high rate of return to drugs by those who have gone through withdrawal makes this a very important problem for anyone trying to understand drug addiction. Perhaps 80 to 90 per cent of those who leave prisons and rehabilitation centers after several months or even years of being "clean" (free from drug use) return to the drug and become addicted again. This fact has led many to conclude that the psychological dimension is as important to drug addiction as the physical. But the recidivism rate is also high among certain kinds of criminal convicts, and only those using poetic license can talk of "addiction" to crime. If we cancel out the physical dependence element, we are left regarding recidivism to crime or cigarettes as a powerful social or psychological habit-formation.

The only way to settle an argument as to whether the psychic or physical dependence is the more critical element would be to find some drug which produced the approximate perceived effect of an opiate and yet was not physically addicting. If such a drug could be found, then psychological dependency could clearly be established independent of the physical dependency. For the heuristic purpose of clarifying the issues in the argument, we can come close enough with marijuana. It often has the overall effect of a depressant, but in the earlier stages is something of a stimulant. There is no physical dependence with marijuana. According to the definition to be used, marijuana is therefore not addicting. However, this would merely avoid by definition the critical theoretical question, if marijuana users have the same pattern and frequency of usage as heroin users. It is the case, empirically, that there is no similarity of usage. After the first experiences, frequency of intake with marijuana is far less than with heroin, even though the individual may continue taking marijuana over as long a time span as the opiate user.

This is an argument against the tendency to give equal weight to psychological proclivity and physical dependence. To be sure, a better case could be made if heroin and morphine could be produced in such a form that there were no physically addicting qualities, but until then, this is the best empirical approximation there is. If we concern ourselves only with psychological dependency, there is very strong evidence that cigarettes are more habit-forming than marijuana. The pattern of tobacco usage is much more frequent and conclusive. Admittedly, marijuana is much more expensive than ordinary cigarettes; but then heroin is very much more expensive than marijuana, and people get addicted to heroin and not to marijuana.

While the psychic and the physical are intertwined in drug use, analytically it is the best tactic to separate the two kinds of dependency, calling the former "habit-forming" and the latter "addicting." One has the cigarette habit, but the opium addiction. That is not to say that an individual can not also be psychologically *dependent* upon heroin. That is clearly possible. The first defining quality of an addict, then, is the definite physical dependence signaled by radical body changes in equilibrium once denied the drug.

Using this kind of conceptualization of the quality of being addicted, I therefore find myself in at least a terminological disagreement with another way of viewing addiction. I have reference to Alfred Lindesmith's earliest work on the subject, *Opiate Addiction*.[4] Lindesmith's book, which deservedly remains one of the most important statements on the study of the problem, incorporates the psychological dimension of cognition into the notion of addiction. Unless the subject *knows* that the withdrawal is caused by the drug, says Lindesmith, he is not addicted. It is clear that at the root of this definition is the attempt to explain subsequent behavior of the opiate user. If the user recognizes the connection, then he behaves in such a way as to alleviate withdrawal, and hence, according to Lindesmith, he is addicted. If he does not recognize the connection, then he can hardly be motivated to take more morphine since he has no reason to suspect that he will achieve comfort from it.

The primary difficulty with Lindesmith's definition is ironically a deficiency in the ability to categorize and explain behavioral alternatives which are called addiction. In what category does one place the actor who recognizes the tie-up between his withdrawal and opium ingestion, and yet refuses to take more opium?[5] For Lindesmith, such a person would not be addicted because, while recognition is said to be a necessary condition, sufficiency is satisfied only with subsequent patterned intake. But suppose we turn the clock back to 1899. The individual maintains himself on a large quantity of morphine over a long period of time because he thinks that the morphine is the cure for his "other" ailments of diarrhea, muscular constriction, and so on.[6] Is he addicted? By Lindesmith's definition of necessary and sufficient conditions, the answer is no. Yet Lindesmith acknowledges that large numbers of such people were indeed "addicted" in the late nineteenth century in just such circumstances. By using the definition of addiction totally in the sense of physical dependency we can circumvent the confusion in Lindesmith's necessary-sufficient psychological-behavioral dimension. The transformations in physiological equilibrium constitute both necessary and sufficient conditions for addiction. How the actor then responds behaviorally is an empirical question, not a logical or definitional one.

If the addicted person declines to take drugs, either selecting cold-turkey or symptomatic treatment, he may be said to have *broken* the addiction. (The physical dependence is broken, and therefore, the addiction is broken.) His possible subsequent return to narcotics use is then primarily a cognitive psychological and sociological issue of great complexity; but it is simply confusing to include in the definition of addiction the psychological dimensions of cognition and predisposition. That dimension is problematic and empirical, as is evidenced by the simple fact that some addicts do not return to narcotics use.

In sum, one is addicted when there is physical dependence to the degree that, due to the lack of the drug, the physiology of the body is thrown into the disequilibrium already described.

The Animal as an Addict

Men no longer impute to nonhumans such things as morality or an introspectively achieved personality. Therefore, the addiction of rats and monkeys should provide some interesting material for study, especially as it relates to parallel behavior patterns usually associated with personality and morality in humans. The rat addicted to morphine does not display personality in the sense of psychic integration, nor does he reflect an awareness of the concept of self. Nonetheless, he does have cognition. That is, there is every indication that he "connects" his addicted condition and alleviation to a specific substance (morphine syringe and not food) and "knows" that substance will bring him comfort from his withdrawal stress.

There have been many studies on addiction in animals. A few have tried to set up a situation for the animal which is as close as possible to the human physical situation. As early as 1940, experimentation with chimpanzees demonstrated pronounced morphine-seeking behavior on the part of the addicted animals.[7] Hungry and about to experience withdrawal, the addicted chimpanzees were presented with two boxes. One had food, the other had a hypodermic syringe which the chimpanzee associated with injection. The animals chose the latter box. However, when the chimpanzees were addicted but in equilibrium, they chose the food box.

An improved research model would have the animal taking his own drugs, as humans often do. Experiments in the last decade have included this. In one such design, rats were addicted to morphine water over ordinary water despite the extremely bitter taste of the former.[8] James Weeks reports an experiment that is even a better approximation to the physical setting in which humans take drugs.[9] Weeks used the technique of "operant conditioning" developed by B. F. Skinner and his associates. The rats are trained to expect a response, say food, from pressing on a pedal. Weeks used morphine injection as the response from pressing the pedal.

The apparatus directed an injection tube into the vein of the rat, and the equipment remained saddled upon him during the duration of the experiment. In the first stages, the rat was injected at periodic intervals by the experimenter until such time as physical dependence was established. Then the experimenter stopped initiating the injections, and the rat controlled the process by pressing or not pressing the morphine pedal. Weeks reports that after dependence was established:

the rat began to press the lever at regular intervals—about once every two hours, more or less, depending on the individual. Some of the rats went into a sort of trance immediately on receiving the injection, sometimes resting on the pedal for a minute. But as soon as they were prodded, they would move about normally without any evidence of the depressive effects of morphine.[10]

It is extremely relevant to this discussion to notice Weeks' caution:

One might be tempted to assume at this point that the rat "liked" the morphine, but it is important not to read human reactions and emotions into animals' behavior. Moreover, although human morphine addicts say they "like" the drug, even in humans it is not clear to what extent the drug is a positive pleasure and to what extent it simply brings relief from the rigors of abstinence. The fact is that the rat may not "like" the morphine at all but has learned that pressing the pedal stops punishment of early abstinence.[11]

In this experiment, the dosage was then gradually decreased, and then stopped completely, so that the rat got no morphine when he pressed the pedal.

When the dose was cut from 10 to 3.2 milligrams per kilogram, the rats responded more frequently in an effort to satisfy their habit. Then I disconnected the syringe completely. . . . There was an abrupt increase in the frequency of responses, which then diminished gradually as the rats developed a severe abstinence syndrome. They became nervous and agitated (but never vicious), breathed rapidly, tried to escape their cages and were sensitive to handling, as if being touched were painful. Gastrointestinal activity increased, the feces became soft and by the next morning the rats had suffered as much as 20 per cent loss in weight. They were very sick rats, but a single injection put an end to all their symptoms.[12]

In a second experiment, Weeks constructed the injection apparatus so that the rat had to press 10 times to achieve one morphine injection. Then, gradually, he increased the number of times the rat had to press the pedal to 20, and then to 32 times in order to get one injection. Finally, the ratio was increased to 50, then 75, 120, 180, 270, and 400 to 1 injection. As would be expected, the rats pressed the pedal more and more often, until finally they received an injection.

In 1964, preliminary reports from researchers indicated that addicted monkeys had kept themselves addicted by self-injection for a period of almost two years.[13] The conditions were the closest physical approximations yet to the human situation. If the simulation were precise enough, we would probably see nonaddicted affluent monkeys robbed by addicted monkeys so that they could get enough simulated money to trade to a simulated monkey peddler. Anthropomorphism is increasingly rare, and though experiments with animals may simulate behavior patterns of humans, it is impossible to impute to monkeys moral reflections upon the goodness or evil of prostituting the self, or self-censure for theft. What we can do with the animal research is to clearly separate the moral-personality issues from the physiological-impulse-cognitive issues. We can do this when we refuse to impute morality, personality integration, and self-reflection to animals.

Predisposition and the Separate Ingredients

The sociological issue is complicated, however, by this primarily physical designation of the "addict." Whether one is a respectable physician in a middle-sized midwestern town or whether one is a rhesus monkey in a pharmacologist's laboratory, one can be addicted to morphine and heroin. The notion of physical dependence guarantees that identification. This is not true of a concept like delinquency. As Cicourel has pointed out, the police may treat the exact same act perpetrated by one youth as delinquency, but regard it as idle and insignificant behavior when engaged in by another.[14] The criteria for classification are *social*.

When it is clear that *physical* dependence is the defining property of addiction, what sense can be made of the addiction problem with a social analysis? Just because the pattern of physical dependence is the same, does it make any sociological sense to lump together in a single category called "addicts" a nurse, a boxer, a succumbing aged person, an exploring working-class adolescent, a physician, a jazz musician, and a professional thief? Clearly, the social differences that exist among the myriad of persons who are addicted are so great that any sociological observer would have an impossible time speaking with confidence about the patterned social properties of addicts, which is one of his major tasks.

The first problem is therefore to clarify what it is that allows one group of addicted individuals to be singled out for differential treatment. It is a problem that the student of delinquency never need face. The characteristics associated with placing boys in this category are basically social in nature, and more easily lend themselves to sociological analysis.

Of the total population of persons who are addicted, only a certain type are known. Because some are unable to maintain themselves on the drug unless they supplement their income by illegal means, this part of the addict population becomes delinquent, and the delinquency is known. Most social and psychological theories of addiction (as well as the response to and treatment of the addict) are limited to this particular part of the known population, and the remainder of those addicted escape analysis. This study is different only in the self-conscious realization that its boundaries do not extend to the total addict population. Every statement about "addicts" should contain the explicit qualification: "socially known."

Who a drug addict is, then, is determined by the physical syndrome described; but only a select proportion of addicts (and that proportion is unknown) are commonly thought about when laymen and behavioral scientists conceive of and theorize about addicts. These are the relatively youthful lower- and working-class delinquents and criminals known to the police for their theft, prostitution, and drug sales. Extreme caution should be exercised in theorizing about the personality of the addict as it is affected by drug use. One should be very wary of assertions that connect "people who are addicted" to generic delinquent behavior, or to statements like "addicts are delinquent types," and therefore take drugs.

Despite all of this, there is now rather common acceptance in lay and professional circles that addicts are addicted primarily because of some psychological problem. The issues here are far more serious than that of a provincial interdisciplinary squabble between psychology, physiology, and sociology as to which discipline is more correct in explaining the drug problem. The way in which men choose to explain a moral issue is a prelude to directives for action or inaction. I am concerned here with the commonly held conception of the nature of addiction. This conception is primarily a psychological one, and this in turn becomes the basis of the way in which addicts are regarded and treated.

Using physical dependence as the sole criterion of addiction, it would be possible to exclude marijuana users, cocaine users, LSD users, peyote experimenters, and morning-glory seed eaters from further discussion of who is addicted. Correspondingly, included in the discussion would be barbiturate and amphetamine addicts, along with heroin and morphine addicts. As indicated, this presents considerable difficulty for an attempted clarification of some of the basic social and psychological issues in narcotics use. For example, barbiturate and morphine users are likely to have somewhat similar social characteristics, while heroin and ghetto marijuana users are likely to be more similar to each other than are heroin and suburban amphetamine users.

Whether a drug is addicting or not clearly has nothing to do with the social context of its use, nor does this information allow one to distinguish differing patterns of individual motivation in its use. Further, whether a drug is addicting tells nothing about the treatment afforded to the user. A barbiturate addict can usually get treatment at a public hospital, whereas a heroin addict usually can not. Amphetamines (addicting) are legally available on the market; LSD (nonaddicting) is not. Illegal use of addicting heroin and nonaddicting marijuana are both felonies, whereas illegal use of addicting amphetamines and nonaddicting peyote is usually only a misdemeanor. Sustained use and addiction to barbiturates is far more debilitating than sustained use and addiction to heroin, yet heroin is illegal in both medical and nonmedical circles. Even more ironic, the undesirable physiological side effects from legal barbiturates are far more numerous than the side effects from illegal heroin. The list could go on, but the point should be made that the addicting properties of a drug have little to do with the social response to its use.

It is essential to make clear that there are varying social interpretations of particular kinds of addiction. To be hooked on barbiturates means something quite different to the general population than to be hooked on heroin. Users of both drugs may be addicted, but they are accorded systematically differential treatment by the society. The psychological question is why certain personalities choose one addiction and not the other. The sociological question is why there is such a different social-legal response to the two physically addicting drugs. If the answers lie in the differing uses and effects of the drugs, there is little pressure to push further. That is not the case here. Since the most common interpretation of addiction is in terms of the choice of individual personalities, this problem will be explored before turning to the second question. As has been stated, addicts are commonly said to be psychologically inadequate and morally weak. *If one has observed that addicts are psychologically inadequate*, the question can be asked, *under what conditions might the observer be forced to conclude that this observation was wrong?* In other words, what would the observer have to see in order to conclude that addicts are not psychologically inadequate?

Once this question is posed realistically to those who hold this position, it is likely that the one piece of evidence they require is that they see the addict give up narcotics usage. To see a man remain on drugs while he simultaneously holds a middle-class occupation, refrains from theft or any illegal activity, is considerate, noble, kind, and just is all irrelevant for the purposes of characterizing the user as psychologically inadequate. The simple fact that he is "using" is regarded as sufficient evidence of inadequacy. This reasoning is circular, tautological, or simply "true" by assertion and definition. Sustained drug usage or addiction is therein defined as the manifestation of psychological inadequacy. "If a human uses drugs, he is psychologically inadequate!" Once such a definition is made, it can never be proven wrong. It follows that all we need to know is whether the person is addicted, and if he is, we know that his personality is deficient. However, if the question is left open to empirical investigation, assumptions we so often take for granted become problematic. For example, if the question is raised as to what it means to be psychologically inadequate (without tying it to drug addiction) the issue usually rests empirically with such problems as "an individual who has a hard time coping 'normally' with the world."[15] However, it is known that if the addict is getting his supply of heroin, he can cope with the world in such a way that the observer regards him as normal.[16] There are addicts with sufficient income to supply their habit without engaging in other illegal activity. This means that if one is economically or financially adequate, one can maintain the appearances of psychological adequacy in coping with the world, and the observer can not detect the difference, which is not true for the alcoholic. If, despite this, one insists that drug usage itself demonstrates psychological inadequacy, it is simply a matter of returning to a definition which equates the two.

The question has significance for the idea of the "decision" to become an addict. Clearly, if one has an inadequate personality, this may explain the drive or the compulsion to narcotics. Conversely, if one has an adequate personality, by the definition of those who take this position, he will not use drugs.

The sociological analysis of the question, "Who *is* a drug addict" revolves around the social identity of the addicted individual. Only when he becomes socially visible is he a problem, since it is only then that he can obtain differential treatment. In the public sphere, most men are treated according to that segmentalized aspect of the person that is most relevant. For example, at a cocktail party the guests are more concerned with sexual attractiveness and sociability than with the demonstration of athletic skill. At other times, the same persons may be more concerned with formal education or income or religion.

Men single out some element of the individual for the purpose of addressing that element more fully. There is a common awareness of this, and usually an acknowledgment that there are many other elements that might also be acknowledged and emphasized. However, there are some categories that have an unusually strong ability to influence the judgment of a total person. These categories are so strong that men often can not see any other part of the individual as independent of it. Such is the case with moral categories, and drug addiction has come to be just such a category in the twentieth century. A moral category provides more than a partial identity for the person so characterized.[17] It is more than simply a way of emphasizing and addressing an individual in particular circumstances and situations. The moral category infuses every situation; it permeates the whole character of the individual and becomes his *total identity*.[18]

Prostitution is one example of a moral category. It carries with it the power of coloring every other way in which a woman might be regarded. As soon as it is known that a female is a prostitute, she is prevented from being partially identified in some other way. The movie *Never on Sunday* was resented and banned in many parts of the United States not just because it portrayed a prostitute, but because the prostitute possessed warmth and compassion, and her morality in every other sphere was quite acceptable if not admirable to Americans. The strongest argument brought against the movie was that it portrayed prostitution in a favorable way. There was no specific scene of a sexual nature that needed to be censored, so the major issue concerned the appropriate way of portraying the prostitute. The quality of the total person was thereby infused with being a prostitute, so that one should not be able to conceive of "such a woman" in any way other than that tied to sexual morality, or immorality, and thus to an immoral person.

The drug addict is presently in the same situation: his being a drug addict is the important category that permeates his total identity. Just as with the prostitute, when the discovery is made that an individual is a drug addict, the typical response is that, "I now know what there is to be known about that person." The essential property of the total identity is that it allows the observer to explain the behavior of the person in terms of that identity. The drug addict is treated as morally capable of theft because he is a drug addict. That he also might be capable of a stable middle-class family life is jarring to the notion of a total identity, and so that is rejected out of hand.

As was pointed out in Chapter 1, simply to be known as an addict is tantamount to being considered a criminal. In order to be a criminal in Western society, the individual must have the intent to commit the criminal act. If there is a pathological state of the mind which calls into question the responsibility of the offender, there can be no crime. The fact that addiction is now conceived primarily in moral terms, with moral consensus directed toward criminal punishment, means that Americans find themselves in a logical bind on this issue. On the one hand, they are forced to impute to the addict criminal intent with its accompanying conscious, rational, willful motivation to commit the act. On the other hand, there seems to be no way for us to understand the willful intent to take drugs (and subsequent addiction) without imputing pathology of personality, or perhaps even mental illness to the individual.

One way to get out of this bind and escape the central issue is to reject the notion of knowledgeability, and to impute naïvete to the unsuspecting preaddict. Such interpretations rest explanations on the malicious peddler who lures the young with free marijuana and heroin, only to later ensnare them. Federal law allows the death penalty for an adult peddler who sells to a person below the age of eighteen. Another path of explanation is to assume that addicts are morally depraved. But being morally depraved and being stupid are quite different, and even the morally depraved (who are knowledgeable, willful, and responsible for their actions) should have sense enough not to become addicted to narcotics. The list of possible descriptions could go on, ranging from being culturally deprived to evil, but the central confusion remains.

On the *"Decision"* to Become a Drug Addict

In the minds of those who have never tried narcotics, there is a great puzzle over the question of how one becomes addicted in the first place. How is it possible, it is asked over and over again, that a man who is individually responsible for his actions could become addicted? Men make decisions on such matters if they are responsible. It is difficult to imagine that at some turning point in his life, the nonaddict made the willful decision to become an addict. That is incomprehensible, and we are left fumbling around for some explanation of the psychic state that produces the desire for drugs. Accordingly, the reigning interpretation of addiction is a psychological one. The language of this interpretation refers to the inadequacy of the personality; the choice is made either from a self-conscious realization and a decision to flee reality, or from a deeply subconscious unrealized motivation.

This point of view acknowledges that social and cultural factors are important at some level, but is willing to place the burden of interpretation upon how the individual is able to cope with these factors. "If one copes successfully, he *decides* to become a nonaddicted law-abiding citizen. If he is unable to cope, he *decides* to become addicted."

The evidence that this point of view marshals seems incontrovertible, namely, the existence of addicts. The trouble with this argument is the same as that with any argument that documents its case by pointing to the existence of men in various categories as evidence for the theory of how they got there. For example, those who are convinced that the poor are poor because they lack motivation or because they are psychologically inadequate can always find "sufficient evidence" for this position simply by citing the existence of poor people.

What exists can always be explained on the grounds that it exists, and then any explanation will do. It can be said just as authoritatively that addicts or the poor are possessed by devils.

We should instead raise the question as to whether men do have the conscious intent to become addicts. For those incarcerated at the California Rehabilitation Center, the answer seems to be negative, as we shall see in later chapters. There is a pattern to the responses which the inmates gave concerning their first contact with narcotics. Almost all of them knew before they ever took heroin that it was addicting. The distribution of knowledge on this critical point is presumably widespread. Almost everyone knows about the addicting potential of heroin, and so it is impossible to argue that men are unsuspecting and ignorant about the effects of the drug and are lured into it by nefarious dope peddlers who speak of it as harmless candy and a one-time shot.

Second, addicts seem to know that heroin in overdose is lethal. This is a more important piece of knowledge than appears at first glance. The strength of any particular purchase of heroin is unknown to the purchaser. It may be weakened many times over before it finally reaches the consumer. The white, powdery substance that he takes may be a certain strength, or it may be four times that strength. Only a chemist with the appropriate measuring instrument could determine the nature of the heroin. Thus it happens that when a particular shipment is not weakened as much as usual one may inject a lethal dose of heroin. This is commonly known even before the first encounter.

Further, the overwhelming majority know before their first experiences with narcotics what the legal consequences of being caught would be. Ignorance cannot possibly be used to explain the first plunge into drug use. The fact that the important and relevant information about the problem is so universally distributed simply reinforces the notion of a responsible man making a decision to become an addict.

The individual user never believes he himself will become addicted. Perhaps we see here the same mechanism that allows a soldier on a battlefield to surge forward and continue fighting while he sees soldiers around him dying from wounds. One can be firmly set in the belief that the self is inviolable, unique, and not subject to suffering, accident, or death. It is unlikely that traditional ground wars could be fought unless men believed that they personally would not die on the battlefield.

A less appropriate but more commonly appreciable analogue is the automobile driver who takes chances on the highway that the observing passenger regards as foolish. But the observing passenger may take the same kind of chances himself when he drives because he believes that the self is indestructible.

This, I think, is the first ingredient that makes addiction possible for those knowledgeable about the legal, moral, and addicting aspects of narcotic usage. It is important to keep in mind that this quality is a common one. Most possess the firm belief that "Nothing like that could happen to me."

Even at this point in the discussion, the "decision" to become an addict is very questionable. One no more decides to become an addict than one decides to die on the battlefield, or for that matter, decides to have a serious accident on the highway. However, there are more particular and detailed problems in the physiology of addiction which illuminate the question of a conscious decision.

As with alcohol, the amount of drugs that it takes to affect the mind varies with the individual. At first contact, some men are affected by one glass of wine and some are unaffected by four. Some are in euphoria on a quarter of a grain of heroin, and some are only mildly affected by twice the amount. Nonetheless, it is possible to assert that most men feel the effects of their first experience with an opium derivative. Those who know the feeling produced by morphine and heroin say that they can no more describe the sensation to the uninitiated than they can describe sound to those born deaf. "To someone who has never tasted a pear, try and describe the taste of a pear." With these drugs, most describe this first experience as rather pleasant, at the least. The body's systems function in a state of balance and equilibrium. When heroin or morphine is injected, the equilibrium is disturbed in such a way that the autonomic nerve centers compensate for its effect with depressant mechanisms. It is this depressant effect which is so pleasurable, in that the subject is no longer troubled by physical pain or even his worldly problems. Physically, the immediate response after injection is usually a tingling sensation in the abdomen, a flushing of the face, and then the pleasant detachment, if not euphoria.

The effects last for about four hours, during which time the user may drift into somnolence, wake momentarily, and drift back again, having constant daydreams. The observer, however, would have a difficult time saying definitely whether one was under the influence or not. A man under the influence may move a bit slower than usual, but not so much as to be noticeable to the unsuspecting observer.

After the first experience wears off, there may be a very slight headache, or slight nausea, but it soon goes away. For the user, it is a small price to pay for the sensation derived from the drug. Still, one may take it or leave it. Many never take it a second time. Many try it again after some days, or perhaps weeks. The "reasons" for the second time are often as normal and social as the first. The physiological response of the organism is the same. Once the drug ceases to be effective, the slight nausea and slight headache may reappear, but this is small discomfort. It is hardly more than the ordinary, mild annoyances that men experience in everyday life. At this point in his career as a user, the individual usually makes a connection between discomfort and the use of the drug. He knows that the nausea results from the drug. In a sense, this knowledge leads him to a conclusion that sends him further along the road to addiction. He reasons to himself that his own body is such that it responds in this way to narcotics. In a word, he makes the erroneous conclusion that the slight nausea and slight headache are his own version of withdrawal.

The user may continue for several months in this part of the syndrome, until finally he understands that he must increase the strength of the dosage to get the same kick that he got originally with a smaller dosage. This is somewhat alarming, but once again, he "knows" what his physiological response to narcotics will be. The stronger dose produces the desired effect, and the penalty is merely a headache and nausea. Because there has been a history of this response, it is treated lightly. The old cliché about the hot tub of water getting hotter with the bather oblivious to the degree of increased heat is appropriate.

After a few more months, the nausea may have progressed to throwing up, and the headache may be intensified and accompanied by fever. There are now hot flashes and cold chills. Diarrhea is common. When the user realizes that he can get quick relief from these discomforts by taking more narcotics, and does so, he is psychologically habituated. This means that he can no longer "take it or leave it," and the willful character of action is suspended. Not a single person, addict or nonaddict, desires a state of affairs where he is at the mercy of an exorbitant market to maintain his body at equilibrium. No one intends or desires this kind of addiction.

Let us turn now to the social situation of the individual when he uses narcotics for the first time. It is rarely, if ever, that a peddler introduces the user to drugs. According to data to be reported later, about two thirds of the time it is a friend who is the first source of contact. The first venture is usually an unplanned affair, where one happens to be in the right place at the right time. A relatively small proportion of addicts made a conscious plan to go out and shoot heroin or smoke marijuana on a given night in the future, or even "later tonight." This description of the spontaneous and communal character of the first contact with narcotics is at odds with the most popular interpretations of the road to addiction. We usually hear that one takes drugs in a psychologically despondent state, fleeing from anxiety and reality, and compensating for an inability to cope with the world.

Addicts report no depressed state when they decide to try dope. To the contrary, they typically report how normal the situation was. A friend, or group of friends, or sometimes a sexual partner knows about the availability, and *on the spur of the moment* (with long-range planning or despondency almost unheard of), they go off with them and find the first experience pleasant.

There is an important difference between males and females in drug usage in general, and on first contact in particular. (As in almost every arena of reported criminal activity, males outnumber females by a ratio of at least 8 to 1).[19] When a man first tries dope, he is likely to try it in a group. Later on in his career, he may be one of the minority users who shifts over and becomes a loner. That is, he may move into a class of addicts that take the drug in complete solitude. Unlike the more typical communal addict who shoots dope with his buddies in a social club atmosphere, the solitary addict shoots a whole load of heroin all at one time, and leaves this world. Although he is atypical, he is the stereotype. He is the more serious addict in several ways. His withdrawal will be more severe, and his need will be more desperate for a single, strong shot of relief. Accordingly, he will be more adventuresome and dangerous in trying to get that relief. The social addict takes dope in smaller quantities at several points, trying to savor both the physiological transformations and the community in which it occurs. Whereas the loner may shoot a half a grain of heroin all at once, the social addict will divide that same half grain into six separate shots within the space of four hours.

This is the male pattern, and it differs significantly from the conditions and manners of female usage. Whereas a friend usually initiates the male, it is usually the lover who initiates the female into narcotics. It can be the husband, the boyfriend, or sometimes the homosexual partner, but it is usually someone with whom the female has an intense emotional relationship. Many women use not because they independently desire the drug, but so that they can please the other person.

The male user is often wary about the possibility that his female acquaintance who does not use will turn him in, or leave him because he uses. Also, he may wish genuinely to share the experience with someone who is close to him. In either case, the motivation is strong to draw the female into the relationship more tightly by getting her to use.

Although women are the small minority of addicts they are among the few who can come even close to the designation of decision-makers on the question of addiction. They are confronted with a choice of action that is usually very explicit. The alternatives are weighed beforehand. Does one risk the loss of the other by refusing to use, or does one solidify the relationship further by engaging in the communal act? Many decide against narcotics when the problem is put in these terms. A few decide to take the drug in a planned, rational frame of mind. However, it is stretching the interpretation to conclude that these women therefore decided upon addiction. Just as with the battlefield soldier and the male preaddict, she concludes that she is an exception, and that she will be able to use and escape addiction. Probably the most common conception of the decision to live a life on drugs is that, after the first experience, the preaddict so likes the feeling that he decides that this is what he wants. This is a reasonable conjecture of what most Americans believe, since they treat marijuana with almost the same horror as they treat opiates, despite the fact that many know that marijuana is not addicting. The great fear is that one will try harmless marijuana and like it so much that the mind and desire will graduate to the more serious heroin.

High-school students are continually warned about marijuana as the first step on the road to addiction. A federal law passed within this decade makes possession of marijuana a crime equal to the illegal sale and distribution of an opiate derivative. Law enforcement officials claim that they never enforce this law on users, but only on sellers of marijuana. Arrests for marijuana usage are not as common as they might be, but the law is on the books, and it specifies equal treatment. This being the case, it would seem that the "decision" to take marijuana is as much of a decision as that concerning heroin. It is clear, however, that marijuana usage far exceeds heroin usage in this country. Some of the supply lines for marijuana feed into the middle-class college communities. Almost every heroin addict has had some experience with marijuana, but the reverse is far from true.

Summary

Not all persons physically dependent upon drugs are known, either to the law enforcement agents or to the small circle of friends around them. Those who are known are likely to be a certain social type, and theories of addiction are thus limited to this specific type. The layman's and the behavioral scientist's view is limited to the kind of addict who has insufficient funds to maintain himself on a supply of drugs without engaging in flagrant public violations of the law. The addict who is criminally delinquent in ways other than simply using drugs is the only addict focused upon in theory and speculation. Because of his association with criminal deviance, there has been a general tendency to regard this addict as "the addict," with his problem as an aberration of personality and morality. As was demonstrated in Chapter I, this is historical shortsightedness of some magnitude. The contemporary known addict is infused with the total identity of an immoral person with an inadequate personality. The interpretation of reasons for immoral behavior is also a directive as to what should be done to the deviant. Americans have now concluded that the way to treat the addict is as an individual with a personality problem curable by techniques that get at the individual psyche. Americans have reified the idea of who an addict *is*, to the point where they can not entertain other alternatives as to who the addict might be. We have ignored the fact that the stereotyped addict comes from a specific and delimited stereotyped social context. But therein may lie an alternative conceptualization of the addict and of the deviant, and thus, as well, an alternative directive for a solution to the current problems, both theoretical and practical.

PART II

Theoretical considerations

CHAPTER 4

Analytic and Empirical Approaches to the Study of Morality

W

E TURN NOW MORE SYSTEMATICALLY TO THE
question of what is variously meant by the term "morality." Two complementary strategies will be used.

The first strategy is the identification and description
of the substance of common-sense theorizing. We look at what people
describe as "moral," attempt to analyze the processes of choice and
rejection, and focus observations upon what is done once behavior is
so characterized. The observer can never look simply at the behavior to
find its moral character revealed. Cheating, lying, stealing, adultery,
and even premeditated murder are conditionally and situationally
identified and approved. Honesty, fidelity, and virtue are situationally
disapproved. Though we must look at the context in order to under-

stand when and why morals are invoked, this is specifically contrary to common-sense theorizing and usage of the term. Morals come down as categorical directives, not infinitely qualified guidelines. Yet, when the very rich steal money, it can not be handled with the same "moral" force as when the poor steal, partly because it makes less "sense." It is this "making sense of" action that provides behavior with its moral or immoral categorization, not the pilfering of the till. (I have already emphasized that it is the "making sense" of heroin, use that made it moral in 1900 but immoral in 1969.) History and logic reveal that there is nothing intrinsically moral or immoral about injecting an opiate into the human body. Yet, many have come to believe that there is, and this problem has been one of the primary concerns of the other nine chapters.

A second strategy involves the observer in the task of separating the foundation of common-sense theorizing about morality from the internal logic or process of that theorizing.

One of the enduring credits of Parsons' work for social science research has been the greater recognition of the necessity of clearly specifying the unit of analysis. After Parsons and others, the analytic unit in the behavioral sciences could be: (1) the individual [personality system]; (2) the community or group [social system]; or (3) the larger culture [cultural system].[1]

The approach to the study of any problem will vary in relation to which of these three units is the intended subject. This is demonstrably true with the study of "morality," where there are three correspondingly different levels of moral issues that might be investigated. It is imperative that they be kept separate in order to avoid conceptual confusion.

The first level focuses upon the individual. In reference to morality, the subject matter pertains to how the *individual* manages a set of principles of behavior. The psychologist of personality might investigate the consequences of the management problem for psychic integration or disintegration. Even though he may take into account the external pressures from the social system to conform, the psychologist's focus is upon the personality as a unit. The pacifist or conscientious objector in a community that supports war and institutionalized killing faces at least the internal moral crisis that results from intro-spection about the meaning of his own behavior in that community. To be sure, there are consequences to his actions that may be viewed by a sociologist as social or communal in nature. If, for example, he burns his draft card or his country's flag, the symbolic gesture may enrage his fellows to the point where they impose severe sanctions. Or, from an anthropological perspective, an observer might raise the question as to why reports of the symbolic gesture enrages a community more than reports of actual human slaughter. (The same men who become emotionally upset at the sight of long hair on males may sit passively at the evening television news reports that "hundreds were killed this week in bombing raids." Whether the bomber was crew-cut or long-haired takes on greater "moral" proportions than his bomb dropping.) However, if it is kept firmly in mind that the unit of analysis is the individual, then the problem does not get twisted into issues that are primarily communal or cultural. Where no reference point of social or cultural values is introduced, the individual's morality concerns the relationships between his own behavior and his beliefs. One difficulty, of course, is that we typically avoid saying that an individual is be-having "morally" when his principles are contrary to our own. We can applaud as a moral man the German of 1938 who stood firmly against the National Socialists. He is said to be "true to his principles, possessed of integrity," and so on. But we have difficulty applauding the contemporary Nazi who "stands up for his beliefs" in a hostile community. Men typically shift the level of their moral perspective to coincide with their own principles. That is, when someone behaves contrary to a community in a manner that we approve, we say that he has integrity and is moral. However, when his principles differ from our own, we usually shift ground and talk about a higher or communal morality which transcends that of individuals, and sharply criticize the individual who holds to "his own principles". In common-sense theorizing, at one point in time it is whether a man is true to his "own"[2] beliefs that makes him "moral," while at another it is the degree to which he subscribes to "transcendent" values that makes him "moral." For the observer, confusion is eliminated by keeping the units distinct and separate.

In the following statement by an American draft card burner, there is a clear illustration of the difficulties of viewing individual action in terms of principles that may be seen either as (1) his "own,"[3] (2) transcendent cultural principles, or perhaps (3) a coalescence of the two. In any case, the subject below is quite aware that his actions may offend the current community moral views.

Those of us who join today in burning our draft cards will be called traitors by some, Communists by others, and "misguided" by almost everyone, including those good friends of ours in the liberal community who agree with our opposition to the war in Vietnam. Yet I hope that some small part of what motivates us may be communicated to our fellow citizens, even in this time of tragedy and of war hysteria.

And what I most want to communicate is that by burning my draft card I am trying to live by the values this nation has taught me. I am trying in the clearest way I can see, to act as a responsible American citizen, true to the deepest and best traditions of this nation of which I am so deeply a part.

Here is the clear act of invoking "the larger or cultural morality" to counter charges that the act of burning the draft card is immoral, because people in the "local" community invoke a provincial communal morality. He begins his case by identifying his actions with "the deepest and best traditions of this nation."

My act is not directed against the American people but against the present Administration. It is the government which would subvert our traditions. As an American citizen I have no choice but to express my opposition to that government. If I failed to do so then I should have failed my duty as a citizen.

He now shifts the grounds of moral judgment to the level of the individual as the unit actor, and asserts that the only moral action for the individual is that which is consistent with the individual's own beliefs.

The present government has openly violated the Charter of the United Nations both in Vietnam and in the Dominican Republic. It has openly, repeatedly, and flagrantly violated the Geneva Accords by its actions in Vietnam. It has openly and ruthlessly violated solemn international treaties with the states of Latin America by its military intervention in the Dominican Republic. There is no responsible man today in the American government who would not admit, in private, the truth of these charges, no matter how strongly he might deny them in public. Our only defense is that our national interests were involved. Such a defense carries us back to the law of the jungle, moving us away from a responsible world community.

The present government has repeatedly distorted the facts about Vietnam in its statements to the American people. The present government violates the values of compassion and decency by its barbaric military campaigns against the civilian population in Vietnam.

As a child in church and in public school I was taught that torture is wrong, that lying is wrong, that wanton violence is wrong. I was taught that aggression is wrong. I was taught that Germans committed a sin by bombing the open city of Rotterdam early in World War II. I believed what I was taught. I believe that I learned values that have merit and by which I seek to live. What can I do now about a government that condones torture, engages in lying, is proud of its violence and is without any trace of remorse for its aggression? As an American I must oppose that government even if it is my own. President Johnson has destroyed solemn treaties. In response I destroy this visible link with this government—my draft card. And by this response I say that the government in Washington which orders the dropping of napalm on villages in South Vietnam is now my enemy, and the enemy also of every American who has not forgotten the religious and moral values he was taught as a child.

Here is the invocation of "transcendant morality" again, combined now with the consistency of individual belief and action. The outcome is termed "moral action" on two grounds. First, the individual is being true to what he believes. Second, he is acting in accord with those cultural values he was taught "as a child in church and in public school."

Second, I act because the values I was taught are not merely American values, but universal values, valid for all times and places. If I condemn the Communists for their murderous actions in Hungary in 1956—and I did condemn them for that act—can I exempt my own government for its even more wanton actions in Vietnam? If I applaud those German troops who refused to obey the orders of Hitler to fire upon civilians, can I do less than to appplaud those American pilots who increasingly doubt that it is right to carry out orders to bomb villages which contain only civilians?

More than simply resting his case on the transcendency of cultural values in Western Civilizations, however, he now sees an identity of his beliefs and *universals*. It is no longer a matter of simply being consistent in belief and action, it is simultaneously a direct responsiveness to timeless morality.

The blind and foolish men cry "my country right or wrong" and mistake that cry for patriotism. But such men do America a great injustice. Patriotism is not measured by blind loyalty to the State, but by determined loyalty to values that transcend even the State. America was not built by conformists—by men of the timid heart, like J. Edgar Hoover, who see treason in dissent, and who secretly fear the turbulence of freedom and the workings of democracy. These were not the men who rebelled against English rule. Our freedom was created for us by men with the courage to dissent, to rebel, to act as individuals. Not a single one of our freedoms was won by conformity to the will of the majority or by loyalty to the State. Every freedom we have—religious freedom, political freedom, the freedom to speak and to write and to assemble—was a freedom won by solitary men or small groups of men who risked their own comfort and in some cases their own lives to oppose the majority when they felt the majority was wrong, or to oppose the State when they felt the State was wrong.

It is to keep faith with these men who won our freedom that I burn my card. We are not the traitors. The traitors are those who preached peace, who were elected on a platform of peace, and who then made war. They are the ones who weaken the democratic process by making a mockery of it. They are the ones who would cruelly waste American lives and Vietnamese lives solely in order to save face, and to avoid admitting their Asian policy was wrong to begin with. In the years to come, long after American troops have been withdrawn from Vietnam and long after the current hysteria has died away, historians will wonder why the American people allowed Johnson to remain in office so long without impeaching him. They will wonder why the Senators and Congressmen were silent when the President was so clearly wrong, both morally and politically. And, in that day to come, the honor of America in these sad hours will not prove to have been defended by the J. Edgar Hoovers or the William Buckleys in our midst. The honor of America will rest upon those of us who resisted what was evil in order that our own sense of justice could survive, and in order that our nation would not be entirely dishonored by silence. It is a sad thing that a man must risk his freedom in order to defend it, and I wish I did not feel the risk was necessary. But, in taking this risk, I do so not as a brave man, which I am not, but as an American who knows that he can only keep faith with his country by keeping faith with himself.

Therefore we stand firm in our resistance to this government in order to be loyal both to those moral and religious values which transcend all national boundaries, and loyal also to this culture, this nation of peoples, this vast land, America.[4]

Americans who read this statement will disagree among themselves as to whether the writer's action is moral or not and their disagreement will only in moderate degrees reflect the extent of their support of the United States role in the Vietnam war. The disagreement about the war is to be understood in terms of the different political commitments, but the disagreement as to whether the writer acted morally is a consequence of confused and inconsistent usage of the concept of morality. A close examination of the statement reveals that the author conceives of his action as an individual statement of sympathy with what he terms the larger and enduring values of his country. (He is very aware that his action will violate the contemporary community's view of moral actions. Indeed he elects to perform his dramatic deed in order to dramatize the difference between his views and the community's.)

At the individual level of action in terms of beliefs, the actor must be described as moral. His violation of the *contemporary consensus* of moral action means that at the community level, his critics can accuse him of immorality. These first two levels are rather easy to address empirically. However, the cultural level is more the subject of debate. In the above example, both the individual and his community claim to be in sympathy with the cultural values. It is not the purpose here to resolve that issue, but rather to point out the sources of confusion over the charge of "immorality" and to illustrate that the characterization of moral action can be tapped empirically so long as the empirical referents said to reflect moral action are kept distinct.

When the question is asked, "Is it moral action?" a reasonable answer cannot be given unless or until the question itself is clarified; moral vis-à-vis what behavioral referents said to reflect the action?

If the question is intended to get at whether or not the individual subscribes to the existing community morality, a quite different answer can be expected than if it concerns only the principles of the individual. Consenting adult homosexuals in the United States may clearly subscribe to all of their own principles of moral conduct, yet be treated as immoral in a community of heterosexuals.

At the first level, an investigation of individual morality might focus upon psychological issues of how the personality copes with some degree of disjunction between the morality of the self and the morality of the community.

The second level moral question to be investigated by behavioral science concerns the community (or social system) moral order. Communities are held together partly by pressures external to actors, partly by a set of beliefs held in common. Sociologists and anthropologists are generally agreed that a sharing of values and beliefs are important elements in the maintenance of community. What disagreement there is revolves around the minimal conditions and the manner of sharing. Even those societies which Durkheim describes as "functionally interdependent" because of well-developed specialization are bound by common orientations towards the world of (specialized) objects.[5] As every social philosopher and theoritician of social order has noted in some form, men grow up in communities learning what is appropriate and inappropriate behavior, then become emotionally committed to those things considered most appropriate.

Introductory textbooks in sociology often go back to the writing of William Grahm Sumner for a description of mores and folkways. For Sumner mores are rules about which community members feel strongly enough to punish severely their violators. Folkways, on the other hand, are simply customs that are enforced, but are not "moral in their implications." Presumably, the empirical test or criterion of how strongly people feel in a given area is the degree to which they are willing to impose punishments. The matter of social system morality quickly gets translated into the behavior of men in the community toward various public or publicly known violations of community rules. There is no need to remain abstract in a discussion of morality. More clearly than in many areas of sociological discourse, the theoretical statement of the concept is directly tied to the empirical issue.

The third and final level of an analytic approach to the study of morality is wholistic. The primary concern is not how the community sanctions and maintains its own moral order. Instead, the focus is upon those elements that permeate a whole culture and to which members generally subscribe in order to persist in that culture.

Here the meaning of morals comes very close to the meaning of values, and if isolated empirically it must be done in the same manner. It is a primary value of an egalitarian democratic culture to state that one man should not be born to a fixed higher social position (such as

nobleman) than any other man. That is more than a communal statement of appropriate behavior, though it can also be regarded as a
moral directive. The wholistic analytic approach to the study of
morality asks "cultural" questions. For example, how the France of
1785 was to survive as a culture was an issue which brought forth moral
questions greater than those relevant to single French communities.[6]
The political issue of a monarchy versus a republic was intertwined with
other issues. Should men be treated equally before the state? Should
reason dictate the administration of justice, or should unquestioned
faith in royal or ecclesiastical judgment be the basis? These are the larger
cultural issues. Men find themselves collectively invested on one side or
the other. Those victimized by a violation of the collectively seen good
have recourse in the greater society. Such issues even concern the question
of knowing and of coming to truth by culturally prescribed paths.
McHugh and Platt have insightfully set forth some of the consequences
of this approach in another context.[7]

This work is concerned neither with transcendant cultural morality
nor with the moral issues relating to individual personality. The two
are discussed here to emphatically distinguish them from and contrast
them with *social system issues* (the moral order), the primary analytic
units throughout. Because the term "morality" means so many
different things to different people, it is fruitful to elaborate what will
not be meant by the term as well as what will be meant. "Morality"
will not mean individual management of one's own principles of
behavior, nor will it mean a set of transcendent directives from a
cultural ethos. Rather, the analytic approach will focus upon the
communal sanctions by those representing, often by fiat, "the community."

An Empirical Basis for Discussion of Morality

The elementary question in this chapter concerns ways in which the
concept of morality can be grasped empirically. In the first chapter,
one was simply urged to accept on faith that certain aspects of life take
on moral character while others do not. The assertion was made that

drug use in the United States in the middle twentieth century is one of those moral areas. Up to this point however, the empirical basis for that assertion has not been firmly established. The focus now turns to this empirical problem.

Partial and Total Identities

An elementary license for membership in a group of men is the presented evidence of cobelief in certain ideas of appropriateness in behavior that are *moral* in their character. The question arises as to why certain kinds of issues achieve a moral status, while others are simply customs of preferred behavior.

All societies have an order of command, whether based on age or sex, whether traditional caste system or open class system, whether highly individualistic and competitive or relatively cooperative. Here is one example of how sociologists have theorized that certain issues might have achieved moral status: Those on the top of any social order usually have a strongly vested interest in maintaining themselves there. If they are to remain on top, they must convince others in that social system that things ought to be that way. Bendix makes this point in discussing managerial ideologies.[8] The men who govern must do so by "right." Any issue which is believed to possibly alter the "right" to be on top is a likely candidate as a moral issue in which men have strong commitments. Theft and murder become primary moral issues in most societies, especially where theft attains a scale to alter the stratified order of men.

The empirical question for the observer of moral order concerns the procedures of how that moral order is invoked and maintained. Variously placed individuals and groups in a community may act either to allow or disallow full membership, rights, and privileges to members of their community. In this there is a continuum from complete acceptance to almost complete rejection. For example, in feudal times, the serfs were largely excluded from participation in the political life. Until the twentieth century, women were also excluded from direct political participation in Western civilization. One could go on enumerating hundreds of examples of how communities through various representatives and interest groups have chosen to include or exclude a portion of their population from *certain areas* of life, with illustrations ranging as far back as slavery in Aristotle's Greece to slavery in nine-teenth-century America to voting rights in contemporary America and South Africa.

There are cases whereby individuals are categorized in a totally dichotomous way through a procedure which grants or denies member-ship in the community. There are kinds of specific behaviors that strategic members of a community regard as thoroughly indicative of the person. A person who exhibits this presumably obvious special kind of behavior (immoral, in this instance) is identified in a complete sense through a particular label; thus generating total identity. The idea of a total identity is not to be confused with the concept of stereotype, nor with prejudice. The man who has the stereotype that "Germans are scientific and militaristic" can still conceive of a German in many other partial terms that have nothing to do with militarism or rational empiricism. While for such a stereotype-holder, Germans may never be able to evade that particular prejudgment about their personalities and characteristics, the very specificity of the categories means that other things about Germans may be held open to question.

Everett Hughes' "master and subordinate statuses" is another way of looking at the problem raised here concerning two different ways of identifying people for moral judgment.[9] Becker has developed Hughes' notions in the area of deviance in much the same way as "total and partial identities" are used here:

Some statuses, in our society as in others, override all other statuses and have a certain priority. Race is one of these. Membership in the Negro race, as socially defined, will override most other status considerations in most other situations; the fact that one is a physician or middle-class or female will not protect one from being treated as a Negro first and any of these other things second. The status of deviant (depending upon the kind of deviance) is this kind of master status.[10]

Stereotypes exist for both totally and partially identified persons, and the same is true for prejudices. One may be highly prejudiced against females as drivers of automobiles, but this partial identification of the character of women may not spill over into other areas of competence or incompetence. The same party who thus feels strongly about women drivers may not be surprised by the fact that a woman could be a nuclear physicist of great competence, a cellist, or even a motor-cyclist. In most areas of life, even where there are strong prejudices and stereotypes, men deal routinely with partial characterizations of other men.

There are few characterizations of men that are total. Those that are tend to be in moral areas.

The person designated as deviant in society may be considered deviant in only one way, but the community reaction to him can be total. For example a pregnant high-school senior may be quite capable of finishing her studies successfully before graduation, but the total response, stigma, and ridicule may lead her to take leave; a homosexual may be as competent as the next person in the government bureaucracy and similar in every other way except for his sexual appetite, but may be treated as though he is *totally* different.[11]

This matter of one's total identity as morally good or evil has been viewed as having roots in a specific strain of Western thought, and more particularly, in the northern Protestant conception of the evil and immoral. Ranulf and Weber are among the many observers who have noted that Roman Catholicism has a more wholistic integrated view of "good and evil" in human action.[12] The Roman Church has always acknowledged both the attainment of virtue and the exist-ence of evil and sin in all men. Perhaps the essence of the problem is demonstrated in the manner in which the southern Catholic countries view forgiveness of sins. Quite the opposite, the Lutheran and Calvin-istic strains make no allowances for sin and are thus "religious doc-trines without forgiveness."[13]

It is commonly acknowledged that contemporary society is secular, but this has blinded social science to empirical investigation of present conditions through study of the nonsecular roots and the powerful centrifugal force of the sacred traditions of the very recent past. The empirical issue is that one need not be a practicing Protestant, believer, or even a churchgoer to have a world-view of the moral order that is a reflection of the Calvinist-Lutheran views. Men in Protestant nations are said to see men as either "good, upstanding, righteous" members of the normal community, or as "bad, evil, and immoral." Such men will typically ridicule the Catholic confessional as a futile exercise in momentary purgation, or at its worse, ephemeral truth overladen with a few layers of hypocricy.

The argument continues that the "deviant" in Protestant nations is viewed in terms of his total evil or total deviance, and it follows that such a strong moralistic conception of the deviant seeks total condemnation and total punishment. It is simply incidental that such nations also desire total rehabilitation, since the essential problem is that this very conception of the deviant in total moralistic terms precludes even partial rehabilitation.

It is this total response to the deviant, be that a pregnant high-school senior or a drug addict, which sets him apart from his fellow-man. It is the total reaction of "normal men" in society which isolates the deviant for such gross and all-encompassing treatment, as though every aspect of his person were infused with the germ of his specific deviancy. Treating deviants as though they were wholly deviant (although in fact the deviance is quite specific) often results in the creation of some very real differences. Becker has this to say about the circle of labeling a deviant:

Treating a person as though he were generally rather than specifically deviant produces a self-fulfilling prophecy. It sets in motion several mechanisms which conspire to shape the person in the image people have of him. In the first place, one tends to be cut off, after being identified as a deviant, from participation in more conventional groups, even though the specific consequences of the particular deviant activity might never of themselves have caused the isolation had there not also been the public knowledge and reaction to it.[14]

The task for the analytic observer of attributions of deviance is to study the conditions under which the imputations of a total identity arise, and once imputed, the conditions under which the moral deviant can be reinstated to normal status in the society.

For the heroin addict, as with others who are accused of moral deviance, the achievement of the status of deviant requires more than a simple assertion by one or several people in the community. It requires first that publicly constituted authorities so characterize him or, that people believe he has been so characterized. Once the designation is public, the individual becomes the subject of a *total characterization*, and is from that point forward eligible to be treated as a single and total identity. The essential ingredient of the total identification is that, with a single attribute, members of the "normal" community know literally "all that they need to know" about the deviant in order to respond to him appropriately.

The female publicly "known" in the community to be a prostitute is known to that community as a totally identified person. She is known as a prostitute, and that characterization is sufficient for all purposes of how to think about and how to treat her. There is nothing of social consequence in the fact one *is* a prostitute, it is all in the fact that one has the *reputation* among ones fellows in the community that calls for moral judgment and differential treatment. There is nothing in actually *being* a heroin or morphine addict that evokes the total identity and the moral response, since there are many who are addicts but who go undetected. To use a more dramatic illustration, the quality of being a murderer is not what produces the moral response, since many innocent men have been hanged and guilty ones have gone to their graves unpunished by their community. For all categories of moral deviance the essential ingredient is the public characterization of the deviance, which carries with it the ultimate sanctions of the community of co-believers.

As Garfinkel has pointed out, any theoretical problem can be fully traced in its implications by restating its basic postulates in terms of the procedures by which the theorized state of affairs came about.[15] The issue is what must be done to an individual in order for the community to respond to him as though he is totally and completely a deviant, or in this instance, a heroin addict. As has been suggested, it is important that law enforcement officials publicly designate him. Once publicly stigmatized, there is no way that the moral deviant can reenter the category of normality insofar as the home or knowledgeable community is concerned. The significance of this for the futility of rehabilitation attempts will become apparent when the focus shifts to that problem.

On the question of partial versus total identity, the degree of permanence to the stigma is an important matter in determining the strength of the moral interpretation. Indeed, this can be one of the

Analytical and empirical approaches to the study of morality

empirical measures of the degree of moral judgment in a given issue. For how long is the stigma attached? For how long is the effective treatment of the offender moralistic? The political scene in the United States provides an example of transitory moralistic treatment. So long as the individual takes a political position at the extreme of his community, he is treated by them as though he were a moral deviant.

However the stigma of moral deviancy in political immorality is not indelible. Those charged with being politically immoral can reenter the community of co-believers simply by renouncing an errant past to the welcoming community. There are countless cases at Berkeley of old-line Trotskyites who have moved to the suburbs of America in every sense. What is of significance here is that having made the move, they are welcomed. Political converts are legion and acceptable. Ronald Reagan could have been a liberal Democrat, but the Right can now vote for him. Russia and China welcome American defectors who have "discovered the errors of their ways," just as Americans welcome Russian and Chinese defectors who "flee an errant past." And if the Berkeley hills have their share of ex-Trotskyites, the Vietnam Day Committee and the Students for a Democratic Society have had more than their share of defectors from the well built-in middle class of American society.

The politically immoral outside of the community of co-believers have a total identity, but that identity lacks complete permanence in that the co-believers conceive that conversion is possible. The total character of the identity is documented by the fact that the politically immoral person is seen as so fully infused by his deviance that "one could not consider seriously having him for a friend." Further, one is dismayed by the discovery that a person for whom one previously had great respect is discovered to be on the other side of the political fence, and the respect for the person is thereby diminished considerably, if not completely. This is the pain of the ardent music lover with contrary strong political convictions who discovers that Gieseking played for Hitler or that Shostakovitch composed for Stalin; it is the pain of the suburban housewife because Dr. Spock wants her country to get out of Vietnam; or the pain of the segregationist Southerners who loved *On the Waterfront* seeing Brando march with the black voter registrants.

If you are a young radical, and you have previously honored a great artist, you are pained by the sudden information that this artist is at politically opposite extremes from you. This is the problem of total identity, the problem that men infuse other men with total qualities that permeate their whole existence, even their music or their expertise on specifics of "no relevance" to the issue.

Some women who revered Dr. Spock for his sane child-rearing advice have written venomous letters to him when they found that his political ideology was different from their own. Some said that they would never take his advice again. Young pianists who respected Gieseking the artist have smashed his records when they came to know that his political position was suspiciously close to a position antithetical to their own. But to repeat, conversion is possible in political communities. One can return to the community of co-believers simply by asserting that the old belief was wrong and that one is willing to accept the terms of the true belief. In this, political immorality and political conversion to a system of beliefs have precise parallels with religious immorality and religious conversion.

The avenue is always open for the Christian to accept the Moslem, the Hindu or the atheist, if he will only renounce his past and join the community of believers. Every major religion provides for the conversion to the faith, and the most religious people are among the most willing to accept the newcomer. The nonbeliever or heretic is totally infused with an identity however, just like the political nonbeliever. In a sacred society, Torquemada could burn the heretics. That action attests to the total quality of the imputation about character. But even in a secular society, the faithful hold the heretic suspect in a manner that transcends a partial identification. The total identification is seen in the necessity of the faithful to completely revise his estimation of the other person once he finds out that the other is, say, an atheist. This is especially true when there has been the possibility of a beginning friendship between two persons. They may find that they are compatible in many areas, on many issues; that they have similar interests in athletics, literature, and music. When the religious question comes up, they may discover an "irreparable" gap. The irreparability of the gap is a direct consequence of the belief that the religious difference between them can not be compartmentalized, but that it informs one of several other aspects of the totally infused person.

In both the political and religious areas then, the nonbelieving deviant becomes a moral deviant to the extent that his identity as deviant is believed to be total. However, because conversion to the community of the normal and moral is possible, because men can move back and forth between the communities, the political or religious deviant is not as intensely responded to as the *finally immoral man*. The final measure of total identity is when the violation of a community's moral dictation has as its result a cutting off of the pathway back to the "normal and moral" community. Along a continuum of ways and methods of assessing the degree of moral strength and sanction, this is the most significant indicator.

With those moral outsiders who simply believe differently (the political and religious are two examples just cited), the community can choose to treat the deviance as something which the individual can himself control, and thereby can reenter the community. Even though heretics are burned and political enemies are bombed, the community retains the hope or the ideal that the violence may be corrective. For those men who believe that homosexuality is (1) immoral, (2) totally identifying, and (3) nonconvertible, the violence against the homosexual has an entirely different meaning. Psychologists and psychiatrists suggest that the gangs of roving Marines who go out on the streets to "beat up on homosexuals" do so more to reaffirm their own identities as men than to correct the ways of their victims, whom they find to be irretrievably lost. The addict, the prostitute, the bank-robber, the murderer; all are stained permanently as total identities in the minds of their fellowmen. We may suspend for the time the question of how the community comes to conclude that one among them belongs in such a moral category. Once so categorized, the individual's movement out of that category is hardly possible insofar as that community is concerned. Indeed, having a record of imprisonment (for most offenses) that is known to the community is sufficient to permanently stigmatize the individual as a moral deviant. Because his reentry into the community is precluded, the whole idea of rehabilitation from prisons is open to the most serious of questions. Rehabilitation or reentry into the normal community is possible only when that community does not know of the history of moral deviance. However because of the strongly believed security risks that a community takes when it receives an exconvict (a totally identified man), all communities force that history out of the exconvict when he seeks to gain a livelihood by almost any kind of employment. Thus we insist upon calling for the very information which makes rehabilitation or a normal return to the community impossible. As will be seen in a later chapter, the high rate of recidivism among addicts is explained as much by this consideration as by the psychological proclivity to deviance or the power that habituation to drugs has over the individual. Unless we are willing to impute a similar proclivity to return to prostitution, bank-robbing, and check-forging based upon psychological habituation, we must be willing to hold as problematic this charge about the addict.

Empirical Approaches of the Study of Morality

The primary concern of this work is with the second level of analysis of moral issues, that which concerns the sanctioning of men in a community. The empirical boundaries for the study of the problem may therefore be delineated in a manner that is more than arbitrary.

Following Garfinkel, a good place to begin the study of sanctions is with those whose task it is to construct or alter the rules or laws. In a very timely piece of research, Blum and Funkhouser have studied the attitudes of members of the California State Legislature on the drug problem in that state.[16]

The expressions of the lawmakers are informative of the kind and degree of moral interpretation of narcotics use that has been outlined to this point. The largest single group of legislators were in favor of confinement and punishment for the handling of the drug problem. Although many expressed their own personal firm convictions that this was the best way to deal with the narcotics traffic and narcotics users, the most frequent argument used was that the public demanded this. Thus, the legislators usually responded as though they were passive public servants, bending to the wishes of the electorate. It was

Analytical and empirical approaches to the study of morality

noted that the strongest and the only effective lobbying was done by those forces who wanted stiffer laws and more punishment.

The more liberal drug bills were consistently opposed by the liquor industry lobby, the police, and church and temperance groups—strange bed-fellows.

Legislators saw as supporters of the treatment-no-penalty approach the Friends (Quakers), American Civil Liberties Union, NAACP, California Democratic Council, and the social welfare people. ... Wryly noting that "the addict has no friends," some observed that not only were the anti-treatment forces much stronger than the pro-treatment ones, but that the latter—for example, the civil liberties groups—were themselves under fire for their "subversive" activities or were decried for their attempts to "break down law enforcement in the state."[17]

Almost every state in the union has passed very strong legislation supplementing or even extending the penalties of the federal narcotics legislation, and California's legislature can be viewed as rather typical on this issue. If there is any difference, it is in the direction of the more liberal and permissive. It has led the movement to separate therapeutic-penal institutions for addicts. Nonetheless, the legal system at its very source is strongly committed to the harshest sanction that it can impose upon the addict, the felony. The fact that the state Supreme Court ruled in the early 1960s that *being an addict* is not a felony is almost irrelevant for the treatment of the addict. The law enforcement agents need only to establish possession of the drug for felony convictions. If one is an addict, he will possess within fourteen to sixteen hours, and the police need only keep an eye on him for the arrest.

An empirical approach to the study of morality must take account of how the community behaves toward the immoral member through sanctions. A look at the legislative operation is not sufficient for these purposes. Rather, it is an informative point of departure, in that men in the community obtain validation for their treatment of the immoral from the public and official arena. When the lawmakers then use the public pulse as the incentive (or at least for the rhetoric of incentive) for strong punitive action, a circularity is achieved from which the moral deviant has no escape. The community's ultimate rationale against heroin or marijuana consumption has been that it is a felony, while the lawmaker's ultimate rationale for strong felonious law has been the public sentiment. What indeed is the public sentiment? What is the reaction of the community to the moral deviant in behavioral terms? Despite the fact that there is no single uniform reaction, it is possible to observe typical ways of responding to the moral deviant, especially in the vital areas of his life. The distinction should be made between the normal, everyday reaction of men to other men that they meet casually, momentarily, or engage only in the most temporary encounters, versus the reactions when men relate to other men concerning vital matters. In the latter case such things would be included as the nature of the restrictions in obtaining employment, housing accommodations, friends, and marital or sex partners.

To study these kinds of moral issues empirically is to study serious sanctioning behavior. Because it is possible to find instances where the behavior of a whole community is expressly in favor of one position while the actual behavior is quite the contrary, there is an important source of confusion, of which sex is a good example. Men may commonly say that they oppose promiscuity and adultery, but they may engage in it. Here one can observe the relationship between publicly visible violations and the degree of sanctioning behavior. In the first chapter, private versus public moral behavior were distinguished. Men do publicly express severe disapproval of adultery, while they privately engage in it. If it becomes publicly known, sanctions are imposed. There are instances where men are caught and punished severely for doing something which members of the community know is commonly practiced. Income tax evasion is a typically cited case in point. Price-fixing by the electrical companies is also a good example.[18] Many businessmen confided later that their only surprise in the electricity trials was the reaction of a few outraged citizens. They certainly were not surprised, much less angered or annoyed, by the conspiracy. Yet these same unannoyed men could have given strong *public* support to the moral principles of the free enterprise system and the positive gains from an openly competitive market. One may "feel very strongly" in one direction and behave in the opposite direction. Again, a good example of this in the West is sexual activity. A strong sexual urge may be overcome or sublimated, on the one hand. On the other hand, one may engage in illicit sex and still feel strongly that he should not have behaved in such a way. In either instance, observation of the behavior may mislead an observer in his conclusions about the "strength of the feeling" of the individual involved. A disjunction of the individual participant's feeling and his behavior may result in extreme guilt, but it should be noted that an interest in guilt feelings focuses upon the individual.

The sociologist of morality concerns himself primarily with sanctioning or conforming behavior. He merely invites conceptual muddiness by failing to distinguish between the two units. As we have seen, when the individual is the unit of analysis, some see morality in terms of the degree to which the individual holds to his own principles. However, when the community is the unit, moral or immoral behavior is viewed in terms of the moral order. There are occasions where an individual may be characterized as moral in the first sense, but where his behavior violates the moral code of his fellow men. In these instances, it is imperative to specify boundaries. For the purposes of this work, "immorality" will be used only with reference to the community boundary. Though its importance is completely acknowledged for other interests, individual morality is not the subject matter here.

Morality has two components: The first is the behavior which is itself subject to communal sanction and control; the second is the nature of the sanctioning and control. The two are interconnected, because an act takes on a moral character in public places as a direct consequence of the way men "normally" respond to it. From a social perspective, there can be nothing intrinsically moral or immoral about a woman smoking a cigarette. If she smokes by herself, there is no issue for the community. However, if she smokes in public, the community may treat her behavior moralistically. It may choose to invoke sanctions to prevent her from continuing. A woman who smoked a cigarette in a public place in 1870 was thus treated as an immoral person. There is nothing abstract, mystical, or empirically difficult to grasp about the nature of her moral behavior or moral treatment. In the example cited, the smoking of a cigarette is *immoral behavior*, while the measures used by the community become *moral control*.

So long as a small minority of a community engage in immoral behavior *publicly*, then moral control of that behavior is effective. However, when there is public knowledge that even a sizeable minority (one fourth or one third) are behaving publicly contrary to a community's "moral" principles, then those principles cannot long persist. When many women began smoking in the presence of strangers, then would-be moral sanctioners could no longer be certain that any other member of the community would be sympathetic. In Mead's terms, the moral order is weakened considerably by the inability of the typical community member to know that any other member feels the same way.[19]

A sizeable minority of deviants thwart social control for another reason. In moral questions, the most extreme sanctions of a community are invoked. Violators are sometimes executed or imprisoned. Where the minority is sizeable, a community cannot use such serious sanctions as these without either (1) depleting the community of much of its human resource or (2) exhausting the resources of the community on punitive action at the expense of constructive development.

Legislation can have a dramatic effect on the course of moral behavior and moral control in those cases where the community generally fears the possibility of the law's enforcement. Thus, in the deep South up through the 1950s, whites who opposed voting rights legislation for Blacks could not have their morality legislated because they did not fear enforcement of the law, even though their acts were public and victimizing. They had reason to believe that the local authorities, all the way up to the governor, would support their local suppression of Negro voting. By the same token, Blacks who insisted on facing police dogs and hoses and electrified prodding by mounted police in the 1960s could not have their morality legislated. They too did not fear the enforcement of the law sufficiently to not register to vote. Instead, they chose prison. When these tactics are routinely chosen by either party to a moral dispute, the old moral order cannot persist.

Where the law is enforced and where men fear that enforcement, public morality can be altered or sustained by legislation. Both components of morality are affected; the behavior itself and the public control mechanism.

There are instances where "the legislation of morality" in this sense has been remarkably effective. It is *law* of the United States which has made it *immoral* in the minds of the citizenry to imprison a man for his religious beliefs. In 1789, most communities probably did not regard such punishment as immoral because they could observe the imprisonment of a heretic without feeling any outrage and without attempting to intervene in the imprisonment. After several score years, however, Americans had swung around until the strength of their moral position equaled that of the law. By 1870, the idea of such powerful state sanction for disbelievers could evoke moral outrage and action on the part of the citizenry.

This is an example where morality was legislated and there were no strong feelings against the legislation. Prohibition is cited however, as the supreme example which proves that legislation is ineffective in influencing morality if the people really want to do anyway what the legislation forbids. But one can just as easily cite sexual desire, sexual behavior, and legislation on sex as a strong example on the other side. We have laws against prostitution and adultery, and there is no clamoring for repeal of these laws on the grounds that men are going to do what they really want to do regardless of law. The key to the puzzle may be the phrase, "where men fear the law's enforcement." Men have never really been punished for breaking the law and going to a prostitute. They have accordingly never feared that law's enforcement. In recent times, they have had little to fear from the laws against adultery, since prosecution is rare in proportion to incidence. The sanctions against a public display of an adulterous relationship have been very stringent in the past. There is a case of desire for activity which the law prohibited, where the legal prohibition was effective in sustaining the moral order of the community even though "men really wanted" to break the law. It is therefore foolish to cite Prohibition continually as a case which proves the ineffectiveness of laws in moral areas where men's desires are contrary to those laws.

One can anticipate the argument that Prohibition is a different case, in that most people felt that taking a drink was not really morally wrong, while people do feel that illicit sex is morally wrong even if desired. There is something to this argument which should be examined more closely. It tells us something more about the relationship between law and morality. Where the ideal-typical member of a community has a conception of the rightness of wrongness of an act, that act takes on a moral quality independent of whether men desire to engage in it or not. In communities where the consumption of alcohol is regarded as wrong, whether or not there is overwhelming desire for it is independent of the moral question. (The same is true for sex in the example above.) Whether laws against alcoholic consumption will be effective or not is therefore less dependent upon how strongly men want it than upon the conception of alcoholic usage as right or wrong.

It then becomes a fruitless chicken-egg argument as to which came first, the conception of right and wrong or the law. Either argument ends in a tautology once the position is stated that one always precedes the other. For example, those who argue that strong moral feelings always predate the law define the terms of the discourse in this circular manner:

Only laws which are in keeping with public morality can be effectively enforced. Laws which are contrary to public morality (e.g., Prohibition) are doomed to failure. If an instance is cited where a law was passed which *seemed* to be contrary to public morality and was effective, then it was not *really* contrary to public morality after all.

The preceding argument is a tautology because it defines effective legislation in terms of a morally sympathetic community. Thus, wherever the law is effective the arguer simply retreats and asserts that it must have been the case that the community was in favor of that law all along. The tautology can be broken by an empirical approach to the study of morality, which sets apart analytically the two elements of morality and traces their relationship to laws and sanctions. The best test of the degree of morality in an issue is the behavior of the men in that community toward violators. If there are no taboos on the behavior, then it is impossible to speak of sanctions or immorality. Only when acts are seen as violations can one come to the empirical study or grasp of moral issues, because it is only with sanctioning behavior that one can assess empirically the moral investments. Logically and substantively it makes no sense to ask the question "Which comes first, law or morality?" It is the nature of the relationship between them that can and should be the subject of inquiry.

CHAPTER 5

Deviance and the reaction of society

GENERAL THEORETICAL APPROACH IN THE sociology of deviance has been undermined by a persistent argument in behavioral science that has polarized two groups. On one side, there are those who advocate the study of pressing social problems as *the* means to the ends of social science. Mills delivered one end of the polemic by implying that to use any other approach was to lose oneself in trivial and inconsequential activity.[1] The roots of this tradition are varied. They range from a reaction to detached, ivory-tower scholasticism of nineteenth-century central Europe to the humanistic origins of the social sciences and the fight against the dehumanizing tendencies of a too-scientific view of human behavior.

On the other side of the pole is the argument that detachment from pressing moral problems is the best assurance of reliable and valid research.[2] According to this view, there is always the danger that a social observer who has a moral axe to grind will use the sharp edge to chop away, consciously or not, at data contrary to the desirable moral position.

Without here trying to resolve in favor of one or the other, it is important to point out some of the consequences of these arguments for the development, or underdevelopment, of theory in the sociology of deviance.

First of all, those who are wary of moral commitments to pressing moral issues and social problems have been professionally hypersensitive in their avoidance of social problems research at all costs. In the desire not to be stigmatized among their scientific peers as choosing and pursuing a problem out of moral indignation or fervor, they have overreacted in the same way some black sociologists and psychologists overreact in avoiding "black" social and psychological problems. Indeed, there is a striking parallel here that is no accident, since young black professionals are strongly advised by the professionally conscious to stay away from the racial data. (The same Black is advised by the "social problems" group to involve himself in research on Blacks and to become actively engaged in the internal moral issue of our time.) The first point is that those most interested in general theorizing are usually those least interested in pursuing research on social problems.

Second, those who have dealt with deviance and "problems" have tended to wed themselves to the particular problem being studied at the expense of general theorizing. There are a few notable exceptions to the preceding generalizations.[3] So there emerges the peculiar development that those typically engaged in the empirical study of social problems have had the least interest in general theorizing about deviance; while those who typically have the greatest interest in theorizing keep arms' distance from deviance research for fear of non-professional contamination.

In fact, of course, our understanding of deviance will advance only (1) when deviance research is emancipated from an exclusive consideration of particular provincial, apolitical social problems and (2) when the overly professionalized sociologist recognizes the necessity of incorporating "problems" into a larger framework. A more general approach would free itself from the stultifying wedlock to criminality, alcoholism, and dope addiction, but unashamedly incorporate these problems for inquiry and analysis as theoretical considerations demand. The reaction of members of a society to particular forms of conduct provides a general theoretical framework for both traditional social problems and other forms of deviance.

Sociologists have had considerable trouble accounting sociologically for the lack of uniform deviation along those social variables selected to explain deviance. If being a young male from an ethnic minority, living in an urban slum, and so on, "explain" the deviance, how does one explain that all others in those categories are not deviants, asks the psychologist.[4] An attempt to address this problem while remaining within a social-structural explanation brought forth the notion of differing access routes to opportunities for deviance.[5] However, as might be expected from the preceding summary of polar camps, such explanations have been restricted in their use to traditional social problems in deviance. Merton,[6] Cohen,[7] Cloward and Ohlin,[8] and Sutherland,[9] have been used almost exclusively in regard to the traditional social problems of juvenile delinquency and highly selected criminal violations. These positions have not been expanded or extrapolated for use in questions of generic deviance.

The notion of societal reaction as a framework for a more generally applicable theory of deviance began to pick up momentum in the last decade and a half. This growth is largely attributable to the seminal ideas set forth by Lemert[10] and Garfinkel.[11] They have been recently applied by Becker[12] and Kitsuse.[13] There are two critical components of reaction that deserve attention in the development of integrated theorizing about deviance. The first is the question of why and how certain actions evoke the social response against the deviant act. Empirical interest is directed toward the process by which members of a group assume the posture of the normal population and the subsequent process by which abnormality is conceived.

The second component concerns the question of how the person or group labeled as deviant responds to others' characterization of his (or its) deviance. These two components are in continual interplay, and it is only in an analytic sense that they can be separated into clearly distinguishable elements.

In the study of deviance, there are several tactics that an observer might use. Historically, sociologists concentrated upon the deviant himself. They drew a lengthy profile of the life of the hobo, the prostitute, the thief, and the delinquent gang member, to name but a few. These portraits were often in case history form. They were extensive, and contributed in their own way to the study of deviance. From the point of view of a theory of social reaction to deviance, the major shortcoming of these studies was that they only implicitly and incidentally touched upon the normal-typical social response to the deviant.

A second tactic in the approach to deviance therefore, focuses upon the reaction of the typical-normal member to the deviant. The method of study is almost never the case history, but instead is broadly based survey research. Hundreds or thousands are sampled from a community and questioned as to their experiences with (and attitudes and behavior toward) men they conceive to be outcasts.

A third tactic would be to focus upon the exchange between the population preempting the title of normal and the population designated as deviant. What is it that happens characteristically *between* them? That is the most difficult approach because it deals with an empirical will-o'-the-wisp, "exchange," and so it must be examined in much closer detail before we proceed to the empirical study for which it may provide a framework.

The Exchange between Deviant and Normal

To use an analogy to the present problem, the discipline of social psychology is concerned with the exchange between the individual and the relevant group in his environment. Analytically, social psychology is concerned with the exchange itself. However, when it comes down to the empirical matter of the actual research, an election is usually made as to which party to the exchange will receive greater emphasis. Thus, there is a wing of the discipline which concentrates upon how the personality is influenced by the group; while another wing concentrates upon how the group structure is changed by certain personalities.

The study of the exchange between the normal and the deviant has similar implications in the choice of emphasis that is usually made. Because the power relationship is so one-sided in favor of the normals, there has been a tendency to look almost exclusively at their effect, via sanctions, upon the deviants. Most of the theorizing in this area has looked upon the degree of effectiveness of the reaction. Durkheim was among the few to look at the other side of the coin when he discussed the integrating "function" of crime and punishment for a social order.[14] By punishing the dissenters and the dissidents, a society reaffirms in clear and decisive action that which is normal and permissible. Punishment not only has the more obvious purpose of reminding other would-be deviants of the undesirable consequences of deviance, but the affirmative statement of what is right and wrong reinforces the beliefs of the participants. If, as in seventeenth-century England, pickpockets are hanged in public, people get support for the notion of what a "bad thing" picking pockets really is.

These are consequences of the exchange; but what of the exchange itself? One must look not only at the process by which the normal sanctioning reaction comes about but also at the reaction of the person designated as deviant.

Whereas men only make an either-or distinction between normal and abnormal in their conception of deviance, in fact there is a long continuum with (a) different degrees of deviance and (b) different times in the career of a deviant when he reaches various points on that continuum. Also, one of the striking things for one who studies deviance is the discovery that most "deviants" usually appear as normal as the next person except in that one area in which they are attributed deviance. In the preceding chapter, the importance of this one area was emphasized because, in the mind of the "normal" man, the "one bad area" of the deviant's life explains him totally as a person. The error of the normal man is profound. Its effect, by stages, in time and by degree, is to make the deviant himself come to believe in his own totally deviant character. But presently the problem is only to outline the form of the exchange between normal and deviant persons and populations.

First, concerning the different stages in the career of the deviant: We have come to conceive of the drug user as one who self-administers some mind-transforming drug and, in that single act becomes "that kind of man." However, as was pointed out in Chapter 3, there are many detours off the road to addiction even after the user has traveled some way. An important theoretical development in the understanding of social deviance would explain at what point members of a society decide that one really becomes a deviant. The answer for the social observer does not lie in the mind of the drug user. (The self-conception of the deviant is of interest to the sociologist for other reasons, which remain to be explored.) Nor does the answer lie in some truth which transcends the social existence of men. We need no more ask the question "Was there sound if no one heard it" than we need ask the question of whether someone is really a deviant if no one knows it.[15] Instead, the answer to the question resides entirely in the time and nature of social knowledge and social response to the deviance. What is of paramount interest in this approach is not what stage the deviant is in, but at what point is he isolated and identified. For example, one may be on his first marijuana cigarette when he becomes socially known as a drug addict,[16] while another may be addicted to morphine and yet have no stigma or identification as a deviant. The difference in the two cases is not a consequence of what they do, but is perhaps an arbitrary reaction by particular persons in the community or society.

In order to illustrate this point let us set up a hypothetical case of two individuals, A and B, who behave alike to the point of having consumed like amounts of marijuana and heroin. Further, let us assume that the one difference between the two is that A's drug use becomes generally known, while B's is unknown. We may now leave the hypothetical world and review developments without straining the imagination. At that point when A's usage becomes known, we must abandon the notion that A and B can continue to behave alike. The reaction to A in the larger society will be hostile and sanctioning. It will as well generate "explanations" of his deviant behavior that are attacks upon A's psyche and his morals. If A accepts these explanations, the reaction of the society will produce in its turn a response that "documents" the explanations and accusations, and "justifies" the sanction.[17]

As for B, the matter of his normality or social deviation takes a quite different road from that of A. The unidentified drug user, B, can live a normal communal life among his fellow men.[18] Despite the fact that this society emphasizes the psychological and sociological character of his deviance, in order to identify the addict, we do not address his psychic or social behavior, but we must resort to the skill of the chemist and ask him for a chemical test. That is an admission of extreme importance to psychological and sociological theories about the deviance of the addict. He cannot be identified as a deviant by either laymen or social scientists observing the quality of his actual social behavior. He is identified instead by a technician who claims no competence and need know nothing about psychic and social matter.

It will be argued by some that this inability to identify the behavior is unnecessary because use of the drug is itself a demonstration that the user needs a crutch. This is a circular and tautological argument, as illustrated by a simple example:

Let us review the proposition that anyone with a scar on his toe has inadequacies of personality and can not cope with reality unless he scars his toe. When my proposition is criticized because it is unbelievable, I simply reply that *I know* that these persons have the psychological crutch of toe-scarring because "if you just take off the shoes and socks any fool can see the scar."

In a similar fashion, there is circularity in the assertion of the personal inadequacy of the drug user. "How do you know?" I ask, and the reply is, "Look at his arm; you see the needle-marks can't you?"

Physical marks or Nalline tests are used to designate the addict, but there would be no need for such tests if the *behavior* of the addict were distinctly deviant. With some forms of mental illness and alcoholism for example, the behavior of the deviant can be identified in and of itself. While there is more agreement on who is a drug addict than any other form of deviance, that agreement rests upon the social knowledge of the physical aspects of addiction and not upon the social behavior of the drug user. Whether a drug user is noticed and labeled is thus dependent not upon behavior caused by the drug, but upon the degree to which the user can prevent the society from looking for the marks on his arm or administering physical-chemical tests. It should be obvious that a drug user or addict with a high income can camouflage his "deviance," while the low-income user is exposed, by circumstances of the market, to law enforcement authorities. Our hypothetical case, B, can thus go along *behaving normally* and remaining totally unidentifiable until or unless chemical tests or arm-punctures (both physical) are discovered. In the following study of drug addicts who are apprehended, we will see how explanations, theories, and characterizations of apprehended addicts make the assumption that this is the addict, and that these explanations account for why the addict behaves in a certain way.

Although there are in fact different stages in the career of the deviant, labeling members of the society do not recognize these variations, either in degree or in time. One either is a moral deviant or he is not, in terms of the nature of society's reaction. One either is a prostitute or not, either a drug addict or not, and so on. That some are said to be "on the road to being a prostitute," is the moral equivalent of being a prostitute. Despite this, the moral deviant himself usually clings tenaciously to the idea that "just a little nip now and then" doesn't make him a full-fledged alcoholic, addict, prostitute, gambler, or whatever the nip happens to be. This early stage can be prolonged in the mind of the deviant for a period extending far into that time when everyone around him regards him as, indeed, full fledged. So long as he remains in this stage, and some addicts do even after they have been caught and institutionalized, he firmly believes that there are avenues through which he can reestablish himself in society. It is suggested here that, as long as deviants hold this belief they might be able to do so, but for the categorical either-or reaction of critical members of the society, which makes their own efforts in this area irrelevant and superfluous (unless they have independent wealth and/or powerful friends, in which case they would most likely not have been institutionalized in the first place). When the deviant abandons the belief that he can return to the society of "normal" men "whenever he wants to;" when he comes to believe that his own deviance sets him apart qualitatively from his fellow man, he has moved into a stage where his rehabilitation can only come about through some revelation or conversion that takes on a quality of the spiritual, supernatural, or messianic. The addicts in Synanon are almost uniformly of the later period, or from another point of view, of the latter type of deviant.[19] Those who have studied Synanon have noted how in some form there is a religious quality in the "conversion" away from the drug evil. In order to join Synanon, one must not only give up drugs, but also renounce all associations that are connected with drugs, be they friend or family or foe. What is more important, he must agree to do things which would probably have been morally objectionable to him before entering. He must go through what Garfinkel has called a "Degradation Ceremony" that strips him of the appearances of his former deviance.[20]

Synanon has been successful with some addicts in the sense that they have not relapsed into drug use for extended periods. However, the organization makes no claim to being effective with addicts in general, and for good reason. First of all, an addict must regard himself as being in the latter stage of deviance described above in order to admit to himself that he requires such a drastic transformation that he is willing to submit to conversion. If the findings reported in the subsequent chapters are at all suggestive of this quality among drug users, it is more common than not to believe that one's self can return to normality without such a transformation. Further, even among those deviants who have the self-conception of being totally different from the rest of the world, only a small proportion would be willing to undergo the kind of voluntary, drastic life-style change that Synanon demands. Therefore, from the vantage point of those who would most like to "rehabilitate" the deviant to an acceptable and normal life, there is cause for pessimism because of the strong and categorical social reaction to moral deviance. The danger lies as well in the categorical response of the persons labeled deviants. Examples are numerous: the stigmatized drug addict who sees that there is no use in his abstinence because he will never be accepted again by nonusers; the slum-dwelling Black who sees that no matter what he does he will be excluded from full participation in the society; the newly migrated lower-class white youth who concludes that the teacher is against him whatever he does. And they all have their parallel reactions: bitterness and hostility directed both outward and inward; the creation of their own groups offering refuge from a hostile society. Black cultural nationalists, tough gangs, and the "hippie" addicts—all are convinced that they have experienced the world in a way that makes them superior to the ordinary, normal man; but alternately they experience doubts about the burden of social deviance, and wonder whether they would live more comfortably if the world had let them be "normal".

Narcotics Use and the Reaction of Society

Drivers suspected of being under the influence of alcohol are required to submit to a chemical test in some parts of the country and the world, in order to determine to what degree alcohol is "influencing" them. This test is not completely valid, because it sets a standard maximum, and individuals vary considerably around that standard in their ability to remain clear-headed. No matter. A test is required. The point that should be emphasized, however, is that only those *behaving* in a suspicious manner are subjected to such a test. (To the extent that breath and other circumstantial evidence point to high alcoholic consumption, that too could qualify as behavior, but it is the driving behavior to which I have primary reference.)

Heroin addicts on parole are also required to submit to a chemical test to determine if they are under the influence of heroin. There is one important difference. There is almost nothing in the behavior of the addict *per se* which evokes this reaction. In short, it is the imputed quality of being an addict rather than the actual behavior of the addict that generates distrust. Thus, when addicts themselves attempt to set up self-help houses or farms, the surrounding communities are hostile and obstructionist.

Addicts who have banded together to try to offer help to each other in the tradition of Alcoholics Anonymous have found remarkable resistance in many urban communities. People give lip-service to self-help, but when addicts band together and try to rent a house, as Synanon has done in several cities, the surrounding community lets out an indignant sound that reverberates for months.

People in these areas excuse their own hostile behavior on the grounds that if the Synanon program is unsuccessful in even a few cases, the addicts will prey upon the community for money to supply their habit. A vicious circle is joined because this attitude itself insures that the addict can never be readmitted to the society of nonusers by any effort of his own. It is consequently not the reaction of the individual addict that is critical to the success of rehabilitation, but the reaction of particular elements of the society.

Any change in the social interpretation of narcotics use will be a result of a change in public policy. Public policy, in turn, is generally a reflection of the actions of the most agitated and aggressive segments of the citizenry in concert with the most powerful. In the preceding chapter, the reaction of legislators in the state of California was noted. In the next section, focus turns to an analysis of some of the views of college students toward the heroin addict.

Some College Students' Views of the Addict

There are many good reasons for using college students as indicators of enlightened public opinion. They are among the most educated 25 per cent of the population. More significant, a nation's leaders are drawn from colleges and universities, with business, banking, government, the military and even the church recruiting their highest ranking personages there. Tonnage has been written on that subject, and no tedious documentation is required to note the significance of the students' interpretation of various aspects of life.

Before they had received a lecture on any material relating to deviance, a class of 120 students in introductory sociology were asked to write a few paragraphs on what they considered to be the major causes of drug addiction.[21] Following are selections from several of the most representative responses:

1. The person who turns to drugs is a person who is incapable of facing the problems of life. It is the insecure person who is experimentative with a medicinal-type "cure-all" that doesn't actually solve his problems but simply makes him less aware of them. Drug addicts are basically cowards and/or

non-conformists. The coward uses drugs to aid him in his flight from facing reality. The non-conformist is experimenting with the forbidden . . .

2. Drug addiction is caused by emotional instability. It is merely one way in which the insecure person attempts to get security and happiness. The degree of addiction in the total population is partly determined by police action and import laws. The main problem, however, lies with the individual's ability to cope with life and with his desire to do so.

3. I feel that a person with a highly disordered mind, lacking the notion of reality and an inability to face, or perhaps conform to his society, will seek an escape through dulling his senses with drugs. The cause of his inability to cope with his life's problems would probably stem from vastly incompleted emotional maturation due to either improper guidance or some kinds of maladjusting features in his childhood.

4. I think curiosity and a desire to escape from reality are two of the major causes of a person becoming a drug addict. Curiosity as to the sensations that are experienced under the influence of narcotics probably is an important factor in inducing an individual to try taking narcotics. But curiosity isn't enough; otherwise many more people would be trying it. There must be, in addition, a desire to escape, if only for a while, from the boring and painful aspects of existence. . . .

5. The major causes of drug addiction are insecurity; search for a thrill; not enough strength of character to realize the end of the means used for a pleasure; selfishness in not realizing the pain it causes others around who care, such as relatives or just people who could use the services of the addict (before he is such); idleness resulting in a lack of alertness to the needs of others; fear of facing the future or simply the present; an attempt to escape what consensus calls "reality;". . . .

6. The major psychological force leading to drug addiction is a desire for escape. The drug addict is one who because of some real situation—either in his environment or in his self—has become too much for him to bear and so he wants to take a vacation from reality in the use of narcotics. . . .

7. In becoming a drug addict it would seem likely that social pressures by one's peers would initiate addiction. The curiosity to see what it is like, combined with the desire to be one of the group might be responsible for an individual's first step toward addiction.

At another point in this work, it is noted that the view of the causes of a problem is also a charter for the problem's solution.[22] For example, if you have a crop that is dying from drought and you believe that the drought is caused by the anger of the gods, it follows that your conception of the solution is chartered into pleasing the gods. Whether you perform a rain dance, offer a goat in sacrifice, or offer prayers simply demonstrates the substantive form that the idea takes. In a similar manner, if someone believes that drug addiction, alcoholism, and prostitution are caused by devils possessing men, then the solution conceived is calling out the devils. Finally, if you believe that drug addiction is caused by weakness of moral character and psychological disturbance, then the solution is equally chartered by that conception.

The different examples listed above are not intended to suggest that one is more real than another, or that all are equally false. The degree of empirical validity in the examples has nothing to do with their heuristic value: the conception of the cause of a problem determines the way in which its solution is seen. Whether the cause is "ludicrous" or "reasonable," is, to repeat, another point entirely.

The preceding statements are verbatim reports of some college students' ideas of how drug addiction comes about. The perpetual theme throughout these, and the other hundred responses, is the view of the addict as one who is fleeing reality. His flight from the real world is seen as resulting from an inability to face problems with equanimity, from emotional immaturity, and occasionally from weakness, cowardice, and lack of morality. The idea of escape is an interesting charter for solution. It will bring with it the idea that the addict's problem will be solved when he learns to "cope" with the real world, adjust to it, and shun the idea of escaping from it.

The attempt to solve the problem is one of the most important of the social reactions to a given form of social deviance.

As we shall see in the next chapters, this idea of escape and the rebuilding of the personality plays a large role in contemporary attempts to rehabilitate the drug addict. This attempt to solve the problem involves one of the most significant of the society's reactions to deviance, and will be explored more fully. In the present chapter, however, the concern is with a different reaction of the society; the normal sanctions in everyday exchanges.

In all but one of the cases listed, the college students place the source of the addict's problem within himself and charge him with the deficiency of some trait that "normal" people possess. The path to addiction is regarded as within the control of the individual. Note that the addict should, by the college students' reckoning, face the realities of his problems even though those realities might be objectively extremely difficult. That is a moral pronouncement, whether one agrees with it or not. Its moral element is the conviction that one ought not try to escape from the problems and challenges of conscious existence. That the explanation for the deficiency is in psychological terms in no way deflects the "ought" quality of the moral pronouncement. "Men should not steal!" When a man is caught stealing, even if his behavior is explained in terms of some psychological disturbance, his theft is treated as a moral act.[23] (This is the dilemma of modern criminal law prosecution in its attempts to place responsibility upon the shoulders of a man who has committed a crime. If he is reasonable and responsible, how is one to explain his crime except by recourse to notions of evil and malice?) The behavior eventually gets labeled immoral; the same can be said for the behavior of the drug addict. As soon as men strongly invest in the idea that it is only appropriate to "face reality" in a certain way, then to avoid or escape will be regarded in moral terms. The need to flee from some deep-seated psychic imbalance does not alter the moral conception or the moral base. Some of the responses are not even phrased in terms of neutral causation. One calls the addict a coward, and another refers to infantile development of the mind.

The conception of the causes of addiction is very much related to the conception of "the kind of person" an addict is. If he is "immature, and is incapable of facing reality," he is certainly not the kind of person that you would want to hire for a job, much less to live near you or marry into your family. There is an aversion to associating with drug users because they are "not the kind of people that one can depend upon." Consequently, the addict is systematically excluded from pursuing the kind of life that "normal" people lead, once his deviance becomes a matter of public knowledge.

The reaction to the deviant is a direct outgrowth of the conception men have of him. This is not only true of his treatment and rehabilitation, as the next chapters illustrate, but also of the kinds of contacts people have with the deviant outside of rehabilitation centers and prisons. In the following study conducted by John Kitsuse and described

in greater detail elsewhere,[24] seven hundred individuals were interviewed as to their responses to certain kinds of deviant behavior. The
respondents were each asked if they had ever known an illiterate, an
alcoholic, a drug addict, a sexual deviant, and other deviants, a total
of ten being named. Kitsuse describes the problem in this manner:

The objectives of the interview were threefold: It attempted to document
(1) the behavior forms which are interpreted as deviant, (2) the processes by
which persons who manifest such behaviors are defined and (3) treated as
deviant. Thus, in the construction of the interview schedule, what the inter-
viewees considered to be "deviant" behavior, the interpretations of such
behavior, and the actions of subjects toward those perceived as deviant were
addressed as empirical questions. Labels such as alcoholic, illiterate, illegitimate
child, and ex-convict were assumed to be categories employed by persons in
everyday life to classify deviants, but the behavioral forms by which they
identify individuals as deviants were treated as problematic.[25]

When the respondent indicated that he had known a drug addict, he
was asked to recall the most recent encounter with that person.

He was then asked, "When was the first time that you noticed (found out) that
this person was a (drug addict)?" followed by "What was the situation? What
did you notice about him? How did he behave?" This line of questioning was
focused on the interaction between the subject of the alleged deviant to obtain
a detailed description of the situation which led the subject to define the person
as (a drug addict).[26]

Following are some descriptions and interpretations from persons in
"normal" or everyday contact with drug addicts:

Case No. 1

Q: Have you ever known anyone who was an opiate addict?
A: Yes.

Q: How did you come to know this person?
A: My husband had an old aunt whom we brought over to a Mrs. —— to
take care of—Mrs. —— was a fine person and we like her very much.
We didn't know where her husband was but she did have a son. When
my husband and I would go over to see his aunt, we met Harry.

Q: How well did you know this person?
A: ... no one could know him well. He was non-communicative. I knew
him when he wasn't in jail.

117

Q: What do you mean by "he was non-communicative?"
A: I mean he slept all the time—and once when he wasn't sleeping, I tried to say hello and be pleasant but he just grunted.

Q: How often did you see him?
A: Once a week.

Q: When was the first time you noticed or found out that he was an opiate addict?
A: I suspected something was the matter because from the very first whenever my husband and I went over there he was sleeping on the couch. Not on his bed—but in the middle of the living room on a couch. This was most disconcerting and annoying.

Q: Did you have any other reasons to believe he was an opiate addict?
A: I didn't think that just because he was sleeping he was an opiate addict. . . . But I first noticed that something about him was different—because he was asleep in the middle of the room—and not on his bed.

Q: Did you notice anything else strange about him?
A: Yes, his eyes, when he was awake, were very glassy and starry. And when he walked he shuffled along.

Q: When was the first time you were positively sure or found out he was an opiate addict?
A: About 6 months after we met him he was arrested for stealing dope.

Q: Who told you, or how did you find out?
A: I read it in the papers.

Q: Will you tell me about it?
A: Yes.

Q: What was the situation?
A: This is what continuously happened. Mrs. always covered up for him. Then when he stole dope she would bail him out of jail to get him back into society, although he was arrested all the rest of the time.

Q: But what exactly was the first situation that made him out to be a dope addict?
A: He stole dope from a doctor's bag and the police found it on him.

Q: After he was first bailed out and home what did you notice about him?
A: He was the same as ever. He was always sleeping and would only grunt now and then. But otherwise he was the same. His mother always said he slept because he was tired.

Q: What was your reaction when you found out?

A: I thought a great deal of his mother, so of course, I was disappointed. She loved him and he was the only thing she had. Here was this woman who had nothing in the world but her son.

Q: What was your reaction toward him as a person?

A: I didn't have any personal reaction toward him because he was an addict; I was just mad at him because it was so disconcerting to have someone sleeping in the middle of the room when one is paying a call or I was also worried about my husband's aunt who lived under the same roof. So—no personal feelings.

Q: Then you had absolutely no personal feeling about him at all but only felt sorry for his mother?

A: Well—I thought him too dumb to do any harm. I felt a dislike toward him only because of what he was doing to his mother. Would you like to know my theory of him? Well, he was an orderly in the army so therefore he could get it easily. I think he probably experimented with it or was curious about it—and it got to be a habit. Or else he is suffering from shock—poor boy!

Q: Why do you think so?

A: I don't know—just a guess.

Q: But what about his friends—how did they react?

A: He had none.

Q: You mean he was always alone?

A: Yes.

Q: How did you personally treat him?

A: Just as I had always treated him before I knew. When he was awake I would always try to be pleasant.

Q: What was it that you noticed most about him?

A: That he slept all the time. He was always in a shell. Very unsociable. Very unsociable. Mrs. never made any apologies for him—I thought this irregular, too.

Q: What did you make of that?

A: It was hard to recognize. I accepted Mrs. but after this started wondering what kind of a person *she* was.

Q: Why?

A: Because she always covered up for him.

Q: Did this change your attitude of sympathy toward her?
A: No—but after a while I began to feel sorry for him.

Q: Why?
A: I don't know—perhaps because he was so pathetic looking.

Case No. 2

Q: Have you ever known anyone who was an opiate addict?
A: Yes.

Q: How did you come to know this person?
A: I went to college with him for a year.

Q: How well did you know this person?
A: Very well.

Q: How's that?
A: We lived in the same dorm and we saw each other quite a bit. We also used to play in a jazz combo together.

Q: How often did you see this person?
A: Everyday.

Q: How's that?
A: Well, if I didn't see him around the dorm I would see him around the band room.

Q: When was the first time you noticed that this person was a dope addict?
A: I can't remember the very first time I noticed it, but I had suspected him of it for quite some time.

Q: How's that?
A: Well he acted peculiar at times.

Q: How's that?
A: Well he just acted like a "junky." His eyes always seemed to be puffed up, and he appeared to be nervous at times.

Q: How did that affect you?
A: It didn't really bother me because I had seen other guys like that before.

Q: Did you actually know that he was a dope addict?
A: Yes, I felt that I had seen enough of it to know when a guy was taking the stuff.

Q: Can you think of an instance where he made you feel that he was a dope addict?
A: No, I just observed him over a long period of time.

Q: What else did you notice about the person?
A: He was very involved in his music.

Q: What did you make of that?
A: Nothing really, because I knew he was pretty wrapped up in his music. I guess all musicians are like that.

Q: When did you find out he was a dope addict?
A: I just asked him one day and he told me.

Q: What did you think of that?
A: It just confirmed my suspicions.

Q: Then what happened?
A: Nothing, it didn't bother me as long as he didn't bother me.

Q: Then what did you do?
A: I just kept my distance from him.

Q: How's that?
A: I only saw him when I had to, during practice and occasionally in the dorm.

Q: When was the last time you saw this person?
A: In 1956.

Q: What was the situation?
A: I was packing my bags to go home from school for the summer and I saw him around the dorm.

Q: What did you notice about the person?
A: Nothing. He seemed the same to me.

Q: How's that?
A: Pretty quiet and to himself.

Q: What did you think of that?
A: Nothing.

Q: Then what did you do?
A: Nothing, he just kept going without speaking so I kept going too.

Q: What happened to the person?
A: I don't really know for sure, but I heard that he was playing in some band in Detroit.

Case No. 3

Q: Have you ever known anyone who was an opiate addict?
A: Yes.

Q: How did you come to know this person?
A: He was a good friend of my father. After he graduated from medical school he moved out of town. It was after he moved that he began taking dope.

Q: How well did you know this person?
A: Well, I knew him through my father. He had moved out of town while I was very young, and he came back for a visit. That's when I met him. I had heard a lot about him from my parents. I guess that he was quite a good doctor.

Q: How often did you see this person?
A: I saw him just that one time that he came to visit us, but like I said, I had heard a great deal about him.

Q: When was the first time that you found out that he was a dope addict?
A: It was last winter. Around the end of January or first of February.

Q: Would you tell me about it?
A: I was having dinner with my parents and we got to talking about various fields of medicine. Then they asked me if I remembered this fellow. When I said that I did, they told me that he had been taking dope and was now in a hospital for the cure.

Q: What did you make of that?
A: I was very shocked, I just couldn't believe it.

Q: What did you notice about this person?
A: He was very handsome and a very good dresser. He was very distinguished-looking. (The subject then interjected that he was between thirty and thirty-five years old.) He was friendly and a good conversationalist.

Q: Did you notice anything else?
A: Nothing bad. There just wasn't anything bad to notice about him.

Q: What happened to him?
A: As far as I know he's still in the hospital, and is still under treatment for his addiction.

Case No. *4*

Q: Did you know your sister very well.

A: No, we were separated when we were young. I lived in Evanston, she lived in New York with a half-brother. We met again when we were older—in 1939 or 40. She came to visit me for a week or so. That's when I discovered she was a dope addict.

Q: How did you discover it.

A: She was sometimes very jolly and other times quite melancholy. I was working while she was visiting, so I didn't see her much during the day. Well, a neighbor told me one day that she thought she must be taking dope, because she went out early in the mornings and came back acting strangely. That started me wondering. So when she was alseep I looked at her arm, and sure enough there were places where she had been getting the needle. I spoke to her about it, but shortly after that she left. I didn't know she was dead until 6 months later when I got a letter from my uncle telling me. It had affected her speech. She had an impediment I guess. How she got it or when I don't know.

Q: Do you mean you don't know how she got the dope.

A: That's right. I didn't see her for 15–20 years. We had only written occasionally. We weren't close at all.

Q: Can you tell me how she acted when she first came to visit you.

A: Wild. Not normally happy, just wild. When she laughed it was almost an hysterical laughter.

Q: Can you give me an example of what you mean.

A: She talked wildly about things she's had in New York that I knew she couldn't have or have done. She told me all the time about how wonderful she was—unusual bragging like that.

Q: What did you think about that.

A: Two weeks wasn't long enough to really find out what the score was. She wanted to play records all the time, and sing and dance—all by herself! She was really wild and loud.

Q: What did you make of all this.

A: I wondered if she really was a dope addict. At first I thought it was her way of life to be so wild. Then I thought she must have lived an awful life, until my neighbor said something. Otherwise she might have gone home without my knowing it. I didn't know what to look for. It hadn't occurred to me that she might be taking dope. The dope must have been the cause of her speech being impaired. I never said anything to her about it. I wrote to her later and never got an answer, so I don't know about why she started it or anything. They did say that's what killed her though.

Case No. 5

Q: Have you ever known anyone who was an opiate addict?
A: Yes, I have.

Q: How did you come to meet him?
A: He was a musician. We used to have jam sessions after school (high school), and he used to come to a few of them . . . not real often . . . I didn't like to use him very often.

Q: How well did you know this person?
(This question brought a good laugh and an air of forced casualness. The subject's speech became hurried and slightly flippant.)
A: Not real well . . . Like we didn't bum around together, if that's what you mean. I had as little to do with him as I possibly could.

Q: How often did you see him?
(The subject started to answer, hesitated, apparently recalling something he'd omitted saying. He stumbled until finally getting together everything he meant to say.)
A: Not very often . . . wait . . . let me change the answer to that question of how I met him. I used to take guitar lessons from him before the sessions I mentioned, so I guess for about a year I saw him at least once a week.

Q: When was the first time you noticed or found out that he was a drug addict?
(Here again the subject seemed to be unusually "casual." He repeatedly laughed throughout his answer and spoke much less formally than he had been, using more slang and jargon that is generally associated with drugs and their users.)
A: He smoked the stuff at first, then he started using the needle. He was about 25 when I was taking lessons. He lived with his parents and I used to go to his house for lessons. He'd always be wearing this T-shirt. One day I noticed the marks on his arm. He never took the stuff in front of me or anything like that.

Q: What did you notice about him?
A: Like I said, I had a lesson. When he came in for the lesson he seemed funny.

Q: In what way?

A: Oh, you know . . . a glassy stare . . . and his movements were kind of jerky.

(The subject's attitude was one of slight irritation. He answered as though it was unnecessary, that I should know how drug addicts acted.)

Q: What happened?

A: We were together about a half an hour . . . he seemed real uneasy and nervous . . . finally he told me that I could make the rest of the time up later, or he wouldn't charge for the full lesson, or something . . . in any case he couldn't finish the lesson now . . . he had to take off.

(He then paused and added something in an "off-the-record" remark with a forced but knowing smile.)

I knew he was going to get a shot. He probably had the stuff in the next room . . . the crazy fool!

Q: You mentioned that you had heard that he smoked drugs before using a needle. Did you know that he was using drugs before you had the lesson you just mentioned?

A: Yes, I think so.

Q: Do you remember the first time that you heard or found that he was using drugs?

A: I don't really remember the first time I might have heard about him, but I think I remember the first time I saw him smoking them.

Q: Would you tell me about it?

A: Well, I'm not sure exactly . . . it was a good six years ago, but it was before the lesson I told you about. I saw him at a jam session. He was smoking it then.

Q: How did you know?

(He seemed very irritated that I should question his ability to recognize marijuana when he saw it. His answer was antagonistic and challenging.)

A: I could smell it! I was real close to him at the session. The stuff stinks, you know . . . smells like raw hemp. I asked the guy next to me and he said it was marijuana. I even casually asked him (the person in question) . . . he said he took it once in a while. It was none of my business . . . I didn't want to get involved with him or the junk.

Q: What did you notice about the person when you saw him then?

A: You mean with the drugs?

Q: Yes.

A: Nothing. He seemed perfectly calm and normal. He just played and was generally quite indifferent. You couldn't tell there was anything wrong with him by looking at him.

Q: What did you do when you found out he was smoking marijuana?

A: Nothing really . . . I just stayed away from him. Like I said I never had much to do with him anyway . . . I just used him for a few sessions . . . I didn't really care what he did so long as he didn't mess up when he was playing.

Q: When was the last time you saw him?

A: About four years ago . . . I just happened to see him teaching guitar at a studio.

Q: Do you remember anything about the meeting?

A: There's nothing to remember . . . I just saw him there . . . we didn't say anything to each other . . . I don't think he even saw me.

Q: What happened to the person?

A: You mean since I last saw him? I really don't know.

Case No. 6

Q: Have you ever known anyone that was an Opiate Addict?

A: Yes.

Q: How did you come to know this person?

A: He was the brother of one of my closest friends.

Q: How well did you know him?

A: Fairly well.

Q: What do you mean by fairly well?

A: Oh, we knew each other to say hello, and well enough to go out and have a beer on occasion. I'd say we were out with each other about every other week.

Q: What did you do when you were out together?

A: Well, we went to shows and had a few beers or something like this. His brother was always along, and occasionally he asked to come along with us.

Q: When did you first notice that this person was an Opiate Addict?

A: Well, when I first saw him he was just a regular guy. We talked about sports and girls, nothing in particular. Well he seemed in a fairly depressive mood when we were talking, because everything seemed to be on the negative side to him. After a while, I was waiting for his brother to come home, he went to the john, and came back a little later as happy as a little lark. Well, at first I thought that something was a little screwy, because a trip to the can doesn't make a person as happy as this one. So jokingly I asked him if he always got this much relief after going to the john, and he just laughed. Then he told me while we were watching television why it was that he got this great feeling. He just came right out and told me that he was taking the needle.

Q: What did you then notice about the person?

A: Well, he didn't seem to be the kind of guy that used this dope, and I really didn't believe him until he showed me the place where he had given himself the injection. Other than that though I would have never guessed such a thing at this time, because he seemed normal to me before he had gone into the bathroom.

Q: What did you make of that?

A: Well, at first I didn't really know what to do. It was one of those things that you read about, or that you see in the movies; but it was something that you really expect to happen to you, but not here. Another thing was that I felt that this guy was a little nutty, and that I didn't want anything more to do with him. The reason for this being that I had always thought of dope as being smuggled in and held in secret, and when I actually came upon a case where a person was using it I felt a little weird.

Q: What do you mean when you said that you felt a little weird?

A: Well by this I mean that I was afraid and that I sensed that something must be a little wrong mentally with him if he used dope.

Q: Then what did you do?

A: Well in the future I avoided him, because I thought that he might convince me that this was really great stuff and that I might just try it someday and end up getting hooked. I also told his brother, and he said that he knew it, but didn't report it because he was afraid of getting the family in trouble with the police. Then I just left the situation alone, because I didn't want to get messed up in itself myself.

Q: When was the last time that you saw him?

A: About the middle of June.

Q: What were the circumstances?

A: Well we were at a party, and he was there. He seemed to be at pretty good terms with everybody, and I was surprised that he wasn't really in the dumps as far as things go with addicts.

Q: How do things go with addicts?

A: Well, it has always seemed to me that the picture painted of the dope addict has always been one of a person that does really crazy things, or who is in such a state of sickness that he can't really do anything.

Q: Well then what happened?

A: About the end of the party he went home, and as I was leaving for a vacation, I didn't see him anymore, but I got a letter from another friend of mine at home saying that this guy is now in jail for stealing money from a store. Probably trying to get money to buy some more stuff.

In its own manner, each of these cases illustrates the point that the observer must use some extraneous indicator to designate the addict. In each case, the "normal" who is reacting to the "deviant" is convinced that he has actually used some valid technique for identifying and addict. In fact, however, such indicators as "glassy and starry eyes" (Case 1) and "puffed up and nervous" (Case 2) are only *reconstructions* that are never used as indicators of addiction before the fact. When asked the telling question of how they actually found out, finally, about the drug addiction of the party, the respondents use such legitimizers as "I read it in the papers," (Case 1) and "I looked at her arm" (Case 4).

There is no instance of self-confidence on the part of the persons reacting to the deviance in assessing the actual behavior of the drug user as being identifiably distinct from the behavior of any normal member of the society. The remarkable feature of instances like the first case is the fact that being arrested for stealing dope is the identifying behavior.

The most significant part is the reaction itself, however, in terms of what the observer does once he finds out. Perhaps the most liberal and tolerant of these cases is the college student (Case No. 2) who simply decided to "keep his distance" and "see him only when he had to." Others range from a categorical dismissal to avoidance as complete as possible.

In one of the examples included, the addict is a person who is a respectable professional (Case No. 3). He has none of the appearances of "the addict" that is the stereotype in the mind of the person recalling his experience. Thus, he is capable of expressing that he was shocked and amazed to learn that this "young, handsome, and professionally successful" person could be a drug addict. The disbelief that was expressed upon first learning of the addiction is an excellent illustration of two important points that have been made so far. First, except for being told by others, the observer can not detect on his own observation whether the addict is deviant or not in his behavior. Second, the moral overtones of drug use have developed to the point that only people who have the appearances of being unrespectable and underprivileged can be thought of as reasonable candidates for the title of drug addict.

The heart of the problem of social reaction to deviance lies in the last case (7). A normal social relationship is undermined by the knowledge of the "deviant" qualities of one of the parties. The girl had a romantic interest in the person whom she thought was "normal," then allowed hearsay and the characterization of others to break off the relationship. There was nothing intrinsic to what occurred between them to reveal any deviance, but the external moral implications of the association were sufficient to cast them apart.

In the remaining chapters, this relationship between moral judgment and the reaction of various segments of the society will be explored in greater empirical detail. The focus now shifts to a study of an institution which is the embodiment of societal reaction to the deviance of the drug addict—incarceration.

PART III

An empirical study

CHAPTER 6

The California rehabilitation center

Material in chapters 6, 7, and 8 was collected while the author was a consultant and research sociologist at the California Rehabilitation Center, Corona, California, from 1964 to 1966.

The views expressed in this publication are those of the author and do not necessarily represent those of the California Rehabilitation Center nor of the California Department of Corrections.

I N POPULATION, CALIFORNIA IS THE LARGEST STATE IN THE union. It has newly arrived to that status as a result of the explosive migration there in the last few decades. The very newness of this vast, mobile population, with its rootlessness and lack of tradition, provided a climate conducive to the development of relatively progressive public programs in the early 1960s. The southern part of the state is sprawling and especially new. Los Angeles, which epitomizes this as a city, has a large population of uprooted lower and working-class Mexican-Americans and Blacks who are unskilled and unemployed. It is close to Mexico with its long, unpatrollable border. These conditions combine with others to effect a sizeable underworld traffic in marijuana and heroin.

It was Southern California which saw the birth of Synanon, a totally voluntary organization for addicts who want to conquer their addiction without legal sanctions or state supervision.[1] It was also Southern California which gave birth to the California Rehabilitation Center, a state-operated institution designed specifically to handle the criminal addict population of the state. Its character was fashioned and styled by the progressivism of the state administrators of the period.

The California Rehabilitation Center (CRC) is strategic for study not only because it is the first large institution of its kind, but also because it has served and will serve as a model for other states with a narcotics problem. At the present, New Jersey has already followed the model of CRC; and Illinois is looking over the program with careful interest. Ideally, the plan is to separate the addict population from other criminals locked up in prisons, and to administer a separate kind of therapeutic treatment designed particularly for the addict. The two federal hospitals at Lexington, Kentucky and Fort Worth, Texas are quite different in that they are primarily voluntary. At CRC, most of the inmates, called "residents," are convicted felons who have been rerouted and committed to this special institution for addicts. During the period that this study was conducted, from early 1964 through 1965, the population was in the vicinity of 1,300 residents. The figure fluctuates by several score in each direction due to the rate of release and commitment and/or return. The ratio of males to females is roughly 6 to 1.

Despite its title and selected euphemisms about its operations, CRC is a prison in almost every sense of the word. Well over 90 per cent of the inmates were brought in after a conviction, involuntarily. As in every prison, the custodial function takes precedence over every other function. The larger society, at all critical points, demands this. Whenever there is an escape, the public's reaction insures that the custodial wing of a prison gets tighter control and more power, while those primarily concerned with treatment must bend and accommodate. The therapeutic part of the program, which is an explicitly stated reason-for-being of the institution, is dramatically curtailed by the very context of the institutional setting.

For example, an important part of normal life outside of prison walls is the decision-making ability and the consequent independent action of the individual. If a prisoner is to be "rehabilitated," he must be "trained" in doing those normal and essential tasks of life as lived outside the prison. It is normal in the world to have the opportunity and ability to express an independent identity through distinctive manners of dress, form, style, and speech. It is normal outside the prison to have an occupation through which one achieves a clear position in the world vis-à-vis others. It is normal outside of the prison to have sexual interests and pursuits, and to have the occasional realization of them.

Before turning to those features of the Rehabilitation Center which are unique, it is important to relate those things which it has in common with other prisons. The normality of sexual contact, the expression of independent identity through appearance, dress, and occupational distinctiveness are all nullified systematically. For the inmate to be given more normal responsibility means that he will not be programmed as carefully. If he is not programmed as carefully, his chances for escape are greatly increased. If the chances for escape are greater, a few will take advantage of the situation and escape. Once the public hears of an escape, all of the forces of reaction are mobilized against the institution in order to force it to strengthen security. This means that the inmate must be watched more carefully and programmed more completely. This destroys his ability to exercise the "training" in assuming the responsibility so vital to his "rehabilitation," and the program therefore contains intrinsic strain that is the seed of its own increasing custody and decreasing ability to rehabilitate.[2] These things CRC has in common with all other American prisons. Later, focus will turn to those things it holds in common with other total institutions, as well as to its uniquenesses on both counts.

Physical Setting

The Rehabilitation Center is located in the Norco-Corona hills, in natural seclusion from the neighboring towns of the area. The administrative and women's units are housed in architecturally interesting structures at the top of the hill. The building used by the administration was first opened in the 1920s as a resort area for a Southern California exclusive social set of the period. With the coming of the Depression, this use lapsed until World War II, when the military took over the whole and constructed rows and rows of army-type barracks in an intermediate valley below the old resort area. These barracks, twenty-three in total, accommodate most of the residents.* After the War, the premises on the hill lay unoccupied for several years. When the Rehabilitation Center personnel moved in during 1960–61, extensive renovation was required. Landscaping, gardening, and work on the exterior have continued to the present, providing work activity for many of the residents.

The 1,100 men live below in the barracks. Each residential unit houses about sixty men. The barrack-dormitory is not only the basic living unit, it is also the basic therapeutic arena. Each barrack has a counselor who works in the barrack eight hours a day, five days a week. During the remainder of the time, the custodial staff rotates and has complete control. Even while the counselor is on duty, the custodial staff is present, and this provides for a measure of strain and conflict built into the system that is to be reviewed.

The 200–250 women in the institution live in a setting more like a college dormitory. They are housed in a brick building across from the administration, and live in small rooms, usually four to a room. Unlike the men's situation, the residential unit does not at all coincide with the therapeutic unit, and the consequences of this for administration and control are remarkably different.

The resident has an eight-hour day in which he is engaged in more-or-less required activities. Four hours are spent in either a work-group, training, or formal education. Work may consist of preparing earth for planting, driving a taxi around the premises, fire station duty, cooking and kitchen help, waiting table in the cafeteria for staff, and so on. The other four hours are spent in group therapy sessions (one hour), cleaning up the dorm, and recreation. While one half of the institution is doing one kind of four-hour activity, the other half is

* The terms "resident" and "inmate" will be used interchangeably hereafter. *Resident* is the term used on the grounds of the institution by the staff.

doing the other. They then shift, and it is possible to observe at any time during the day a large number of residents playing football, handball, or baseball while another large group is watering, mowing the lawn, digging, or working with a ground crew. It is during this eight-hour day that the counselor is in the barrack.

Getting Committed to CRC

A little more than half of the inmates of the institution have been convicted of a felony in a County Superior Court (often robbery, sometimes narcotics sales), and after conviction, the judge suspends criminal proceedings and refers for civil commitment to the Center. He may do this if there is evidence that the felon was either an addict or in "imminent danger of becoming" an addict. For a convicted felon, commitment to CRC is certainly not a bad deal. First of all, his sentence there is one to ten years, and the chances are good for release within two to three years under extended parole for the remaining period (assuming good behavior). Second, the atmosphere is more liberal and the freedom of movement for inmates is greater than at any of the medium and maximum security prisons.

Officially, CRC is for the rehabilitation of addicts. However, any observer familiar with the administration of justice in the United States will recognize that the structure of this situation places great bargaining power in the hands of the prosecuting attorney. An armed robber who would ordinarily face say, a twenty-year sentence, can now be offered a deal. If he informs on his contacts in the narcotics black market, the prosecution may guarantee his civil commitment to CRC in return for the favor. Certainly, a plea of guilty is more easily won in these instances because the stakes for the convicted man are clearer. With a twenty-year sentence, he can not be eligible for parole until at least one third of the time is served in prison. That means a minimum of seven years. However, with a civil commitment to CRC, we have seen how his one-to-ten-year investment may allow his parole after twelve to fifteen months. Cooperation in the bargaining with the prosecution is thereby increased even more than in ordinary circumstances.

The deal is not so good for those convicted of a misdemeanor. The maximum prison sentence for such offenses is one year in any case. They have little time to gain by having their convictions suspended and the civil commitment to CRC invoked, since the latter carries with it the one to ten year situation just described for felons. Approximately 20 per cent of those inmates at CRC are in such a circumstance. Many of these are the prostitutes (prostitution is a misdemeanor in California) who were discovered to be drug users or addicts. While they were convicted of prostitution, they effectively serve their time as drug addicts. There is a serious question of a civil liberties or constitutional violation in these cases, and it will some day soon get a review in a high court. These are undoubtedly the bitterest residents in the institution. They have the strong feeling that they have been tricked by the law enforcement people, and have an excess of venom for the whole system, including the therapeutic community conception of the institution. In this investigation, they proved to be the group most hostile to the institution and its goals and programs.

The remaining 25–30 per cent of the inmates are commitments without a court conviction for a crime. Typically, either law enforcement authorities or family members bring such cases to the attention of the courts.

Despite the range of types of commitment sources, the inmates at CRC must be described as predominantly a population with a criminal history. The arrest list for many reads like Pepys' diary, underscored by the fact that the inmates have an average number of three jail terms behind them for narcotics or narcotics-related offenses prior to their commitment to CRC.

Group Therapy and the Therapeutic Community

For one hour, the residents gather for a session of "group," "grouping," or "group therapy." The officially designated time set aside for this purpose is a relatively small part of the day, but the stated policy of the treatment staff is that everything which goes on in the day should have therapeutic purpose and value. The one hour spent in the group session is thus seen as arbitrary focusing on the central reason of the whole program. The work crews, the classroom, the recreation are all considered to be elements of the therapeutic community, and the treatment staff feels that it can not, and should not be set apart. Problems that arise in the rest of the day are to be brought to group, freely and openly aired, discussed, faced, and resolved where possible. The counselor leads each group session. For the men, the group consists of those in the living unit, the barrack. Thus, sixty men come to group at the same time to discuss, challenge, squeal, argue, support, destroy, build, and devastate. The counselors have latitude in deciding how they will run the group sessions. Some require that all residents of the unit attend, and some make no official note of attendance. Some counselors are aggressive and domineering in the sessions simply by force of personality, and they tend to sway the group and control it. Others are relatively passive, and allow the session to go very much its own way.

The women also come together in a central location for group sessions of about sixty under a single counselor. However, an important difference is that the women's group is not living together in a single barrack, but has separate rooms of four inhabitants. The staff readily acknowledges that for the women, the group is therefore far more an artificially constructed one-hour experience than a living part of the ordinary day. For example, if a male complains about something that is going on in the dorm, every other person in the sixty-man group is likely to be part of it by his presence in the larger unit. If the reason for the complaint persists, many members of the group session are likely to become involved in the living experience. However, if a female has a complaint about what is going on in her small living unit of four, and brings this up in a group of sixty, the others are more likely to treat it as a private problem which need have no effect upon them.

Despite the wide divergence of temperaments and strategies of the counselors who guide the groups, there is a common theme that threads throughout these sessions. The theme emanates from the institution's approach to the problem of narcotics addiction, an approach reflecting the reigning interpretation of addiction in society. The common feature of the group sessions is the focus upon the psychic makeup of the individual addict, and the central issue at hand is the motivation of the actor. Sometimes there is an attempt to explain past behavior, but there is increasing emphasis in both the rhetoric and the guidance of the counseling staff to explain present behavior. This concern is appropriately termed the "here and now," parlance borrowed from current usage in psychotherapy. The self-conscious progressivism of the institution and its treatment staff must be contrasted with traditional prisons and traditional institutional treatment in order to be appreciated. Prisons typically deny the inmate any responsibility, autonomy, or decision-making about even the most minute aspects of his personal life. The prisoner is told not only when to get up in the morning and when to go to bed, when to eat and what to eat, what to wear, how long the hair can be, and other routinized features of prison life, but as well, he is told that there are specifically legitimate channels of grievance to handle every conceivable problem. However, at CRC there is an attempt to allow the residents to solve selected problems in an emergent manner within the community. For the men, this means that they may want to bring up in group a problem such as the distribution of towels and soap. Unlike most prisons, where towels and soap are distributed individually to inmates by the staff, in CRC, a counselor may place sixty towels in a dorm and leave it up to the community to solve the distribution problem. If someone hoards, or takes even a small bit more than his share, the sanctions are left to be administered internally. It is the hope that this strategy is more rehabilitative in the sense that it forces participation and communal involvement.

The one-hour group sessions provide the arena for the realization of such a strategy, according to the treatment staff. The towel hoarder must confront the group, during which time he is called individually to account before those with whom he must live a daily life, as a peer. Because the living unit is coterminous with the group for the males, the connection between what goes on in group and daily activities is a close one. The men can bring to bear collectively the implementation of the group session. The extent to which spatial arrangements and ecological patterns determine the nature of the control relationships among people is clearly demonstrated when this situation is contrasted with that of the women. After the women finish with the group session of sixty, they return to the specific problems which attend to group life among four. There is thus a tendency to treat the group as a separate theatrical performance which need have no forced or sanctionable connection with life in the institution.

For example, one male may be the object of intensive scrutiny in one of the sessions, where barrages of questions are fired at him examining his psychic integration and the motivation for his social relationships in the barrack. One of the complaints against him may be that he takes the ping-pong paddle back to his bunk and stores it under his bed. Not only does this behavior affect everyone else in the barrack who wants to play (it would have the same effect among the women), but it can also be *observed and sanctioned* by any of the other fifty-nine. For the females, the probabilities of control are limited to an additional three.

This is not to say that the men do not feel that they are very much on stage when they are the focus of the group's attention. It is to say that the performance in group for men has more of a consequence after its completion. This is remarkably at variance with traditional prisons, to the point of being opposite. The common saying which captures the spirit and practice of the ordinary prison is "Do your own time." That is, when the prisoner arrives, he learns immediately that the best way to get his time off for good behavior is to stay out of the way of other inmates and to avoid fights, squabbles, and the like. If he minds his own business, he is acting in the maximally efficient manner. There are, of course, times when his own business may coincide with the business of others, in the form of deals for favors, cigarettes, induced or extorted homosexuality, and so forth. However, these activities are always hidden and are never part of the explicit policy that guides the official destiny of the inmate in the prison. He is not supposed to be doing any of these things, and if these things remain officially undiscovered, as they usually do, they have nothing to do with his good behavior and his likelihood for early parole. For a man with a twenty-year sentence, one third off is the critical reality which impinges upon his prison behavior. When it comes to how he relates to the institution, then, it is characteristically accurate to say that he will do his own time.

This is in sharp contrast to the CRC resident's pet phrase, which en-capsulates how he feels about the quickest way to get out of the institution: "If you wanta walk, you gotta talk." The residents are poignantly aware that one of the most important criteria for being released is to demonstrate in group sessions that one is aware of the psychic disturbance that the staff feels brought about the narcotic delinquency, and what is more important, that one is able to express in some kind of searching, groping, or perhaps articulate fashion that this is the case. The staff must see some outward sign that the ex-addict is struggling with and mastering his psychic integration problem, the essence of that which is said to have resulted in his addiction. The resident can display this in a number of ways, but he knows that one way is minimal: "you gotta talk" in the group sessions.

Here it will help to clarify the addict's subjective feeling that there is pressure to be expressive if the pathway out of the institution is examined. The staff here has much more to say about when the resident is to leave than in an ordinary prison. In the latter, the inmate knows precisely how much time he must "do" and what "good time" and "good behavior" consist of in behavioral terms. If he has a twenty-year sentence, he must serve at least one third in the prison. The other two thirds is determined by whether he stays out of fights and whether he obeys certain prison rules that are explicit and known, formal and informal.[3] That is, the whole emphasis in the ordinary prison is upon structuring with great clarity those activities and inactivities which lead to early parole. What one may think of those activities, the lack of humaneness in them, the degradation, the shortsightedness; all of that is a different order of question. The point is that the behavior which leads out is clear, and the individual knows how to do his own time. This is not the case for residents at CRC. A good analogy is the difference between undergraduate and graduate training in the United States.

Matters are very clear for the undergraduate. He knows that if he takes certain courses and passes the exams in them, he will move to the next level. He knows that as he passes through four levels, for a period of four years, he will graduate. He knows because the catalog tells him so. There is a public statement of activities of which he is aware, and which administrators and faculty must honor. Just as with the prisoner in the typical prison, things are relatively fixed. The professor has latitude only in so far as it refers to his single course. The cataloged character of the requirements restricts the malleability of interpretation for all parties, whether it is a prisoner in a penal institution or a student in an educational institution.

Contrast this with the situation of the graduate student, the counterpart of the CRC resident. Graduate studies are specifically ambiguous. The graduate student has no guarantee that his completion of the required course work will lead to a degree. There are activities in which he is required to engage, but there is no assurance that these activities are sufficient. The faculty retains the right to make a judgment about the preparedness of the candidate for an advanced degree—as to whether he is ready. This means that the graduate student must try to figure out what it is that the faculty wants over and above the publicly stated criteria. To be successful, he must find this out in a subjective and intuitive way. There is no catalog publicly honored. The dissertation must demonstrate "individual creativity and scholarship." But the interpretation of what is creative and scholarly is left to the faculty. It is not a matter for public perusal, where anyone can see that an exam has been passed. At what point does the dissertation meet those requirements? As for the preliminary qualifying examinations, when does one ever really display a grasp of a whole field of inquiry? The answer is that this resides in the judgment of the reviewers, and the judgment occurs at some future time, ambiguous and unknown to the actor acting in the present. The same is true for the CRC resident.

The CRC staff is in the position of the graduate faculty. It is not behaviorally clear and demonstrable as to what is meant by demonstrating maturity, or displaying a grasp of one's own essential personality problems. It is not at all clear to the staff, much less to the resident. If it were clear to the staff in terms of some specific behavior, then it could simply be recorded and published for the residents to read and so accommodate their behavior.

The graduate student is ridden with a kind of anxiety that the undergraduate never experiences in the pursuit of his studies. The CRC resident is ridden with a kind of anxiety that the ordinary prison inmate never experiences in his quest to leave the institution. If it is possible to find parallels in the production of anxiety, it should also be possible to find parallels in the behavioral response. To the extent that a graduate program is not fixed, graduate students spend that much more of a proportion of their time trying to convince the staff that they are committed, or some other such attitude with which they can display to indicate that they should be chosen. Surely enough, CRC residents spend that much more of their time concerned with the appearances of commitment than do prisoners who are doing time. The group session is the part of the day when such commitment activity is most appropriate. To talk, to engage others in reflective and penetrating probes is to display a commitment in the direction that is believed to be most rewarding. It is the path out, and whether it is thought to be most rewarding because of its use as a technique to fool the staff or its use to understand the self is not at issue here. The point that is to be emphasized is that the residents feel the pressure to actively engage in the lives of others via the communal character of the group and group life. It is a shift from the traditional method that has some dramatic consequences.

One of the striking things about the institution has been the enthusiasm of the staff members for the desirability and effectiveness of the group-therapy program. There is typically a great deal of cynicism by staff members in other total institutions (regular prisons, mental hospitals, army barracks) as to the desirability and effectiveness of the program. The treatment people at mental hospitals and prisons often seem to have doubts as to the good, much less the effectiveness, of what they are doing.[4]

In these first years, the treatment staff of the Rehabilitation Center has been very committed to the group-therapy program. They rely heavily upon psychological interpretations of the residents' behavior, and their commitment seems to be based on the belief that this interpretation is the key therapeutic device.

After the first three weeks in the institution, the new resident takes an examination to determine his scholastic achievement level. If he tests out at a grade of over 8.5, which is the equivalent of about a high school freshman, he may choose to go into vocational training provided by the Rehabilitation Center. In the early stages, this consisted of training in upholstering, certain kinds of carpentry, some painting, and allied pursuits. There is a plan to expand the alternatives of the training. If the new resident scores below 8.5, he is strongly urged to go to the school within the institution for classroom instruction. The educational program is tied in with the local public school system, which allows the successful student to be granted a diploma from that system. The student attends classes daily, and pursues studies in a manner which is an attempt to approximate the normal classroom.

CRC and the Rehabilitation Issue

Following Goffman's usage, the California Rehabilitation Center is a total institution.[5]

When we review the different institutions in our Western Society, we find some that are encompassing to a degree discontinuously greater than the ones next in line. Their encompassing or total character is symbolized by the barrier to social intercourse with the outside and to departure which is often built right into the physical plant, such as locked doors, high walls, barbed wire, cliffs, water, forests, or moors. These establishments I am calling *total institutions* . . . .[6]

One of the essential characteristics of large total institutions is that masses of people (1,300 in the case of CRC) must be systematically mobilized through bureaucratic organization to do such things as eat, sleep, and wash, in a coordinated and orderly fashion. From this, other things follow. The first problem of the administration of the institution is to accomplish these massive tasks with some efficiency. As Goffman points out, the staff is therefore very much concerned at the very outset with surveillance, in seeing to it that everyone behaves in the properly coordinated manner. The trouble-maker is the individual who spoils this mass social ordering of behavior by being late, or in any way by being individually deviant in these essential efficiency-producing procedures. The point is not that the staff is replete with intolerant personalities. The point is strictly sociological: the structure of relationships forces a degree of intolerance of individualistic behavior in basic matters of everyday living. It is a structural problem that all total institutions have in common, CRC not excepted. There is always the staff-inmate split which transcends the mere roles of the two parties. It is more than simply a difference between two groups who have clearly different positions to maintain.

The entrance of the inmate into the institution meets several of the conditions of a successful degradation ceremony.[7] The individual is stripped of the most typical appearances of a unique identity and is confronted with a proliferated set of rules that are to be mastered immediately. His early success is measured in these first encounters, or other situations covered by procedural handbooks. As he proceeds in the institution, the resident learns that as long as he stays within the boundaries specified in the rules, it is the treatment staff that he must primarily deal with and not the custodial staff. That is, the treatment staff has a superior structural position so long as the life of the resident does not cross over normally routinized parameters of everyday life.

The fact that the treatment staff has the upper hand in this regard produces an interesting response on the part of many, if not most residents. Simply stated in summary form, it is issued as a challenge: "If I am psychologically sick and you are so smart in matters psychological, cure me!" Here we find the first important conflict of ideologies between staff and inmate populations. If one is sophisticated in contemporary psychotherapeutic matters, he knows that someone with a psychic problem can be cured only to the extent that he is receptive to the idea of his own committed participation in the therapy. For the therapist to be effective, he must have the cooperation of the subject at least to the point that the subject is willing to conceive of the problem in the same terms.[8] The subject, according to psychotherapists, must be willing to introspect, then express. Whether the procedure followed is directive or nondirective is not critical to this basic point. But as Hollingshead and Redlich have pointed out, sophistication about psychotherapy resides primarily in the middle and upper classes.[9] The lower and working classes are skeptical and even hostile to treatment that is not more clearly organic. For the lower classes, if one is sick, one goes to the doctor who knows about the sickness. The doctor prescribes the appropriate medicine, and the pill or liquid either works or does not.

The inmate population at the Rehabilitation Center is overwhelmingly working and lower class. The treatment staff population is overwhelmingly middle class. In the Hollingshead and Redlich study, middle-class therapists administering therapy to middle-class patients find relatively little difficulty with the initial point of contact in coming to terms with the problem. The patients accept their role as introspecting and expressing patients, and would be alarmed at an attempt to treat their mental problem organically with, say, pills. Quite the contrary, the middle-class therapists had severe problems of communication with the lower classes of patients, who regarded the psychotherapy as evidence of incompetence, or stalling, or charlatanism, or worse. Where, indeed, is the pill? After a series of such encounters with the patients, the therapists began to prescribe organic treatment systematically for the lower classes. This helps to account for the fantastically distorted proportion of organic treatment of mental illness among the lower classes.[10]

There are two important differences between CRC and the mental hospital situations reported by Hollingshead and Redlich. First of all, the CRC resident has a far more forced and continuous relationship with his group therapist. Second, there is a general enthusiasm within the CRC treatment staff for the group-therapy program. Parenthetically, there is no middle-class clientele with which the treatment staff can compare the CRC residents. The treatment staff confronts the resident with only one possible conceptualization of the path to cure, that of the individual's introspection and then expressive communication in the group therapy.

The resident's statement, "Cure me!" is an assertion of ideology. The staff's reply is steeped in its own ideology: "Enter into the therapeutic community in order to cure yourself, and I will watch closely to assess what progress you make." The staff–inmate split inherent in any total institution is thus reemphasized in an additional sphere at CRC. However, there are structural properties peculiar to the institution that produce accommodation rather than conflict. Obviously, the typical inmate wants to get out of the institution. For reasons that have been cited elsewhere, the approval of the treatment staff is critical for early departure, and this approval comes primarily from "good behavior" in the therapeutic community. Whether or not the inmates really believe what they are saying about themselves and others in the group is not at issue here. The important thing is that they realize that they are forced to maintain the appearance of a strong commitment to the therapeutic principles. In the first stages of the resident's entrance into the institution and therefore into the group sessions, he is likely to be hostile and cynical. Afterward, he is likely to take one of two paths. Even if one starts out "playing the game of therapy," a continual daily dose of it can affect the participants greatly. About one third of those who said that they started out cynically about the program later said that they came around to accept the positive and helpful aspects.[11] About 40 per cent indicated that they remained skeptical of utility of the program for themselves, but interestingly enough, most of these said that they thought the program might be beneficial to others.[12] To the extent that the first one third are being helped by their acceptance and belief in the program, this is a remarkably accurate perception of reality for the more skeptical and cynical.

There is a peculiar consequence of each pathway taken by the inmate. If he remains cynical about the program, he is relatively detached and analytic in his approach to it. From this posture, it is not very difficult to develop some ability to practice skillfully those responses that are asked for by the treatment staff. It is ironic that the detached can be far more expressive as a direct consequence of the glibness that comes from the detachment. The sincere are sincerely struggling and are often reluctant to express an intimate, personal, and potentially self-devastating piece of information before fifty-nine other men, some of whom are covertly hostile to the whole proceedings. This problem comes up significantly in the discussion of the criteria that the treatment staff employ in deciding when a resident is ready to leave the institution.

The Creation of Community, Identity, and Total Identity

A drug intended for one purpose may be quite successful in achieving that purpose, but it often is accompanied by undesirable side effects. The critical problem before the drug researcher is how to develop a pure drug, one free from deleterious side effects that are sometimes more serious than the problem the drug was trying to cure. For example, chloromycetin is a cure for the streptococcic infection, but it also is known to produce the side effect of aplastic anemia in a dangerous number of cases, and aplastic anemia is often fatal.[13]

A social institution faces a similar problem. It may be intended for one purpose, but it may have side effects that are deleterious in and of themselves. In fact, they may be as deleterious as the fatal side effects of some drugs. The trouble, of course, is that while it is very clear when a drug has side effects, the side effects of institutions are very subtle, compounded, and often obscured. The explicit purpose of CRC is to provide an enforced drug-free environment for the rehabilitation of the addict. As has been pointed out, the program is designed to meet the specific problem of the addict, and so he is separated from other prisoners and placed in an all-addict community. The rehabilitation of the addict is seen in terms of his return to normal life outside of the correctional facility, free from drug use or other trouble with the law. This smooth return to normal life is contingent upon two kinds of acceptance. First, the general population must be willing to accept such a return as possible and legitimate, if not normal. This alone is a critical problem that is the subject of much of the rest of this work. There is a second kind of acceptance that is of equal importance: namely, the addict himself must regard his return as possible and desirable. It is with this issue that the therapeutic community becomes so interrelated. The hope of the treatment staff is that the therapeutic community provides the addict with the strong motivation to stay off narcotics, and therefore to stay away from the addict community.

However, the very existence of CRC as a separate institution for addicts, and the very notion of a group session of addicts, reinforce the idea of the addict as a separate kind of person, thereby creating unanticipated and very undesirable side effects. To a lesser extent, this occurs with every prisoner, addict or not, but it is greatly exacerbated by two practices current with the addicts. Ordinarily, the great diversification of a prison precludes the possibility of a consciousness of kind, or a community developing. The Rehabilitation Center emphasizes consciousness of kind because it is a separate structure for addicts. What is more important, the group-therapy sessions have the explicit function of developing a community of men involved in elaborate introspection about themselves as a special and different case. The importance of an identity as an addict is set against the "normal" or nonaddict world.

Addicts are trained to conceive of themselves as a class of men apart who have something very binding in common, namely, the personality weakness of which they are continually reminded. A side effect of the success of this program may be to instill in the ex-addict a sense of his identity as an addict who best belongs among others of the same type—other addicts. It may be that the ex-addict comes to believe that "squares are really different," that there is something about one who takes drugs which does make a qualitative difference. The unanticipated consequence of such a community, whether it is a therapeutic community or a living community, is that the members may come to feel a kinship with each other which supercedes their involvement with those outside the community.

The best parallel example comes from the sociology of minority relations. One of the effects of ethnic segregation in a "dominant" culture, whether the segregation is voluntary or forced, positive or negative, is the emergence of primary identification of ethnic members with the successes or failures of members. For the drug addict, the crisis of identity may not be as clear to the outsider, but it may well be worth more serious consideration and deliberation by "segregationists."

Thoughtful consideration of the nature of individual and group identity would be fruitful to an understanding of the community issue. Most people may shift from one social setting to another without a carry-over of "who they really are" being the sole determinant of how people will react to them. When a lawyer meets a corporation executive or a judge socially, he may choose to consider chess-playing ability as the focus of their identities. It is a simple, necessary, and common fact that one be able to parcel out the relevant identity of the person with whom one is dealing at the moment. For most, there is no one partial identity that is sufficiently important to color the total person with such completeness so as to become what the person always is. There are exceptions, and being a social deviant is one of them. The moral interpretation of the individual infuses into every aspect of his being. The public's conception of what a drug addict is revolves around the imputation of immorality of the total person. To place a number of addicts into the same highly structured living community is to reinforce the separateness as well as the totality of the moral identity. It is easy to see how a group of men who are regarded as immoral, when herded together into a single community, might develop a consciousness of kind or kinship to the newly created community and a feeling of real separateness from those outside the community. The development of this kind of community can only undermine the rehabilitation of the addict. He may feel that he cannot, or has no desire to enter a world where men are so totally different; namely, where they are nonaddicts and complete squares. The issue of total versus partial identity cuts both ways. The addict, too, may begin to see the nonaddict as being so completely different that communicating or relating is undesirable, if not impossible. The whole program of rehabilitation in the institution is officially designed to make the ex-addict's reentrance into the normal community smooth and successful. Yet, the use of the community to achieve that purpose has built into it a side effect that is detrimental to its aims.

The treatment staff makes a judgment as to when the resident is ready to leave the Rehabilitation Center and return to the community. As has been indicated, there is no clear set of actions that are known to be the pathway out of the institution. One critical factor that is commonly acknowledged is the readiness of the community to which the addict is returning to provide a place for him that maximizes a drug-free life. The primary indicators of this for the staff seem to be (1) the existence of an occupation and (2) the newness of surroundings and the nature of acquaintances. It is especially important that the acquaintances are not users. The treatment staff makes a decision to release the resident based largely upon their imputation of what the receiving community is like. This means that the staff must have some conception of what a good community is, and this conception will greatly influence its judgment of who is ready to leave the institution. The staff–inmate split, as we have seen in another context, coincides with a social-class split. The differing views of what constitute appropriate relations in the community may follow these class lines, and therefore some of the staff's criteria may be irrelevant to the living conditions that inmates face when they leave. For example, middle-class treatment staff may regard it as perverse when the inmate refuses to engage in a certain kind of free and open expressiveness in group. He should, according to the treatment staff, participate in the group's uncovering of a delinquent culprit among them. If he does not, then he needs more rehabilitation. However, from the point of view of the community to which the inmate is to return someday, this training is hardly preparatory or rehabilitative. The lower- or working-class community will heavily sanction the free and open and expressive cured addict who helps to uncover antisocial and antimiddle-class culprits in the working-class community. If he takes as his own the set of directives for living that he learned in the institution, the translation into action in a lower-class community will bring him continual trouble.

Within the institution, there is strain that is built into the two types of relationships that the staff has with the resident. It has been pointed out that the treatment staff is separate from the custodial staff. The former work an eight-hour day for five days of the week, while the latter must be on duty for twenty-four hours of a seven-day week. *That information alone is an accurate reflection of the locus of the public's concern.* When the counselor from the treatment staff is on the job, he has the larger measure of control over the resident. However, when he leaves at five in the evening, authority lapses automatically to the custodial staff. All recognize that there ought to be some continuity between the rules laid down by the treatment and custodial overseers. Strain is therefore siphoned into the internal staff relations. The custodial staff works eight-hour days also, but in three shifts. The counselor may leave some directives for residents and some strong suggestions for the custodial men who are to see that they are carried out. However, the custodial men are responsible directly to the custodial line officers, not to the treatment people. Their rewards and promotions come from the custodial wing, and a certain amount of resentment develops when directives originate from a source to which the line officers are not responsible. The manner in which the inmate interprets and exploits these strains is the source of a separate study. This introductory profile of the institution is continued in the next two chapters, though the direct focus shifts to an empirical study of the inmate himself.

CHAPTER 7

The moral implications of psychic maladjustment in the deviant

THE PRESENT-DAY PHYSIOLOGIST HAS A RATHER EASY TIME making a clear separation between physiological illness and moral judgment. The known fact that a man is suffering from cancer or diabetes does not affect his standing as a responsible, respectable, or "good" citizen. (It has not always been so. Within the last century, those with certain physical illnesses were believed to be possessed by devils and were shunned and ostracized by "decent" men.)[1] The present day psychiatrist or psychologist has a much harder time purging the analysis of certain psychic illnesses of implications of moral judgment. Whether he wants it that way or not, his assessment of certain normal mental adjustments is intricately interwoven into the community's conception of what constitutes a good man. For example, to say that one is unreliable, can not bear to face reality, "retreats into a world of fantasy, gives up, runs away from problems," is perhaps to accurately assess his psychic state and behavior, but it is simultaneously to characterize him in terms that undermine his status as a moral and responsible citizen.[2]

The reason is simple enough. A "moral" or "good" man in Western society is responsible, independent, respectful of the rights of others, and in the conventional wisdom, able to face the reality the rest of us have come to know.[3] At this juncture the intention is not to challenge the professional integrity or accuracy of one who might so judge a specific social deviant, in this case a drug addict. Instead, the goal is to point to a side effect of such a judgment that has its own consequences: that to question the ability of the individual to face reality without a crutch is also to impugn his right to take his place in a community of normal men—*men who in their turn see that ability as moral fibre and courage*. In Chapter 4, the problem of moral judgment was separated into three levels of analysis: the individual, the community, and the larger culture. Placing the present discussion in that framework, the community consensus of appropriate behavior is the standard by which individual adjustment or maladjustment is set. Whether we are talking about the American who adjusts to his tribe's ritual expectations that he grow grass around his suburban home, shave every day, and support napalm bombing, or whether we speak of the Tchambuli's adjustments to the vicissitudes of his tribe's rituals and hostilities, the psychologist's measuring stick of adjustment must be within the context of the existing social environment. That is necessary because his unit of analysis is the individual, and varying the culture simply changes the substance in the issue of adjustment. Unless or until the psychiatrist and psychologist raise the issue of the moral order at the second or third level, then " . . . a citizen of the Third Reich was well-adjusted in his lack of rebellion and hostility to authority when he did not seek inquisitively and skeptically into why authority purged his neighborhood of the Jews." Yet the moral resistance to admitting to the psychological health in this instance is understandable even in "value-free" scientific circles. Studies of a certain kind of personality (authoritarian) emerged to explain the pathological character of the adjustment.[4]

But to the extent that the authoritarian personality is capable of an analysis approaching culture-free dimensions, to that extent it has nothing to do *per se* with adjustment. Adjustments are made to social and cultural conditions and systems. Despite analyses of personality types that successfully leap above the substantive issues, the point remains that a well-adjusted individual is one who does not defy the community consensus of appropriate behavior. It follows that to be well-adjusted is also to be morally acceptable within that community. What has been less well appreciated and explored is its opposite, that to be maladjusted is in this sense to defy consensus and often totter on the perimeters of morality. It is to this problem that attention should now be turned.

We have seen that the dominant interpretation of addiction regards it as a consequence of some defect of the personality. In discussing the "inadequate personality" of the addict, Ausubel quotes the following passage from a Mental Health publication on the inadequate personality:

By the time an individual reaches late adolescence in our culture we can normally expect certain evidences of goal maturation to take place. We can expect him to aspire to a status that he attains through his own efforts rather than to one that he holds merely by virtue of a dependent relationship to his parents. We can expect him to formulate his own goals and reach decisions independently; to be less dependent on parental approval; to be able to postpone immediate pleasure-seeking goals for the sake of advancing long-range objectives; to continue striving despite initial set backs. We can expect him to aspire to realistic goals; to be capable of judging himself his accomplishments, and his prospects with a certain amount of critical ability; to have acquired a sense of moral obligation and responsibility.[5]

Ausubel then goes on to describe failures of the inadequate personality and tries to tie it in to the behavior of the addict:

The inadequate personality fails to conceive of himself as an independent adult and fails to identify with such normal adult goals as financial independence, stable employment, and the establishment of his own home and family. He is passive, dependent, unreliable, and unwilling to postpone immediate gratification of pleasurable impulses. He demonstrates no desire to persevere in the face of environmental difficulties, or to accept responsibilities which he finds distasteful.[6]

This description treats "immaturity" as a total quality of the personality rather than a selective one which emerges in some situations and not in others. Yet, using the criteria listed above, all of us are mature in some situations and immature in others. Where lies the compelling set of criteria which determine why certain situations are more important than others in indicating whether *the personality* is immature or inadequate? From the account above, the set of criteria used comes from a single social class's view of appropriate behavior: note the use of "financial independence, stable employment, and the establishment of his own home and family." There is remarkable bias here toward labeling of one social segment of the society as mature and adequate at the expense of another. Sociologists have long since established empirically that the most important determinant of a man's social, financial, and educational status is his father's occupation.[7] The child from a financially stable home is far more likely to find himself financially independent at age twenty-one than the child from the slums. The same goes for stable employment. But there is an apparent contradiction between the relationship between the "inadequate personality" and drug use if we recall the history of the problem. In the first chapter it was pointed out that the upper and middle classes had more addicts than the lower classes from 1870 to 1904. It was not until the 1920s that the shift in the predominance of those known to be addicted moved from the upper to the lower classes. Is this to be explained by some dramatic transformation in the personalities of the privileged classes in this short decade, and an equally strange transformation in the personality make-up of the lower classes? Did each class inexplicably take on the characterstics of the other in so short a time? Hardly. Rather, the explanation lies more closely to the fact that the social meaning of addiction changed, as did its detection.[8]

Ausubel is quite correct in his implication that it requires a psychologist to explain why certain persons in a given social group with equal exposure choose or refuse drugs.[9] That has never been at issue in this work. What has been heavily questioned and criticized is the conclusion that men have drawn from this, namely, that therefore the psychological interpretation of drug use can be used to provide solutions to the cultural and social problems that emanate from the cultural and social meaning of drug use. The anthropologist or sociologist must raise a different order of question, not of the propensity to addiction of given individuals in certain classes or groups, but of the meaning of addiction in the culture, of why certain classes of persons use drugs more than others, and why differential sanctions are used on these populations. I have suggested and have tried to demonstrate that when the center of society (the middle class is the solid base of social morality in America and the West) engages in a form of behavior, it is safe from strong negatively sanctioned moral judgment. Morphine use in the United States from 1870 to 1900 is an example. But when it is commonly believed that such behavior is the property of those outside the center, it is susceptible to negative moral judgment. With LSD, we are now witnessing a certain manifestation of this. Because it is being more frequently used by university students from the middle classes than by high-school drop-outs from the working classes, LSD use is only attacked as a "dangerous drug," and its use is not treated as an act which qualitatively sets apart the user as a different kind of moral person. One could easily venture the suggestion, however, that had LSD use begun with the less-privileged classes of youth, it would have been categorically treated as a character-defining act. There is something of this in the tendency to castigate the users as bearded hippies, but the fear is now widespread that even the clean-shaven will be tempted.

Background and Qualifiers

There is a hidden danger in attempting to describe and analyze the drug addict who has been apprehended by authorities. Even though one may issue many warnings that the description applies only to known addicts, it is almost inevitable that the cautionary note will be forgotten or repressed in the mounting pressures to explain and understand the general problems of addiction. The warning is worth repeating even for this manuscript, where the term "the addict" is used to signify "the typical addict known to authorities." The following study pertains only to apprehended addicts. It is possible that they are less than one tenth of all addicts.[10] The purpose of this study is not to describe *the drug addict*, but to realize some greater understanding of the consequences of the moral interpretation of addiction on *a select group of addicts*. This select group is of particular relevance and interest because it constitutes an addict population that is the target of a program that tries to work with the commonly believed cause of addiction. The California Rehabilitation Center is explicitly aiming at the psychic problems of the addict. Up to this point, the central thesis has been that the legal shifts, the consequent market conditions, and the social vulnerability of the visible addict in the twentieth century have transformed his problem into a moral one. The moral interpretation of narcotics addiction, it has been argued, is stronger than any other, and greatly influences the psychological and physiological view of the addict. Now we reach a point of direct empirical investigation of this matter to see to what extent the moral versus psychological and physiological views predominate in the treatment of known addicts.

Following is a summary review of what are commonly regarded by the CRC treatment staff as the causes of addiction. Rather than try to obtain a single formal statement of the way in which the CRC treatment staff conceives the causes of narcotic addiction, an examination of the written directives and clarifications of the treatment program will provide a clearer picture. These programs reveal the nature of the staff's conception of the addict in a penetrating manner. Following is an excerpt from a Treatment Model drawn up by one of the staff members, describing what are commonly regarded by the staff as the characteristics of the adult addict:

1. He withdraws from stressful or difficult situations, gives up, retreats, runs away.
2. He feels inadequate, worthless.
3. He can not relate comfortably with authority figures, is fearfully distrusting and hostile.
4. He is very dependent on others.
5. He blames others for his problems.
6. He attempts to manipulate everyone to serve his own ends.
7. He doubts his manhood.
8. He has difficulty in verbally expressing his feelings, especially about himself.

9. He rarely feels or exhibits interest in the welfare of others at the expense of himself.
10. He is fearful of others.
11. He sets up situations that get him punished or rejected.
12. He identifies with delinquent values, delinquent behavior, and rejects those who pursue socially acceptable adjustments and behavior.

I reprint these items of the treatment model not because they are exceptional or unique views of the addict, but because they represent the more typical treatment staff's conception of the problem. It is taken for granted that the addict is a psychologically abnormal individual with a personality disorder:

We try to keep a few psychotic patients on hand if they fit into the program somehow so that they can be used as teaching subjects for both staff and for the "resident" body. For the most part, however, we are dealing with a whole diverse number of personality disorders running the whole gamut of this classification from the schizoid personality to the several categories of sociopathy and passive aggressive personality.[11]

The following statement is from a staff position paper as represented to a legislator who visited the grounds. Acknowledging that performance in the group is an important part of the judgment of his ability at self-help and coping with his own problems, the position paper went on to say:

Not just by what he does in treatment group . . . A man may look like a real winner, sitting there and talking a lot, but does it follow through on his job? What sort of work traits does he have? Has he availed himself to the educational opportunities in the institution? We try to find out what is happening with the family ties. Is he receiving visits; what are his plans regarding his children? Has he had any disciplinary action? How is his conduct outside the group? How has he been running his life here in the institution? Can he adhere to our institutional regulations?[12]

Not only does the correctional counselor in the living unit write a report on the resident and his conduct in the group sessions and in the dormitory, but written reports come from a variety of sources:

Work supervisors, for example provide reports: a man might get on a work crew—a laboring crew outside, working on ditch-digging, planting lawns, clean-up crew, or something like that. His work supervisor will submit a report on his performance at least quarterly. Too, we follow the normal semester curriculum and we have school grades by the instructor in addition to comments about the man's conduct in the classrooms.[13]

It is made clear to the addict that his life in the institution is under constant surveillance as to his rehabilitation and adjustment. He is not permitted to simply "play the game of therapy" in the group sessions, but he must also demonstrate that this therapeutic aid relates to other aspects of his daily life. The causes of his addiction, as the treatment staff presents the problem to him, are in his psychic disturbance, unnatural and abnormal dependence, and inability to manage the world without drugs. To demonstrate that he is ready for release, he must show evidence to the staff in the many areas of his institutional life that he understands these problems being pointed out to him, that he seriously accepts the analysis, and that he is committed to the task of working out himself the psychic difficulties which afflict him, for which he is responsible, and which he must conquer.

Aims of the Study

The major purpose of the study to be reported here is to ascertain to what extent the moral interpretation of narcotics use exists in a setting where the participants are self-consciously and deliberately committed to a psychological view of addiction. The next purpose is the answer to the question of how the moral interpretation, or lack of it, affects the addict's self-conception, the treatment he receives, and his relationship with the society.

Another purpose of the study is to produce a social profile of the resident addict population at the Rehabilitation Center. The task is to detail such things as the age range among the addicts, ethnic and racial identification, family status, and occupational and sex distributions. After finding those places in the social order where addiction (or apprehension of addicts) is most likely to occur, the next problem is to achieve some explanation of why those particular places in the society should be overrepresented. It may be that further insights into the problem of addiction can be obtained from observing why certain

The moral implications of psychic maladjustment in the deviant
categories are most frequently represented among apprehended addicts. Perhaps a basis of explanation of why particular social categories appear while others do not can be established. From a social profile, patterns and recurrent themes emerge, and the burden of the analysis is to find these patterns and arrange them in a coherent form.

The Sample

The universe for this study was the resident addict population of the California Rehabilitation Center, from early 1964 through the spring of 1965. Because of some continual entries and departures from the institution, there is no static population figure. However, the institution stabilizes around the figure 1,300 for the period of the analysis, with some few score fluctuations over time in both directions. The first study was carried out on a random sample of approximately 10 per cent, stratified for the male–female distribution.[14] A total of 155 were included in the sample for the purpose of being interviewed in the first segment of the study. There are approximately 1,100 males in the institution and 200 females. In the sample, there are 103 males and 52 females. The greater proportion of females selected for the study than in the institution was required in order to have enough cases to compare with males. Sex was chosen as an important variable because of the systematically differential treatment accorded male and female addicts both within the institution and on the outside.

The second segment consisted of a sample of about half of those interviewed. Information was collected from the files on seventy of the interviewed residents. These files were reviewed for the purpose of collecting information that could be used to cross-check some of the responses given in the interview, and also for an independent evaluation of the interviewed residents by the staff. At short periodic intervals, the counselors submit reports and evaluations of the residents. These reports assess progress in the program and indicate the counselor's evaluation of (a) the likelihood of successful rehabilitation and therefore (b) a possible recommendation to the evaluating board for release.

The recommendation is typically honored, and is therefore an important documentary piece for research on the substantive issues in release to the community.

Finally, in the third segment there is summary census data collected and presented on the total population of the study, 1,303 residents of the Rehabilitation Center during the last months of 1964. The research report will therefore contain three different populations: (1) the total population of the institution, (2) the 10 per cent interview sample, and (3) the cross-check sample whose files were analyzed against the interview material. The assumption is made that the samples are representative of the universe of the study (total resident addict population), but no claim is made about the generalizability of the findings to the total addict population of the United States, or even of California. Quite to the contrary, as has been pointed out earlier, the total addict population across social classes is unknown and unknowable, and the shortcomings of many theories of addiction are traceable to the refusal to acknowledge this critical point. The empirical basis for any theory about addiction is limited to observable behavior. This is truer for social deviance of this kind than for ordinary and typical problems in society (e.g., striving for higher status) since deviants have stronger reasons for concealing themselves.

Methods of Data Collection

THE INTERVIEW

The most important single method of collecting data for this segment of the study was an extensive and intensive interview. All questions were open-ended, although many required only simple responses of one or two words. A cursory review of the schedule reveals that several questions required probes of some depth and considerable skill in eliciting a response with substance. Trained interviewers were therefore necessary, even in the exploratory stages of the research. A serious problem presented itself. Trained interviewers asking residents questions about drug use would clearly be seen by the residents as aligned with the staff. In an earlier discussion, a portrait of the institution suggested how vulnerable residents feel about the staff's judgment and evaluation. The vulnerability is caused by the ambiguous quality of what is meant by psychic integration, coping successfully, and so on, as the resident sees these things existing independent of specific situations in which he finds himself. An inquisitive staff-approved questioner is obviously to be seen as a threat to parole chances, regardless of the objective conditions in the past or the present. The point is simply that the resident can never "know" the specific criteria because they are never given to him as rules (or criteria) that apply across-the-board.

With staff-aligned interviewers ruled out, there was the serious problem of obtaining even remotely reliable data by the interview method, since whoever conducted the interview would be correctly perceived by the residents as staff-appointed and therefore aligned with the staff and its interests and goals. Strategic reasons therefore impelled the research in new directions. Equally important to the strategy problem was the theoretical-methodological issue of how to best establish and maintain rapport with a subject population of men regarded in the society as moral deviants. Part of the answer came from reviewing selected successes of the Synanon program, and part was dictated by traditional sociological knowledge about the behavior of in-groups and reference groups. What success Synanon has enjoyed is based upon the rapport between men and women who are, or have been drug addicts. A basic principle of social exchange is that those in communication have a common point of reference. These are compelling arguments in favor of using addicts themselves as the interviewers. Eight of the residents were selected for training as interviewers. The principal investigator conducted these training sessions, familiarizing the interviewers with the larger aims of the questions and the study and instructing them on how to probe intensively in selected areas. These sessions were invaluable not only for the reason that the interviewers could find out precisely the nature and source of the questions from the person conducting the research, but also because the latter could modify and rephrase questions which the residents (as prospective interviewers) could indicate as ambiguous, or have a different meaning than the one intended. As only one of many such examples, one question asked if the respondent had ever peddled drugs. The resident interviewers pointed out that many who had actually sold drugs to others from time to time might answer this question negatively. The reason is that dope peddling is seen by addicts as a total occupational identity. From this addict point of view, one can no more be said to "have peddled drugs" from occasional sales than one can be said to "have been a fireman" because one has put out fires many times in his life.

Male residents interviewed the males in the sample and females interviewed females. The only exception to this was the series of twenty regular interviews conducted by the principal investigator, who interviewed both sexes.

All questions were presented to respondents with no forced choices. The interviewers were thereby able and were urged to explore interesting and novel directions of a particular response. These explorations were channeled to the extent that they were related to the interests and orientation of the research project as discussed in the training sessions.

One of the pitfalls of this kind of research is the assumption that the respondent and the interviewer mean the same thing when using the same term. For example, one question asks whether the respondent feels morally inferior to nonaddicts. Before beginning to answer the question, the resident might ask what the interviewer means by "morally inferior." The interviewer's response was to explicitly deflect the question and instead explore what the resident himself conceived as moral. The reason for this rests in the fact that the subjective experience of moral inferiority can not be tapped unless the respondent is allowed to express his own interpretation of the terms of the question.

In addition, the interviewer must guard against subtle variations in meaning that are not even questioned by the respondent, and therefore never raised as issues for discussion. It is hardly possible to ask every respondent what he means specifically by particular phrases. However, as Aaron Cicourel has suggested, there are some adequate techniques that can be used to minimize the difficulties of multiple meanings.[15] Following Cicourel's suggestion, the principal investigator conducted an additional ten separate interviews not included in the sample proper.

The moral implications of psychic maladjustment in the deviant

The purpose of these interviews was to clarify some of the problems of communication between interviewer and interviewee that are otherwise ignored.

Characteristics of Total Population: *1,303*

The ratio of males to females in the institution is almost 6 to 1. It is also a very young population, with more than 75 per cent being under the age of thirty. (Table 7-1) These two characteristics are similar to

TABLE 7-1

AGE AT ADMISSION OF INMATES OF THE CALIFORNIA
REHABILITATION CENTER (AUGUST, 1965)

MALE

Age at Admission	Number	Percent
19 years and under	**55**	**5.0**
17	1	0.1
18	13	1.2
19	41	3.7
20 years–24 years	**509**	**46.0**
20	69	6.2
21	112	10.1
22	116	10.5
23	104	9.4
24	108	9.8
25 years–29 years	**281**	**25.4**
25	73	6.6
26	58	5.2
27	48	4.3
28	56	5.1
29	46	4.2
30 years–34 years	**150**	**13.5**
30	25	2.3
31	29	2.6
32	37	3.3
33	30	2.7
34	29	2.6
35 years–39 years	**70**	**6.3**
35	19	1.7
36	21	1.9
37	16	1.4

TABLE 7-1 (*Continued*)

Age at Admission	Number	Percent
38	9	0.8
39	5	0.5
40 years–44 years	**26**	**2.3**
45 years–49 years	**9**	**0.8**
50 years–54 years	**4**	**0.4**
55 years–63 years	**3**	**0.3**
TOTAL	1,107	100.0

FEMALE

Age at Admission	Number	Percent
19 years and under	**10**	**5.1**
18	3	1.5
19	7	3.6
20 years–24 years	**80**	**40.8**
20	7	3.6
21	16	8.2
22	21	10.7
23	25	12.7
24	11	5.6
25 years–29 years	**57**	**29.1**
25	15	7.7
26	13	6.6
27	12	6.1
28	10	5.1
29	7	3.6
30 years–34 years	**27**	**13.8**
30	1	0.5
31	12	6.1
32	5	2.6
33	6	3.1
34	3	1.5
35 years–39 years	**15**	**7.7**
35	4	
36	1	
37	4	
38	4	
39	2	
40 years–44 years	**4**	**2.0**
45 years–49 years	**1**	**0.5**
50 years and over	**2**	**1.0**
TOTAL	196	100.0
Median age in years	25.7	
Percent under 21		8.7
Percent under 25		45.9

most other reports on the qualities of the known addict since about the year 1920. (As was pointed out in the first chapter, before that time most known addicts were middle-aged and female.) The same pattern holds for ethnic, geographic, and occupational variables. The tables show that the ethnic minorities not only have disproportionately high numbers of the addicts at CRC, but that they actually are a numerical majority of the inmates.

The most dramatic of this finding is the large number of Mexican-Americans apprehended as addicts. Among the males, half are Mexican-American. (Table 7–2) Negroes appear in relation to their number in

TABLE 7-2

ETHNIC GROUP OF INMATES OF THE CALIFORNIA REHABILITATION CENTER (AUGUST, 1965)

MALE

Ethnic Group		Number	Percent
White		450	40.7
*White, Mexican descent		546	49.3
Negro		109	9.8
Japanese		1	0.1
Hawaiian		1	0.1
	TOTAL	1,107	100.0

FEMALE

Ethnic Group		Number	Percent
White		118	60.2
*White, Mexican descent		45	23.0
Negro		33	16.8
	TOTAL	196	100.0

*These categories are those used in institutional records.

the population. Thus, in comparison to other studies of narcotics use, they are unexpectedly under-represented.[16]

The city is the breeding ground for almost all known addicts, and in California, one city is far and away the leader. Two of every three persons in CRC come from the county of Los Angeles. (Table 7–3)

These findings then bear out or reflect the generally known facts about apprehended addicts: that the problem primarily exists among the young, among males, in the cities, and among the ethnic and racial minorities. It is also true that the inmates at the rehabilitation center are predominantly working and lower class. In fact, white-collar or middle-class occupations for the inmate or the inmate's family are notable exceptions. More than 90 per cent of the inmates could be identified with either working- or lower-class occupations, or a history

TABLE 7-3

COUNTY OF COMMITMENT OF INMATES OF THE CALIFORNIA REHABILITATION CENTER (AUGUST, 1965)

MALE

County of Commitment	Number	Percent
Southern California		
Los Angeles	711	63.9
Imperial	11	0.9
Kern	4	0.4
Orange	63	5.7
Riverside	9	0.8
San Bernardino	41	3.7
San Diego	44	4.0
San Luis Obispo	2	0.2
Santa Barbara	6	0.5
Ventura	34	3.0
SUB-TOTAL	925	83.1
San Francisco Bay Area		
Alameda County	33	3.0
San Francisco County	48	4.3
Contra Costa	13	1.2
Marin	3	0.3
Santa Clara	26	2.3
San Mateo	6	0.5
Sonoma	9	0.8
SUB-TOTAL	138	12.4
Balance of State		
Sacramento Valley counties	6	0.5
San Joaquin Valley counties		
Fresno	19	1.7
Marced	1	0.1
San Joaquin	15	1.4
Stanislaus	1	0.1
Tulare	1	0.1

TABLE 7-3 (*Continued*)

County of Commitment		Number	Per Cent
Other counties			
Calaveras		1	
Monterey		3	
San Benito		1	
Santa Cruz		2	
	SUB-TOTAL	50	4.5
	TOTAL	1,107	100.0

FEMALE

County of Commitment		Number	Percent
Southern California		165	84.2
Los Angeles		138	70.4
Imperial		1	
Kern		3	
Orange		8	
Riverside		1	
San Bernardino		4	
San Diego		5	
Ventura		5	
San Francisco Bay Area		26	13.3
Alameda		8	
San Francisco		8	
Contra Costa		3	
Marin		1	
San Mateo		2	
Santa Clara		3	
Solano		1	
Balance of State		5	2.5
Sacramento		3	
Fresno		1	
San Joaquin		1	
	TOTAL	196	100.0

of no employment.[17] When this is contrasted with the fact that the 1960 census for the United States revealed that over 50 per cent of the country's labor force was white-collar, one can get a sense of the gross overrepresentation of the working classes among the apprehended addicts.

Miller has suggested that the lower-class environment is one in which the conditions for "getting in trouble" are very great.[18] Whether he is right or not it is certainly true that there is something in the lower-class situation that makes its members more susceptible to arrest, prosecution, and conviction than the middle classes.

TABLE 7-4

NUMBER OF PRIOR JAILS BEFORE DRUG USE OF INMATES OF THE CALIFORNIA REHABILITATION CENTER (AUGUST, 1965)

MALE

Number of Prior Jails Before Drug Use	Number	Per Cent
Unknown	25*	
Total known:		
None	1,009	93.2
1	46	4.2
2	17	1.6
3	4	0.4
4	1	0.1
5	2	0.2
6	3	0.3
TOTAL	1,082*	100.0

FEMALE

Number of Prior Jails Before Drug Use	Number	Per Cent
Unknown	6*	
Total known:		
None	184	96.8
1	3	1.6
2	2	1.1
9	1	0.5
TOTAL	190	100.0

One of the most important findings from the study of the total population is that 93 per cent of the male inmates at CRC had no jail history prior to offenses for their use of drugs. (See Table 7-4) This figure refutes the often heard claim that the drug addict population is a criminal population before it turns to drugs. This argument, from the arsenal of the Federal Narcotics Bureau, would have it believed that drug use is simply another form of criminal activity engaged in by persons who have already been established as criminals by their other

The moral implications of psychic maladjustment in the deviant

violations of the law. In fact, if we look even at the history of prior juvenile commitments of the CRC inmates, 85 per cent reveal no juvenile record. (See Table 7-5)

TABLE 7-5
NUMBER OF PRIOR JUVENILE COMMITMENTS BEFORE DRUG USE OF INMATES OF THE CALIFORNIA RE-HABILITATION CENTER (AUGUST, 1965)

MALE

Number of Prior Juvenile Commitments Before Drug Use	Number	Per Cent
Unknown	25*	
Total known:		
None	924	85.4
1	133	12.3
2	24	2.2
3	1	0.1
TOTAL	1,082*	100.0

FEMALE

Number of Prior Juvenile Commitments Before Drug Use	Number	Per Cent
Unknown	6*	
Total known:		
None	181	95.3
1	9	4.7
TOTAL	190*	100.0

TABLE 7-6
INTELLIGENCE OF INMATES OF THE CALIFORNIA REHABILITATION CENTER (AUGUST, 1965)

MALE

Intelligence	Number	Per Cent
Unknown	55*	
Total known:		
Very superior	2	0.2
Superior	47	4.5
High average	268	25.5
Normal	554	52.6
Dull normal	162	15.4
Borderline	18	1.7
Defective	1	0.1
Median	Normal	
TOTAL	1,052*	100.0

TABLE 7-6 (*Continued*)

FEMALE

Intelligence	Number	Per Cent
Unknown	11*	
Total known:		
Superior	13	7.0
High Average	79	42.7
Normal	78	42.2
Dull normal	12	6.5
Borderline	3	1.6
Median	Normal	
TOTAL	185*	100.0

TABLE 7-7

MARITAL STATUS OF INMATES OF THE CALIFORNIA REHABILITATION CENTER (AUGUST, 1965)

MALE

Marital Status	Number	Per Cent
Single	349	31.5
Married and common-law	439	39.6
1 marriage	338	30.5
2 marriages	83	7.5
3 marriages	18	1.6
Divorced, separated, or annulled	313	28.3
1 marriage	216	23.6
2 marriages	41	3.7
3 marriages	11	1.0
Spouse deceased	6	0.6
1 marriage	4	0.4
2 marriages	1	0.1
3 marriages	1	0.1
TOTAL	1,107	100.0

FEMALE

Marital Status	Number	Per Cent
Single	23	11.7
Married and common-law	92	47.0
1 marriage	46	23.5
2 marriages	39	19.9
3 or more marriages	7	3.6
Divorced, separated or annulled	79	40.3
1 marriage	41	20.9
2 marriages	30	15.3
3 or more marriages	8	4.1
Spouse deceased	2	1.0
1 marriage	2	1.0
TOTAL	196	100.0

The moral implications of psychic maladjustment in the deviant

TABLE 7-8

INDICATION OF OPIATE SALE ACTIVITIES OF INMATES
OF THE CALIFORNIA REHABILITATION CENTER
(AUGUST, 1965)

MALE

Case History has Indication		Number	Per Cent
No		781	70.6
Yes		326	29.4
	TOTAL	1,107	100.0

FEMALE

Case History has Indication		Number	Per Cent
No		161	82.1
Yes		35	17.9
	TOTAL	196	100.0

TABLE 7-9

AGE FIRST USED MARIJUANA, INCLUDING PRESENT
OFFENSE, OF INMATES OF THE CALIFORNIA RE-
HABILITATION CENTER (AUGUST, 1965)

MALE

Age First Used Marijuana		Number	Per Cent
Denies or no use		113*	
Used–age unknown		27*	
Total unknown :			
Under 12 years		15	1.5
12–13		135	14.0
14–15		276	28.5
16		156	16.1
17		142	14.7
18		80	8.3
19–20		81	8.4
21–24		60	6.2
25–29		18	1.9
30 and over		4	0.4
Median age in years		16.4	
	TOTAL	967*	100.0

TABLE 7-9 (*Continued*)

FEMALE

Age First Used Marijuana	Number	Per Cent
Denies or no use	73*	
Used—age unknown	6*	
Total known:		
Under 12 years	1	0.9
12–13	12	10.3
14–15	37	31.6
16	21	17.9
17	13	11.1
18	9	7.7
19–20	10	8.5
21–24	10	8.5
25–29	3	2.6
30 years and over	1	0.9
Median age in years	16.4	
TOTAL	117*	100.0

TABLE 7-10

AGE FIRST USED "HARD" NARCOTICS, INCLUDING PRESENT OFFENSE, OF THE INMATES OF THE CALIFORNIA REHABILITATION CENTER (AUGUST, 1965)

MALE

Age First Used Hard Narcotics	Number	Per Cent
Denies or no use	8*	
Used—age unknown	27*	
Total known:		
Under 12 years	1	0.1
12–13	6	0.6
14–15	73	6.8
16	85	7.9
17	98	9.1
18	157	14.7
19–20	255	29.8
21–24	270	25.2
25–29	85	7.9
30 and over	42	3.9
Median age in years	19.9	
TOTAL	1,072*	100.0

TABLE 7-10 (*Continued*)

FEMALE

Age First Used Hard Narcotics	Number	Per Cent
Denies or no use		
Used—age unknown	6*	
Total known:		
Under 12 years		
12–13		
14–15	15	7.9
16	9	4.7
17	22	11.6
18	21	11.1
19–20	35	18.4
21–24	52	27.4
25–29	24	12.6
30 years and over	12	6.3
Median age in years	20.6	
TOTAL	190*	100.0

TABLE 7-11

PRIOR COMMITMENTS SERVED OF INMATES OF THE CALIFORNIA REHABILITATION CENTER (AUGUST, 1965)

MALE

Prior Commitments Served	Number	Per Cent
None	152	13.7
1 or 2 jail or juvenile	396	95.8
3 or more jail or juvenile	360	32.5
1 prison only	12	1.1
1 prison plus misdemeanor	132	11.9
2 prisons	39	3.5
3 prisons	13	1.2
4 prisons or more	3	0.3
TOTAL	1,107	100.0

FEMALE

Prior Commitments Served	Number	Per Cent
None	64	32.7
1 or 2 jail	78	39.8
3 or more jail or juvenile	41	20.9
1 prison only	3	1.5
1 prison plus misdemeanor	7	3.6
2 prison	3	1.5
TOTAL	196	100.0

175

TABLE 7-12

TYPE OF DRUG USED PRIOR TO COMMITMENT OF INMATES OF THE CALIFORNIA REHABILITATION CENTER (AUGUST, 1965)

MALE

Type of Drug Used Prior to Commitment	Number	Per Cent
Unknown	10*	
Known:		
Opiate	1,057	96.4
Marijuana	13	1.2
Dangerous drugs	27	2.4
TOTAL KNOWN	1,072*	100.0

FEMALE

Type of Drug Used Prior to Commitment	Number	Per Cent
Unknown	2*	
Known:		
Opiate	193	99.5
Marijuana		
Dangerous drugs	1	0.5
TOTAL KNOWN	194*	100.0

TABLE 7-13

OFFENSES OF INMATES OF THE CALIFORNIA RE-HABILITATION CENTER (AUGUST, 1965)

MALE

Offense	Number	Per Cent
Homicide	4	0.4
Manslaughter	4	0.4
Robbery	16	1.5
1st degree	5	0.5
2nd degree	9	0.8
Attempted robbery	2	0.2
Assault	1	0.1
Assault with deadly weapon	1	0.1
Burglary	82	7.4
2nd degree	81	7.3
Attempted burglary	1	0.1

TABLE 7-13 (*Continued*)

Offence	Number	Per Cent
Theft except auto	**46**	**4.1**
Grand theft	9	0.8
Petty theft with prior	30	2.6
Theft of credit card	1	0.1
Receiving stolen property	6	0.6
Auto theft	**15**	**1.4**
Grand theft auto	5	0.5
Operate without owner's permission	10	0.9
Forgery and checks	**59**	**5.3**
Forgery	51	4.5
Fictitious checks	3	0.3
Fraud, nonsufficient fund checks	2	0.2
Fraud, possession of completed check	3	0.3
Sex	**2**	**0.2**
Rape, statutory	2	0.2
Narcotics	**438**	**39.5**
Sale to minor	2	0.2
Possession	256	23.0
Possession with 1 prior narcotic felony conviction	2	0.2
Possession with 2 prior narcotic felony convictions	2	0.2
Possession for sale	17	1.5
Sale	113	10.2
Sale with 1 prior narcotic felony conviction	1	0.1
Forgery or fraud of narcotic prescription	20	1.8
Sell substance in lieu of narcotics	2	0.2
Maintain place for narcotics	1	0.1
Driving under influence of narcotics	22	2.0
Marijuana	**126**	**11.4**
Possession	93	8.4
Possession with 1 prior narcotic conviction	1	0.1
Sale	29	2.6
Possession for sale	3	0.3
Dangerous drugs	**6**	**0.6**
Provide dangerous drug to minor	4	0.4
Driving under influence of drug	2	0.2
Other felony offenses	**14**	**1.3**
Escape from jail	2	0.2
Other	12	1.1

TABLE 7-13 (*Continued*)

Offense	Number	Per Cent
Misdemeanor charges	229	20.6
Narcotic addiction	179	16.0
Possession of hypodermic kit	29	2.6
Other narcotic misdemeanor	11	1.0
Disturbing the peace	2	0.2
Misc. traffic violation	5	0.5
Not classified misdemeanor	3	0.3
No criminal charge	69	6.2
TOTAL	1,107	100.0

FEMALE

Offense	Number	Per Cent
Robbery, first degree	1	0.5
Burglary, second degree	5	2.6
Theft except auto	9	4.6
Grand theft	1	0.5
Petty theft with prior	7	3.6
Receiving stolen property	1	0.5
Auto theft	1	0.5
Forgery and checks	18	9.2
Forgery	16	8.2
Fraudulent checks, no funds	2	1.0
Narcotics	72	36.7
Possession	43	21.9
Possession for sale	3	1.5
Sale	16	8.2
Forgery or fraud of narcotic prescription	6	3.1
Driving under influence of narcotics	4	2.0
Marijuana	15	7.6
Possession	12	6.1
Sale	3	1.5
Other felony offenses	2	1.0
Drunk driving	1	0.5
Conspiracy	1	0.5
Misdemeanor charges	62	31.7
Narcotic addiction	46	23.5
Possession of hypodermic kit	7	3.6
Other narcotic misdemeanor	3	1.5
Miscellaneous sex offenses	5	2.6
Not classified misdemeanor	1	0.5
No criminal charge	11	5.6
TOTAL	196	100.0

The moral implications of psychic maladjustment in the deviant

Findings from Interview Study

Whereas no claim is made for the generalizability of these findings to the addict population outside the institution, the results from the interview should be representative of the total addict population at CRC.

Findings from an interview study such as this are subject to two important and recurrent criticisms: (1) How does one know if recall is accurate? and (2) even if the memory of the respondent is complete and correct, can we take his statements as anything more than the superficial, self-conscious realizations of his condition and personality? It should be stated at the outset that neither of these questions need be raised in order to develop an explanation of the patterns of social relationships that exist. For example, when we know empirically that people at the top of the social world say that the world is a just place and people at the bottom say that it is not, there is no need to pose the question as to whether people "really feel that way" in order to explain and predict how such statements vary with social position. Further, when we can observe that the well-to-do in any society tend to vote more heavily to conserve the existing social order, explanations do not stand or fall upon the ultimate reality of whether the voters "know" they are acting in terms of their self-interests, either short- or long-range.

As for challenging the recall ability of a set of respondents, that problem is most critical when there is reason to believe some motive for systematically telling lies. Where a set of say one hundred respondents show a pattern of recalled events, there is a built-in check unless (a) there is room to suspect collusion, or (b) the question probes into an area known to be socially sensitive or taboo. For example, questions about abortion, sexual failures, or informing to the police touch areas where one can expect systematic falsification. However, recall ability of the number of rooms in the home of a friend, and so on, is at the opposite extreme.

In these interviews with addicts, both kinds of questions occur. An attempt has been made to avoid giving the impression of the ultimate reality of responses to certain questions even though they may be of use in other kinds of explanations. On the other hand, ability to remember whether one's first experience with marijuana was "alone or in a group situation" was treated as having face validity.

THE PATH TO ADDICTION

In an earlier discussion, some issues were raised concerning how it is possible for knowledgeable men to become addicted to heroin. The outsider finds it incredible that any individual in possession of all his faculties would knowingly take the path to addiction. It was suggested

TABLE 7-14

"[WHEN YOU FIRST TOOK DOPE], DID YOU BELIEVE THAT YOU WOULD BECOME HOOKED ON IT?"

	Number	Percent
Yes	28	18.1
No	125	80.6
Can't remember	2	1.3
TOTAL	155	100.0

that part of the explanation is to be found in the idea of the indestructibility of the self.[19] The prospective addict sees himself as an exception to the pattern of addiction around him. Notice that over 80 per cent of the respondents said that, when they took a narcotic for the first time, they were sure that they would not become hooked (Table 7-14). Of the few who said that they did believe that they would become addicted, only a fraction maintained this position upon probing. It usually developed that even though they realized the possibility of becoming addicted, they refused to believe it would actually happen to them.

The naïvete or lack of information of the beginner user about the danger or risks in drugs should be cast aside as an explanation for how one starts with drugs. In this group, virtually all claim to have known teat heroin was addicting when they first used it.

The first source of contact with the drug was usually a friend. (Table 7-15) Contrary to popular mythology, the professional dope-pusher (one who himself does not use but deals only for the profit)

The moral implications of psychic maladjustment in the deviant

almost never contacts the novice and entices him for his first trial. Instead, a friend, who is himself an occasional user *but not an addict*, invites him to a gathering where the drug is available. Those who are themselves addicted possess a strong moral code that acts as a barrier against initiating novices. Infrequently the code is broken, but the situation is one where stress is great due to the impending onset of withdrawal.

TABLE 7-15

"WHO WAS THE SOURCE OF YOUR FIRST CONTACT WITH DRUGS?"

	Number	Percent
Wife or husband	3	1.9
Brother or sister	4	2.6
Mother or father	1	.6
Other family member	3	1.9
A friend	99	63.9
A group	28	18.1
Sexual partner (If this category and friend overlapped, the stronger was chosen)	13	8.4
Physician	4	2.6
TOTAL	155	100.0

In the circles where the CRC inmate grew up, marijuana was easily available. Any of a number of his acquaintances might take him to a party where pot was being smoked, and any of a number of these might be an occasional heroin user. It is a serious mistake however, to jump to the conclusion that marijuana leads to heroin.[20] The only point here is simply that the widespread use of the drugs in a person's normal everyday environment means that he will come into contact with it in a normal and everyday manner. It is not the dejected, depressed, and withdrawn moment that can be identified, nor does it appear to be true that there is some critical turning point in the decision to experiment with drugs the first time. For these addicts, the available evidence suggest nothing pathological in the way of a moth-flame compulsion. Quite to the contrary, the addict seems to be drawn into a normal set of social relations and normal kinds of social behavior when he experiences the drug for the first time.

For the female, the case is a bit different. She is more likely to be

TABLE 7-16

"WHO WAS THE SOURCE OF YOUR FIRST CONTACT WITH DRUGS?"

	Male	Percent	Female	Percent
Wife or husband	0	0	3	5.77
Brother or sister	1	.97	3	5.77
Mother or father	0	0	1	1.92
Other family member	3	2.91	0	0
A friend	72	69.90	27	51.92
A group	25	24.27	3	5.77
Sexual partner (If this category and friend overlapped, the stronger was chosen)	1	.97	12	23.08
Physician	1	.97	3	5.77
TOTAL	103	100.00	52	100.00

TABLE 7-17

"THE FIRST TIME YOU USED DOPE, WERE YOU ALONE, IN A GROUP, OR WITH ONE OTHER PERSON?"

	Number	Percent
Alone	9	5.8
In a group	94	60.6
With one other person	52	33.6
TOTAL	155	100.0

pulled into drug use because of her close emotional attachment to a single other individual who uses heavily, or is addicted. The attachment may be to a lover, to a husband, or sometimes to a homosexual lover. The pull to drug use seems to be through some single other person. (Compare tables 7-15, 7-16, and 7-17.)

The moral implications of psychic maladjustment in the deviant

In the whole sample, only eight cases were cited where a family member drew one into narcotics use; and in seven of the eight cases, the person drawn in was a female. It is equally striking to notice how females differ from males when we look at the sexual partner as the initiator to the drug experience. While almost one fourth of the females started taking drugs with a sexual partner, less than one male in a hundred began in this way. Much of the explanation lies in the power relationship between males and females in the society in general, since women are more dependent upon the financial need to hold the support of men with whatever means they can devise.

TABLE 7-18
"THE FIRST TIME YOU USED DOPE, WERE YOU ALONE, IN A GROUP, OR WITH ONE OTHER PERSON?"

	Male	Percent	Female	Percent
Alone	3	2.91	6	11.54
In a group	66	64.08	28	53.85
With one other person	34	33.01	18	34.61
TOTAL	103	100.00	52	100.00

It should be carefully noted that neither males nor females report that their first experience was when they were alone. Indeed, the first experience is usually in a group situation for both, rather than a single other party (Table 7–18).

These findings suggest that the social dimension of the early experimentation with narcotics is more than a simple desire to conform to a deviant subculture or to rebel against middle-class authority and morality. It seems instead to be a configuration of events that unravel in a normal sequence. It achieves its insidious anti-bourgeois, anti-authority character from the response that later comes from the authorities, agencies, and institutions committed to a different moral-legal view of drugs. Explanations of the rebellious nature of the drug user are very much like explanations after the fact in prison riots, wildcat strikes, and spontaneous student unrest. The most trivial and unpredictable of events may set off a prison riot.

Once the riot starts, however, the rioters start writing up a list of legitimate grievances with the institution, a list which authorities and newspapers then treat as the cause of the original disturbance. In fact, every grievance on that list has usually been going on for decades, often in a more insufferable way than at the point of the riot. But the list is used as the basis of explaining why the riot occurred. The same thing happened with the Berkeley student revolt in 1964. The immediate source of the student rebellion was the response to specific and individual injustices to an arbitrarily selected group of students.[21] Yet, when the analysts finished explaining what had happened, one would have thought that the list of grievances drawn up by the students was the real source.[22] In fact, Berkeley students (as all other American student bodies) had up to that time and have since that time, lived complacently, obediently, and peacefully under the very conditions described in that list as the cause of the revolts. Why then the rebellion at that moment?

There is a parallel to the discussions of the rebelliousness and curiosity of the drug user. He lived peacefully for decades under conditions similar in form to those now described as the indicators of personal inadequacy.[23] When the law shifted the legal conditions, the addict's list of grievances, liberally supplemented by the experts, was suddenly treated as the explanation of his addiction.

Marijuana is usually the first narcotic that the individual tries, but it is by no means the only path to heroin usage. Unlike many American college students, the CRC inmates are very likely to have been exposed to both marijuana and heroin traffic. They could more easily make the choice. Thus, those instances where they did not go on to heroin use are all the more significant in questioning the popularly cited relationship between the two drugs. The ethnic and racial differences in patterns of heroin versus marijuana use are quite instructive for a discussion of the path to addiction. First of all, there has been a dramatic upsurge in the incidence of marijuana usage and heroin addiction in the Mexican-American communities of Los Angeles since 1950. Marijuana especially has recently become very much a part of the life of the lower and working-class Mexican-American adolescent's world. The precise reasons for this development are subject to explanation at several levels. In simple traffic terms, one clear explanation is the large

The moral implications of psychic maladjustment in the deviant

flow of marijuana into the Mexican subculture from across the Mexican border. It is a long border that is only a few hours away. The communal ties and old primary associations facilitate distribution. In this light it is interesting to note that, for the modal case, Mexican-Americans in CRC began using marijuana at about age fourteen or fifteen. The most frequent age at which they began with heroin was eighteen. Blacks begin both marijuana and heroin usage much later. Most Negroes reported that their first experience with marijuana was between the ages of eighteen and twenty, while heroin contact did not begin for most until the middle twenties. One popular explanation for this is that the bulk of the black community in Southern California has been more recently settled. Because these youths got there much later in their lives, it follows that they begin everything a bit later, including deviance. That is only partially true for this sample, since a large proportion of the Negroes had resided in the California county from which they were apprehended prior to their tenth birthday. Another current explanation is a modified frustration-withdrawal hypothesis. Blacks continually confront situations in which they are the objects of discrimination. For some, this builds up into frustration and hostility. For some, this turns into resignation, alienation or withdrawal. Narcotics provide the withdrawal. This sequence takes time, however, and that is why black youth tends to start with drugs much later.

One part of this interpretation fits very well into what is known about ethnic and minority conditions. First, the black community is not a subculture in the same sense as the Mexican-American. There is no separate language, no distinctive kinship structure, and fewer customs and traditions which set the Negro apart from the dominant group. The Mexican-American can more easily achieve a distinctive cultural identity precisely because he has a separate language, a familial lineage system that differs from the dominant society, and distinctive traditions. There is, however, one more important factor explaining the differences in the path to addiction by the two groups. The two minorities have a different way of looking at the world of objects and of men. If it were simply a matter of dress and costume and of tradition, or a matter of the way one holds a knife, effects a dialect, or carries a stride, men could readily communicate and blend cultures. It is far more important that these things which are different in their outward appearances often carry with them a way of conceiving of things, for example, a different view of the sexes and their places, and a conflicting posture toward issues treated as the basis for moral crises.

For the Mexican-American, extended kinship is an essential fact of existence. For the native white American, and for the black American especially, extended kinship is often problematic, confusing, and conflicting. To simply assert this sheds only a glimmer of light on the finding about Negroes and whites drawing family members into addiction upon occasion, while Mexican-Americans rarely if ever do. However, if one is to understand that finding and others like it in the largerc ontext of varying cultural paths to addiction, the nature and role of kinship must be examined. The nuclear family is the primary kinship unit in the United States, as it is in every culture where technology has undermined large communal family life as an important economic base. In a society that is so specialized that one member "goes to work" to provide for everyone in the household, the household had better have five or six members, not twenty-five or thirty. So the older people of Sweden, Germany, the Netherlands, and the United States can all be heard to present the common complaint of being cut off from the nuclear family unit. Mexican-Americans in this country, especially the Southwest, are far more likely to retain an identity and ties with a traditional culture that does not see the nuclear family unit as a separate one. Contrast both of these situations with that of the Negro, whose slave past purged him not only of an extended lineal kinship, but rendered problematic the nuclear family itself. For two and a half centuries, the tradition of the Negro in the United States was to deny the nuclear unit on the simple expedient that he could control neither offspring nor spouse.[24]

In the single area of kinship structure, things are quite different for Blacks and Mexican-Americans in ways that vary even to the manner in which they conceive of filial relationships. All of this has bearing on the relative degree to which the Mexican-Americans have a distinctive subculture. The family unit and its relative importance in the culture is but one area where documentation is possible. This cultural distinctiveness helps to account for a variety of otherwise confusing differences that can be found between Blacks and Mexican-Americans in the addict population. For example, it is possible to make sense of the fact that though both are minorities, Negroes wait longer (until age eighteen to twenty) to begin narcotics use. At least from the base point of the frustration-withdrawal hypothesis cited earlier, the cultural context adds new meaning. When Negroes experience discrimination, they have a less coherent cultural base to relate to, but return again and again to the dominant culture to meet more of the same. They may delay the withdrawal and alienation until they have experienced a good deal more frustration. Interviews with black addicts at CRC provided some support for this notion, but interpretation should be cautious because of variable regional conditions.

The moral interpretation of narcotic use and narcotic addiction is the primary focus of this research, as has been elaborated in the earlier sections. How this moral view varies with ethnic and age groups should be instructive in finding out the effects of select cultural experiences on social patterns of addiction. Those groups of addicts who are most likely to confront a strong moral reaction from the society should be those whose addiction is most abhorrent to the dominant society. Youthful middle-class whites *scandalize their immediate community*, the juvenile authorities, and the courts by their narcotics usage much more so than early-adult working-class Blacks. It follows that the strength and intensity of the moral reaction to the former will be stronger. Although the three qualities of age, class, and ethnicity have been combined for the purpose of the example above, each operates independently. The moralistic reaction to an adolescent's drug usage is predictably stronger than reaction toward an adult; the reaction to drug usage by the middle class toward one of their class is stronger than the corresponding reaction in the working or lower classes, and so forth. Men come to expect different behavior from other men who have different positions in the society. The banker's son who is a known user violates expectations far more strongly than the factory worker's son, or the son of a mother on public relief. The former is a violation which produces the response of indignant action. Accordingly, it is predictable that addicts from a middle-class background, addicts who are white, and those who were addicted at a relatively young age should express the strongest feelings about how morally different they are from others in the society.

The CRC addicts who are convinced of their own general moral inferiority resign themselves to a more peaceful relationship with the world. They make little effort to rehabilitate, even in the terms of satisfying the requirements of institutional commitment. This is reflected in the evaluations and judgments filed on individual resident addicts. A content analysis of these files revealed that those respondents

TABLE 7-19

"DO YOU REGARD YOUR USING DRUGS AS SOME-
THING WHICH SETS YOU APART FROM THE REST OF
SOCIETY? (THAT IS, DO YOU REGARD YOURSELF
EITHER MORALLY SUPERIOR OR INFERIOR TO NON-
USERS?)"

		Number	Percent
Superior		29	18.7
Inferior		68	43.9
Don't know		43	27.7
Equal		15	9.7
	TOTAL	155	100.0

who judge themselves most harshly in moral terms tended to be less successful in the eyes of the treatment person making the assessment of their progress in the institution. It is no accident that the staff made generally more positive prognoses of those inmates who would not say that the staff felt morally superior to addicts. There is some difficulty here in deciding which comes first, the prognosis or the refusal to cast the staff in these terms. The interesting empirical problem is the extent to which these judgments vary along socially patterned lines.

Each respondent was asked if he felt that his use of drugs was some-
thing that set him apart morally from the rest of society. (Table 7–19) Two thirds could say that they felt that it did. Four out of every five addicts could assert that nonusers regard themselves as morally superior to narcotics users. (Table 7–20) In light of the self-conscious attempt by the staff at the Rehabilitation Center to recast the problem in therapeutic terms, it must be noted that the residents impute to them

The moral implications of psychic maladjustment in the deviant

an almost equal measure of feelings of moral superiority. (Table 7–21)

That is, despite the fact that the treatment staff uses the language of psychology and psychiatry in dealing with the addicts, the latter still feel that the primary way they are being looked upon is moral. Some of the residents who see this as inevitable reasoned that it is a conse-

TABLE 7-20

"DO YOU THINK THAT NONUSERS REGARD THEM-
SELVES AS MORALLY DIFFERENT FROM DOPE USERS?"

	Number	*Percent*
Superior	128	82.6
Inferior	2	1.3
Don't know	23	14.8
Equal	2	1.3
TOTAL	155	100.0

TABLE 7-21

"WHAT ABOUT THE STAFF AT CRC? HOW WOULD YOU
SAY THAT MOST OF THEM FEEL IN RELATION TO DRUG
ADDICTS?"

	Number	*Percent*
Superior	102	65.8
Inferior	2	1.3
Don't know	38	24.6
Equal	12	7.7
Some superior	1	.6
TOTAL	155	100.0

quence of the staff's greater power position in the institution. That is not necessarily true, since in an educational institution, students rarely (except facetiously) impute to the administrators or the faculty, who have more power, convictions of moral superiority. Or in an institutional setting such as a modern corporation, the lower line position of an individual carries with it no firmly predictable feelings of moral difference. While it is true that the army and the church, as institutions, are heavily laden with moral censure aligned to position, this is very much a function of the substantive properties of these institutions.

Soldiers, priests, and treatment staff come to a world that has been preinterpreted for them in very moralistic terms.

Most of the addicts at CRC report that they feel morally inferior to nonaddicts. From probing in the interviews, there is evidence that they believe this to be a constitutional element of their character, not subject to change either by treatment or their own will. For example, many residents indicated that they wanted to respond better to the program, but that the situation they found themselves in was hopeless because of the different world view of addicts and nonaddicts. A quality of semi-bitter despondency was apparent among them. Many felt that the power in the world is held by moralists who make arbitrary decisions about the morality of others. Nonetheless, these same respondents granted legitimacy to derogatory characterizations of addicts. An unexpected theme that persisted through many of the interviews was the anger, resentment, and even indignation which resident addicts displayed toward other addicts *as addicts*. Sociologists have come to expect fervent anti-Semitism from Jews located in certain social positions, and they have come to expect caustic anti-Black expressions from certain Negroes. It is still surprising, however, to hear a man express contempt toward a whole group of men incarcerated in the institution with him ostensibly for the same kinds of offenses against the society.

Sometimes this hostility toward other addicts integrates the pejorative and the psychological. Some said, for example, that "There ain't nothin' worse than a goddamn junkie. He's immature, always tryin' to rationalize for what he does, always tryin' to blame others. He can't take the world, so he takes the coward's way out." Just a shade underneath this analytic layer is contempt: "I've known hundreds of hop-heads in my life and I know, they're *no good to themselves or to anyone else*; they're the most selfish people in the world."

When men come to believe that they are morally different from other members of their society, and when they believe that the others agree with this and are justified, their deviant behavior and its sustenance over time is both predictable and explainable. The primary issues in the treatment and rehabilitation of such individuals concern the ability to breach the large gap of moral interpretation between addicts and nonaddicts. It is a mistake of some magnitude to assume that addicts as deviants can be changed as an independent population. The reaction to addiction in the society is interwoven with the addict's moral conception of himself. So long as he retains the conception of his own moral difference, he has a justification and explanation for his own morally different behavior. The ability to change that conception can not be separated from the ability to change the moral reaction which produced, and produces, that conception.

There may be a few individual cases of successful return to society in a large population of addicts, just as there are individual successes in a program such as that of Synanon. But the gross problem in the society is not mitigated by a few individual successes. If we speak in terms of the typical case, *any rehabilitation program of social deviants is doomed to fail in its own terms by its own criteria* ("rehabilitation") *so long as the larger society treats rehabilitation as passage between two moral categories.* The typical addict at CRC sees himself in terms of moral inferiority. He also sees other addicts as inferior in kind and character to the rest of the population. His perceptions are simply reflections and mirror-images of the dominant attitudes toward addiction in this country for the last three decades. In sum, rehabilitation between two moral categories can not succeed by directing attempts at change only toward the category of the "morally inferior." Even if a treatment staff was completely free of such feelings, and even if every ex-addict left an institution personally and morally committed to change his behavior (both of which are empirically untrue), the moral interpretation of addiction in this society is so strong that return to the old communal ties is predictable for the typical addict.

CHAPTER 8

Perspectives on the addicts' world view

IT IS TYPICAL OF THE EARLY EXPERIENCE OF THE ADDICT-
to-be that he knows or knows of people who use narcotics and
who get away with it. They get away with it in the double sense
that they are neither addicted nor are they known to the police.
This double victory is witnessed by probably every individual who
knowingly uses heroin illegally for the first time. It is as important a
model of the consequences of drug use as that provided by the double-
loser addict whom the newspapers and slick magazines sensationalize.
Because the heroin novice has the opportunity to see for himself that
it is possible to be an occasional user, there is further reinforcement of
the tendency of ego to treat the self as exempt from the experience of
personal disaster. This property was discussed in greater detail in an

earlier section on the individual's path to addiction.[1] It is documented by the findings from this study, where four out of five believed they could use heroin and escape the hook of dependency.

Once hooked, they lose many of their negative attitudes about being addicted. A good many reflect upon the positive aspects of drug use, emphasizing the uniqueness of their experience as one which subjectively sets them apart from typical man's dull and routinized daily life.

Yet, there is in the addict an ambivalence on the meaning and the desirability of drug use. For example, while he may extoll its effects in elegant poetic metaphors, he tends to feel strongly against tempting or luring a square (nonuser) into drugs. Not only does he feel this way personally, he acknowledges that it is a strong principle among friends and acquaintances in the addict world. The arrogance and the swagger that emerges when he speaks of his own experiences with drugs shift to thoughtful deliberation, caution, and sometimes even passionate moral conservatism when contemplating his own role in spreading addiction. He can certainly feel that it is wrong to lure a square into addiction under the present circumstances of the illegality of drugs, yet he can approve of the idea of drug use in an abstract or ideal world. Thus it can be seen that there is no real or objective inconsistency, since the approval of drug use is only in an abstract or ideal world, and he merely warns against the kind of real life one would face if addicted in a world of hostile, power-wielding squares. The salient matter is that the addict here *senses* inconsistency and is probably ambivalent on the subject.

Contrary to the popular view, the veteran apprehended heroin addict commonly reports that his use of heroin is primarily to allow his body to function at equilibrium; he does not use it for euphoria or kicks. The using for kicks appears to be much more likely in the early phase of heroin consumption. That is true at least for these studies, where kicks is a motivating force, reportedly, for only a small minority of those who are fully addicted.

The claim is made by more than half of the addicts at CRC that the person they consider to be closest to them did not know that they were starting to use drugs. That the addict sees it as good strategy not to inform his "closest contact" of his decision to use drugs reflects an accurate awareness of the social meaning of narcotics use. The other information may be regarded as a measure of reaffirmation of the position stated at many other points: that if the user so wishes, the detection of the physical and physiological consequences of the opiates is difficult if not impossible to the naked eye. We have seen that this is true of the professionals who work with the addict as part of their routine job (and who must nevertheless rely upon chemical tests), but it is even true of the spouse or best friend or lover who has the opportunity to observe the myriad of moods outside of a strictly professional relationship.

The addict is himself aware of this possibility, and occasionally[2] regards himself far superior to the alcohol consumer whose motor facilities are dramatically disturbed by drinking. The great majority believe that, while under the influence of heroin or morphine, they can competently drive a car, ride a bicycle, and perform other tasks that require coordination and some dexterity.[3] Taken in combination with their knowledge of how the world regards, treats, and compares the alcohol user vs. the drug user, one can appreciate the source of their bitterness about the rational and just character of social life. Even under circumstances that would seem to maximize their tendency to say the opposite,[4] a full 40 per cent believe drug laws should be changed and narcotics made available to the addict through legal channels.

This bitterness about the perfidy of social justice gets expressed in many forms, from cynicism about the liquor lobby's campaign against marijuana to feelings of persecution that are often justified about the way the courts selectively handle the addict. To begin, the apprehended addict is likely to have had contact with authorities whose job demands unethical treatment. What the police really want from him is the name of the big supplier, the big seller in heroin. For this prize they are willing to subject him to continual harassment and even passive torture prior to his arrest. In an earlier section, I cited a Chicago state's attorney's defense of the practice of holding and detaining suspected addicts for long periods, openly admitting to a violation of their civil liberties.[5] According to the culture of the addict, it is during this detention period that the police allegedly bribe with heroin, knowing that after any fourteen-hour period, the addict's body will begin to go into with-drawal if unrelieved by the drug.[6] Since the police are legally permitted to hold a man for twenty-four hours on suspicion, there is plenty of time to break an addict down. Wretching on the floor of his empty cell in the city jail, he sees himself taunted with the alternative of heroin within his grasp and informing about his contact. At the first level, it is an ugly picture he draws of law enforcement.

But there is still more irony in it. In the following statement an addict reports how agents from the Federal Narcotics Bureau roughed him up before turning him over to the local authorities:

They came after me with a certain amount of relish. I didn't say "Sir!" and they were happy to have an excuse to hit me, saying I was disrespectful. What they really wanted to know about was *The Man*! When I wouldn't talk, one of them hit me hard, saying I was still being "disrespectful." I dropped my head down in self-protection and the other one said, "You're fleeing an arresting officer when you do that," and hit me so hard on the side of my head that my ear flesh is still mending from it. Then when they brought me here to this place (CRC), one of the first questions these counseling therapy guys wanted to know was "why was I so hostile to authority figures?" You get it man? You get it, don't you . . . they bust my ear, slam fists in my guts, then ask why am I so hostile to authority?

Of those addicts about which most is known, those apprehended and incarcerated, almost all have been through a court of justice. Because these people come almost entirely from the less privileged classes and can seldom afford the prohibitive fees of a private lawyer, they encounter the workings of justice in a way that further undermines their respect for the legal authorities of the society.[7] Officially, of course, they have the right to counsel, and the public defender is there to serve this function. In practice, however, the public defender is typically an accomplice and confederate of the prosecuting attorney. As Sudnow's remarkable study of the public defender's office points out, the structure of the enterprise encourages the collusion of the two attorneys with the conclusion of the police reports.[8] In no sense does that structure encourage a critical posture and a serious legal defense of the accused, since a defense of each accused man would tie up the workings of the court with backlogs for years. Sudnow demonstrates that the public defender approaches the accused with the belief that he is guilty, and that the task is simply to get him to confess, plead him guilty—and on to the next case.

Findings from this study corroborate Sudnow's work. First, one fourth of the residents did not have any lawyer when the courts committed them to CRC. Of those who did have a lawyer, almost 70 per cent had a public defender. The interviewer explored the defendants' perception of the situation as it might have compared to a legal defense by a private attorney. Most saw it as an extension of an arm of the police and the courts. They did not regard the public defender as one actively engaged in the fight to protect their legal and constitutional rights as a citizen in an egalitarian republic. The public defender wanted a confession. Just as one would expect from Sudnow's description and analysis, the defender gave his client many reasons why he should plead guilty ("It will go easier on you," "We know you did it," and "Don't put on any innocent and pure act for me, the police aren't buying.")

But the relationship with the prosecuting attorney provokes even more selective persecutions for the addict, because it is more specific and particular to the addict. Every lawbreaker from the lower classes has a good chance of running into the public defender situation described, but the prosecuting attorney's interest in the big contact man behind the heroin black market makes his interest in the addict intense. Every single addict may be the important lead or link to proliferated racketeering and syndicated control. The deal that the prosecution is willing to offer him is more bald and more attractive than that offered to other law-breakers, like armed robbers who act alone. At the same time, the negative side of the deal is all the more difficult for the addict to face. He must inform on the illegal activities of others, and there are few stronger moral taboos to be violated in one's dealings with a legal authority.

Double Standards of Morality

Once inside the gates of a prison for the rehabilitation of the drug user, the addict has more opportunities than ordinary prisoners to see the operation and irony of a double standard of morality. Even in ordinary prisons, authorities refuse to let convicts do such things as swear and shout, while men normally do this when brought together in groups. (I do not mean to include such things as restrictions upon smoking and drinking. There are some admissible justifications here, for the regulation of time and place rules exist in any large, bureaucratically controlled institution. Reference is here made only to instances where the purpose is to make the individual a "better" person.) The very petty theft of a fourteen-cent ballpoint pen may be treated with gravity in a rehabilitation center, while it is scarcely noticed or is shrugged off in a school, a dormitory, or a church. To lose a ballpoint from your work desk is seen as simply one of the normal hazards of living a normal life among normal men. But after a CRC correctional counselor lost a ballpoint pen from his desk he described this consequence:

I brought it up the next day in the group (a therapy session of about 60 men). I told them that it was among them, and that it was their responsibility to return it to me. I use that pen to sign progress reports, and I let them know that I wasn't going to send out a single progress report until the pen was returned. You know that if the report isn't filed, they can't get out. Well, the internal pressures built up, and the pen was back on my desk within four days.

The counselor went on to say that it obviously was not the money, but the principle:

I couldn't have cared less about the pen. I just wanted to show them that they have the power to solve their own problems internally, and that they are a community that shouldn't permit one to get away with something like that.

It is unfair to conclude that the counselor is deluding himself into thinking he communicated some moral lesson. One can doubt that this was his interest. Nonetheless, the emphasis is upon what one "ought to do" in a community. That is a far cry from what is expected of even the staff, since "everyone knows" that you shouldn't leave your bicycle unlocked at the nearby shopping center. Few outside of prison walls would treat the violation with such concern, but while there is clearly a double standard, it is unclear to what degree the inmates subscribe to it. One female inmate recounted the following experience concerning one of her roommates:

They caught —— out back with one of the guys who comes up here to work on the grounds. They were just over in the corner flirting and maybe kissing a little bit, but you would have thought they had committed a crime that none of the counselors could have thought they themselves could perform. They were both "written up" for it, and it cost them each at least three months more in this place. The thing that gets me and a lot of the girls is that they (the staff) behave the same way. We know they play around with each other, flirting and probably a lot more, but if we dare do it, we get penalized and lectured too as though we were abnormal.

The staff defends its position that the double standard is in operation, but necessary. The rationale is that the inmates need greater discipline than normal people, and that the addicts have forfeited their right to normal freedoms by their antisocial and criminal past. But there is an inherent paradox and dilemma here. Presumably, the path back to normal social relations is through the experiencing of them, yet the Rehabilitation Center (and indeed, all prisons) preclude the possibility of such normality. Normal sex is not just normal sex, it is the occasion for serious admonition. Petty theft is not just petty theft, it is a signal of a serious failure of the whole rehabilitation process. In one group-therapy session that I witnessed, the principal subject was a woman inmate who worked in the kitchen as a cook. She had the practice of giving out an extra apple or orange to her friends, and of taking bread and fruit and cheese to her own room for evening snacks; additionally, she used this as a personal dispensing station of goodwill. In this particular session, all this was uncovered for the staff counselor for the first time. The counselor turned the problem back to the group for analysis and discussion. At first the group was cautious and protective, but the dam of resentment of the less-favored who got no apples finally broke, and many joined in on the revelations. The woman began by denying the charges, and at that point an interesting thing happened. Some of her friends turned against her "because she lied" about her activities, and reported the truth of the charges. The counselor kept directing the attention of the group to the question of *why* she took fruit. As might be expected, some of the analysis was glib, some obsequious, some laced with hostility, and some was penetrating and sensitive. (The problem most imminent then was simply to decide upon the legitimacy, the cogency, or the viability of any given analysis.)

After the session was over, I joined a post-session group of about ten of the sixty, including the counselor, who discussed what had transpired in the group. Since I was a visitor and thus in their view a "detached observer," they asked for my views. In sum, I said that the group had held the woman and themselves to standards which were far higher than those outside of the prison's walls. There was a sudden, unexpected, spontaneous clamour and shouting of agreement. "Right on!" "Right on!" *That* was correct, they said, and that was true about "everything else" in the institution. The counselor defended the standards on her own grounds, then turned back to the small group and asked them to analyze why they had erupted so spontaneously.

But the double standard is even more striking in areas that are not touched by the group session, most particularly the judgments by men in administrative positions that are not subject to group-therapy review. One case will illustrate the point. Certain rules define the boundaries where residents may walk. A female resident, while on duty as a canteen worker, once absent-mindedly carried some coffee a few yards outside of a boundary. (The boundary is not marked physically with lines, nor does it have a sign posted. One is simply supposed to remember not to walk past point X.) An administrator saw her, and submitted a report on the incident which, if honored by the releasing committee, would have delayed her release by several months. Happily, the report was not honored, but no one seriously raised the question about that administrator's "need" to submit such a serious indictment for so trivial a matter. The double standard of morality which some of the incisive addicts observe and poignantly feel lies therein: Using the very criteria of the institution for free and healthy development of the psyche, why should the psychic needs of the staff escape analysis and attention? In the eyes of the resident, this is more hypocrisy. The coffee incident should have been talked about in group just like any other.

The addict sees the double morality of the larger society in the same way as he sees the staff, and he is right. Once publicly labeled as an addict, his prospective employer, prospective friends, and so on, demand of him a stricter form of moral puritanism than of others. If he is late once or twice for the job, it is seen in terms of his lack of gratitude to the employer who surmounted the barrier of prejudice to hire him while he was on parole. If his temperament is surly and without the proper deference and humility, he displays that he is still "one of them" and not at all regretful of his past. If, on the other hand, he is too humble, he has been "beaten down into something less than a man" by his drug experience. What I am suggesting is that the society demands that he toe a precise and highly circumscribed line which, if the members of the society itself were so forced, they would reject out of hand as authoritarian and irrational. For the addict, the public chant that he is a coward fleeing a reality he can not bear to face is a special kind of mockery. There may be those for whom this is an accurate explanation of their earlier behavior leading to addiction. That is another matter for another book. But once addicted, the reality that addicts must face monthly requires a personal fortitude as strong as that demanded of ordinary men in a lifetime.

The Normality of the Deviant's World

Despite the agedness of the cliché, men are still both surprised and amused to learn of honor among thieves. That is because men persist in regarding social deviants as though they were totally different persons who should thereby possess totally different values. And so they find it surprising and funny too that drug addicts should regard a petty thief with an amount of indignation, resentment, and moral consternation equal to that possessed by the middle-class, suburban housewife. The symmetry is achieved when we discover that the petty thief regards the drug addict with equal moralistic derision. This is a parallel to white Protestants and Catholics who are surprised to find that Blacks share their own anti-Semitic prejudices. As Raymond Mack has pointed out, such whites would exclude the Negro from equal participation in the culture even to the extent of holding back his share in the nation's byways of bigotry.[9]

One strain in sociology has tried to raise the argument of a different kind of culture for the deviant, with a separate set of values,[10] while another strain represents deviance (of youth) as a purer form of adult values.[11] In some aspects of the life of the deviant, each of these is undoubtedly true, and cogent arguments are contained in the essays by Miller and Matza. It is easy to lose sight of the congruency of values and morals between those who usurp for themselves the role of normals and those whom they then castigate as deviants. Even with so seemingly remarkable demarcations as the deviance of the mentally ill and the normality of mental health, there are strong congruencies.[12] For the drug addict, the similarities between his views of the larger rights and wrong in the world, of the sources of dignity and respect, of what is proper and appropriate in relationships between friends, siblings, bureaucrats, and so on—the similarities of his views to those of the "normal" nonaddict are so close as to be interchangeable. We can take the view of the family as one example, and more particularly, the conception of the responsibilities of parents toward their children.

Some of the women residents in CRC are mothers. Their children are taken care of by relatives and friends on the outside. The identity which these women have as addicts is not nearly as strong as their identity as mothers. The conception of self as mother is typical enough, and the actual child-rearing practices (when the resident was with her children) are the common, expected, and normal practices of any other mother. Cicourel conducted a comparative study of the uniformity of the mother's role and her child-rearing practices of populations in Argentina and the United States.[13] In both societies, he interviewed a range of social classes and types for the comparative basis in his data. As part of the data collected in the United States, he conducted interviews with female addicts who were mothers. His findings support the notion that the latter engage in the same behavior, and conceive of their own roles as mothers and of themselves in the same manner as other mothers from the same general classes and ethnic backgrounds who are not drug users.[14]

Chein and his associates note the same phenomena of the typical or normal views of the addict with respect to young adolescent populations.[15] Nyswander and others record the normality of the addict's views of self as a special health case[16] and the present study reports the normal character of the addict's social world and his view of it as he embarks upon first usage.[17] True enough, Becker[18] and Finestone[19] emphasize the "outsider's" view which the addict takes, but neither makes his case in such a way as to challenge the position here stated: that the outsider's view incorporates, digests, and actually manifests the views of typical man insofar as it concerns life beyond the perimeters of the outsider's own narrowly conceived (i.e., by the self) deviance. As soon as we leave the specific arena of the deviance, the chances are very great that we are dealing with a typical man with values, interests, and commitments that are typical for the remaining categories and subcategories that may be used to describe him. To lose sight of this in the stampede to total identification of the deviant is to court failure at every turn, from first apprehension to final release from parole. If we keep it uppermost in our minds, however, it will force us to raise questions at the very outset which challenge the whole process of apprehension, generic treatment, and total surveillance upon parole.

The Counselor On the Addict's Attitude

A segment of this study was concerned with the correctional counselor's judgment of the addict's readiness for normal society. This problem involves not only the view of readiness, but also includes the counselor's conception of what does and what should constitute normal society.

For each resident inmate of the Rehabilitation Center, a rather complete file is maintained from the day he enters the program until his release. His counselor files periodic reports on his progress, or lack of it, detailing such items as attitudes toward work, responsibility, deviance, and of course the group-therapy sessions. These files were analyzed for more than half of the subjects who were part of the intensive interview study. A consistent finding was the importance of the initial impression that the inmate makes upon his counselor. It typically remains intact for several evaluations at least, and often follows him throughout the time the counselor in question has contact. The turnover of counselors provides an interesting phenomenon for contrast. When a new counselor enters the scene, there is no reliability that his judgment of the character and potential success of the inmate will be consistent with that of the old counselor. It should surprise no one but the counselors themselves that the consistency within the long file reports of a single counselor are higher than the consistency of file reports between counselors on the same inmate. That finding may raise no eyebrows, but it does raise face-valid questions about judgmental reliability.

If a resident joined some group, that is to say, informally "hung around" with a select bunch, that was the single most important factor in the counselor's judgment of him. It tended to override all other characterizations with ease. One gets the impression that the counselor knows his own dormitory very thoroughly, for he writes with confidence about the deviant cliques and the responsible cliques, the jokers, the immature, and the troublemakers. The nature of the group joined was, of course, critical, but also of importance was the point in time in which the group was joined. For a resident to join a deviant group within a few weeks of his arrival placed an indelible mark upon him that could hardly be erased even if he later renounced that group. However, if he waited a few months, joined a deviant group, then renounced it, he was considered "saved." The explanation which seemed most reasonable of the counselors' view was that the early noncommital behavior of the addict reflected a searching for identity that was later misplaced into the wrong grouping. For the "original" deviants, however, the immediate identification with a deviant group was treated as the "homing" activity of a through-and-through deviant.

The counselors' reports were analyzed in a search for the kind of reasons that the counselor believed led the inmate to narcotics, the kinds of cure or treatment he considered best for the individual case, and the chances he gave for the success of the CRC program. These data were then compared to the data collected in the interviews with the inmates themselves.

First, with regard to the kinds of reasons that the counselors believed led to drug use, social factors played a surprisingly dominant role in their written reports. The role of the peer group, a sense of belonging, conditions and structure of the family life, and the like are constantly cited. Factors of individual personality are also noted, but to a much lesser extent. This finding was surprising because (a) it does not coincide with the verbal expressions which the counselors and other staff give when asked about how the addict becomes addicted, and (b) when we turn to the kind of cure recommended, personality changes are seen as the predominant vehicle. The larger explanation for this inconsistency will be taken up later when we turn to how men shift their interpretation of deviant and criminal activity depending upon the stage of the judicial-legal process in which it is seen.

The cure or treatment which the counselor recommends, then, is group therapy and the reorganization of personality. That is understandable enough in that this is institution policy, and these are written reports to superiors. There are occasional reports that group therapy seems ineffective for a particular case, usually because he "just isn't mature enough for it" or because he is "lost" to salvation. However, there are a few forthright admissions that the treatment program will not be effective on an individual. The greatest measure of doubt comes in the assessment of the likelihood that the resident will be successfully rehabilitated by his experience at CRC. That is, it seems that the counselors have great self-assurance that they know both the source of the motivation for drug use and the best kinds of treatment, but have reservations about the success of the program in rehabilitating the ex-addict for normal return to normal society.

The explanation for this lies very close to the second aspect of the problem of the counselor's task that must now be examined, namely, the counselor's conception of the community to which the ex-addict should return. As noted earlier, the very nature of the occupation of counselor makes its occupant a member of the middle class. That does not mean that he will necessarily carry his class bias and his class view into his professional job, but this is a likely occurrence at the very least unless consciously checked at every turn. Thus, for example, if we ask what ought a typical man do with his salary, we would expect to get different answers depending upon whether the respondent was working class, middle class, or upper class. So long as this is merely a judgmental matter of opinion, there is nothing nefarious to be noted in these differences. When, however, one class member is in the position to pass judgment on the life chances and the freedom of some one from a different social class, ethical and value premises arise. Such is the case with the Rehabilitation Center, where almost all the inmates are working class and all the treatment staff is middle class. It is the middle-class treatment counselor who has the dominant and commanding view of the way normal life should be lived in the outside community: An inmate who announced in group that he "lived only for the weekends" was cited for this in a counselor's file report as "socially irresponsible and immature." An inmate who "spent too much time with a small clique" of friends rather than developing some individual "strength and independence" was cited for this as revealing an inability to maintain himself "on the streets" without help "from the wrong elements." Inmates who see the police and all legal authorities as their enemies are cited in the file reports as recalcitrant and socially maladjusted—despite the fact that we know from other sociological studies that this orientation to the police is highly class-related, with the middle class seeing the police as their protectors and the working class perceiving the police often as hostile and harassing.[20]

Thus, the counselor's highly class-biased views of what constitutes appropriate behavior in the community of normal men infuses his judgment of the readiness of the inmate for release. That the inmate is working class explains a great deal of the counselor's skepticism about the degree of rehabilitation that has taken place and the possibility of successful return to the community. What is less appreciated is the fact that the inmate is likely to return to a working-class community, not a middle-class one. His "rehabilitation" may therefore specifically maladjust him for the return. Those who look for more reasons to explain the high recidivism rates from these institutions might do well to consider this point.

The counselor in the institution is not the only authority who experiences this frustration that seems to be built in to the system of handling incarcerated addicts. The parole officer who takes over the surveillance outside the prison walls experiences it even more strongly. In the following section, we will explore some of the common problems of the parole situation that arise when men succumb to the total identification of the addict as a deviant.

The Parole Agent as the Keeper of Middle-Class Morality

In the intricate and complex relationship between law and morality, nowhere is the interplay clearer than in the role of the parole agent. He exercises significant authority with a great deal of latitude. The situation is in striking contrast to that of the policeman, whose activities are much more restricted by explicit rules of legal procedure. True enough, the policeman must use discretion on his job. However, he is only given an inch, and so he must take his mile. The parole agent is given a mile to start with, and what he can take is proportionately greater.

The police officer must apprehend the "criminal" before his formal conviction. He is restrained in his handling of suspects because the law guarantees that a man is officially innocent until proven guilty by due process. If the officer makes a mistake in the sometimes long and tedious process from suspicion to apprehension to arrest, a lawyer for the defense can free the accused with skillful legalistic footwork. This makes the policeman's job a study in role conflict. The public demands that all crimes be solved and that all culprits be brought to justice. Simultaneously, the public (or perhaps better, the courts, the ACLU, some civil libertarians, and the Constitution) demands that suspects have their rights as private citizens protected until convicted.

Once convicted, the law violator loses most of his rights. If he is sentenced to prison for a felony, he cannot vote, he has no more right to privacy, and he may legally be the subject of continual invasions of his domain, his personal property, and even his person. When he leaves the prison on parole, he is still technically serving his sentence and has not regained his rights. At this point, the parole officer takes charge of the case. To a greater degree than the policeman, he can exercise his own judgment as to whether the parolee belongs back in prison, or whether he should remain out on parole. The breadth of his discretion and latitude in the exercise of moral judgment means that he has the decisive voice about appropriate, acceptable, and normal behavior. It has just been noted that the treatment staff in the rehabilitation center acknowledge a double standard of morality, and argue that the law violator has lost the right to pursue normal life with its immunity from minor transgressions in rules and laws; that instead, the convict must prove that he is a better person than those on the outside.

Many parole agents feel the same way about their case subjects. Ex-drug addicts on parole are typically not permitted to drink alcohol to the point of being "high." They are given strict curfews, permitted only certain kinds of acceptable jobs, are required to report periodically and systematically, and are required to hold steady employment. To be unemployed is obviously no crime, but it is a serious parole violation for which the parole department may send the parolee back to prison. There are many reasons for this regulation, as there are reasons for other stipulated activities which have as their official justification the creation of a climate for "staying out of trouble with the law." However, in their own right, these rules reflect a certain view of the appropriate life of the individual in society. One ought to have a job, philosophizes the parole department, whether or not he need do so for subsistence. One ought not get drunk, whether this has anything to do with the ex-addict's heroin or not. So we find deeply imbedded in the idea of parole violations themselves the tendency to specify the appropriate life for the parolee, an appropriateness that can be divorced from the consideration of law violation.

As noted, this differs greatly from the role and concern of the police, especially in the degree to which it is possible to impose appropriate behavior. The police may know that adultery is being committed, but unless there is a plaintiff and strong evidence that will stand up in a court of law, nothing can be done to the known culprits. However, if the parole agent knows of the adultery of the parolee in the same way as any normal member of the community might know (heresay, gossip, circumstantial evidence), there need be no *flagrante delicto* for corrective action. When the parole agent finds out that his colleague in the office has been "playing around with someone's wife," he may be very annoyed, but it is dangerous and shaky business to act upon that knowledge. There are points of law, proof, and slander. The very same parole agent is capable of *effective* indignation when his parolee is "playing around." The legal issue of legal proof is not a question. Here is a case of the use of a conception of natural law. "The adulterer deserves to be punished." The fact that he is, say, an ex-drug addict on parole makes him accessible to the punishment he "deserves." So, the adulterous drug addict is sent back to prison by his parole officer not because he relapsed into heroin usage, but because of his affrontery of sexual morality. Adultery, indeed, is against the law. However, it is critical to the point being made that "everyone knows" people don't get sent to jail for adultery. They may get beaten up, they may be subpoenaed to the witness stand or sued for alienation of affection; but they are rarely imprisoned for adultery in American society.

Nonetheless, the parole officer feels thoroughly justified in his action. His rationale is intricate, but much of it can be summarized in the notion that a parolee is engaging in immoral behavior which signals that he lacks rehabilitation to society's demands.

There are better examples than adultery, however, to illustrate how the parole officer acts as the keeper of middle-class morality. Adultery is illegal. Going to the race track and betting is not. Yet a parolee who had remained spotless as far as the law was concerned was returned to prison for refusing to "accommodate to a style of life that is conducive to law-abiding behavior." The primary documentary evidence for this violation of appropriate life-style was repeated adventures to the race track, and only occasional employment.

It will come as no surprise that parolees from middle-class backgrounds have a much easier time complying with the rules of keeping in good standing with the parole office. A stable home life is usually an important plus for the parolee, as are the kinds of friends with whom he associates. Since the parole agent is himself middle-class or aspiring thereto, he typically and perhaps naturally favors the kinds of parolees who can sustain friendships in that class. More important, the quality of the friendship and the nature of acceptable activities that are pursued are critically related to social class. The ideal is one who saves his money and adjusts his life and his aspirations to those with power and prestige in the society. Setting a portion of one's income aside for a future when one can move to a better residential area is in this context a positive act. But if one comes from a lower or working-class background, the chances are so much greater that more immediate pleasures on the weekend and flashy clothing give the real currency to living.[21]

For the parole officer, this "unwise" use of hard-earned money is a point which allows him to call the whole rehabilitation of the ex-convict into serious question, and parole violations for such persons take on a new dimension of seriousness.

As a direct consequence of this, the period on parole is a time where the ex-convict ex-addict is most resentful of the selective treatment directed towards him. Other criminals on parole are far more likely to get away with minor transgressions such as seeing old friends and taking a drink if they simply avoid trouble with the police. The ex-addict on parole sees himself quite correctly in a different situation. His minor transgressions of the same dimension (in his eyes) are treated by the parole agent as a lapse into "drug-prone" behavior. The increasing sophistication of the agents concerning the concepts of a total social environment for the addict produce a stronger impulse for surveillance. This in turn makes the addict feel himself relatively deprived and the return to old friends and the return to drug use becomes increasingly imminent.

Relapse and the Addict's View of It

Of the many factors that account for the high rate of relapse into drug use after parole, the addict himself counts two most heavily. These are the harassment-benevolence of squares and outsiders, and the hearty welcome and comfortable atmosphere of the old friends who are still using.

Led by the Nalline testers and the parole agent, the society at large invades the life of the paroled addict to a degree that he usually experiences as persistent harassment if not persecution. He must report regularly for Nalline tests, which serve to inform authorities to their own satisfaction that he is or is not using. (There has recently been some controversy about the fallibility of Nalline testing, but that is another point.) In addition to these regular appointments, he must expect some surprise visits from authorities who at any moment may take him in for more tests. The most feared and the most hated harassment, however, is the spot visit at 3 A.M. that always hangs over the paroled addict, even though he may experience it only once during several months of parole. This is simply something of a bed-check by the authorities to see to it that the parolee is not only living where he is supposed to be living, but also that he is keeping to the curfew that has been set. For the parolee who is tottering on the edge and may be pushed either way, this is experienced as a degradation ceremony (especially if he is not living alone) and sensed as harassment, even though some will be moved to begrudgingly state that it is a necessary evil for others.

Alongside of those who subject the addict to what he feels is harassment are those who are charitable and who give of themselves to him, but who do so in a style and manner which he comes to resent as benevolent at best. Very commonly and ironically, it is the employer who "condescended" to hire him that the addict parolee comes to resent most.

They never miss a chance to remind you that they did you a big favor by giving you a job, even the lousiest dish-washing job, and that you should be eternally grateful for it. If you are two minutes late, or leave a speck of a spot on the floor, they may not say it, but they look at you as though they wonder if they ever should have done you that big favor . . . just like they weren't paying you a god-damn pittance for nine hours of labor.

In one sense, the employer of the parolee seems unable to win such a battle. Even if he keeps quiet and goes out of his way to show special attention to the sensitivity of his employee, he is regarded with a dubious eye. However much truth there may be in a particular charge, the remarkable sensitivity and tenderness of the addict's ego on this point turn his vision to one of persecution.

In any case, the potential harassment of the parolee at any juncture makes it impossible for him to conceal from those closest to him (physically and emotionally), from employer to friend to lover, that he is a parolee. Because they thereby know who he *is* (total identification), he imputes to them a series of feelings and attitudes about his past that makes it very difficult for them to pursue a normal and relaxed social or personal relationship. Thus the very structure of the parole situation, which sets up a quasi-normality for the parolee, acts as a push in the direction of relapse, because the parolee after a time seeks the more relaxed and comfortable, taken-for-granted atmosphere of his old addict cronies. They demand little else of him than that he join them for a social evening. This is not to suggest that his persecution is delusion and paranoia. Some is and some is not. The point is that the distinction between the two is neither meaningful nor made from the addict's view because the structure of his social situation makes the distinction for him irrelevant. He finds that the only people who, in his terms, "accept him for what he is" are the old addict friends. They welcome him back with the cynical assurance that once an addict, always an addict. But they express this in the most congenial manner, and he feels no moral condescension from them, for they themselves are "hop-heads."

But the structure of the parole situation gets even more diabolically ironic at this point, because simply being with old addict friends is a parole violation of serious dimensions. With his own justification, the parole agent treats the return to the old circle for the sociological significance that he begins to invest in it. Any warning that is forthcoming about a situation that does not directly involve the use of heroin is treated by the addict parolee as more unnecessary harassment. That, in its turn, impels him further on the way to more serious violation and complete relapse.

To understand the relapse into drug use, it is critical that one understand the way in which the ex-addict makes a separation between the moral meaning of drug use and the moral meaning of other illegal activity. He does not regard the consumption of morphine or heroin itself with moral approbation; but rather it is those things which addiction to drugs drives one to that he regards as morally reprehensible. The moral degradation of the man's self-conception comes when he must steal to supply his habit, *but it is not the habit itself which he abhors* for its moral turpitude. Thus, when he is feeling harassed by the world of authorities and squares, it is no big thing to return to the needle-wielding friends, and, indeed, to the needle.[22]

The popular conception of the ex-addict's return to drug use is in error, therefore, when it conceives of a significant and remarkable breakdown of a structure of positive attitudes. The chances are that the ex-addict never came to the point where he conceived of drug use in character-transforming terms. The decision to use cannot then be explained as a character-transforming decision.

On the "Failure" of Rehabilitation

In a world where the typical public relations or advertising man is paid more than twice as much as the typical hospital worker, men will find ways to turn disturbing ideas into more comforting euphemisms, and indeed, to phrases that signal positive development. I have just said in the last chapter that the rehabilitation of the deviant is doomed to failure by the very criteria of the institution that is set up to rehabilitate him. Just as there are ways of avoiding the issue of why the care of the sick should be less rewarded than the construction of the right jingle, so are there ways of avoiding the word *failure*.

Ordinarily, a high rate of return to a prison (recidivism) is regarded as the failure of the institution to successfully rehabilitate the convict. A prison may be successful in punishing a criminal and successful in keeping him off the streets, but if he returns to a life of crime he has not been rehabilitated. For reasons that have been detailed elsewhere, the blame is more on the society, but failure is failure, and like Juliet's rose, the change of name does not alter the scent. The California Rehabilitation Center has rephrased the problem to avoid the term *failure* even on the question of rehabilitation. The CRC solution begins with the use of an analog: In an ordinary hospital when a physician sends the patient away from the hospital on an out-patient basis, he does so because he believes that the patient can manage outside of the complete dependency of the hospital. If the ailment flares up again, he is called back, examined, and perhaps retained for more treatment. The original treatment is not called a failure.

So it is with a Rehabilitation Center. Those who return are "not regarded as failures of the treatment program, but as interim patients that come and go as their adjustment to the community reveals a need for more treatment." Even if the whole treatment staff at CRC can completely accept this interpretation, the returning addict cannot. True enough, the relationship between the individual and the prison may be intricate in its psychic dimensions. Any individual addict may be diagnosed as having a pathological need for the total embrace of a total institution that suspends his responsibility about individual decision-making. (However, even in such cases, the admission to the self that one needs that total environmental control is clearly separable from the view of one's self as a "success" in a world which treats such return to prison as failure.) Those addicts who are returned to CRC because of a minor transgression of parole rules and not for heroin use feel cheated. They know that outside of CRC the return is regarded as a failure. Yet they get the label without having had the indulgence in the very activity that has been used to identify them totally as failures.

But the implication should not be drawn that a dramatic change or reversal in the attitude of the addict about his own failure or success would ameliorate the problem of his rehabilitation. Rehabilitation is a two-sided transaction, and the receiving society must take the first step. The society must begin first not just because "it started it," but because no other solution is possible. One or two individual addicts in one hundred may manage to stay away from relapse and failure. However, because one or two black slaves in one hundred escaped to freedom, the success of those few with the underground railroad did not prove that all it takes is individual will power and a strong personality to escape. Those slaves escaped in spite of the system of controls on runaway slaves, and they escaped as much as by propitious circumstance as by force of personality. The perseverance or fortitude of a Dred Scott or any other runaway did not reduce the likelihood of his being caught, beaten, and returned. From a sociological point of view, the apprehended addict is as totally identified as the slave. No matter what his personality, so long as the society honors a system that catches, supervises, harasses, and degrades him, only one or two in one hundred will escape.[23] It is then a travesty to use those one or two addicts who do escape as evidence that all other addicts could manage as well if their psyches were well put together. This has the same illogic as pointing to a successful runaway slave in 1850 and saying to the other hundreds of thousands of slaves: "He did it, why couldn't you?" A century later, we can look back and see that it was the institution of slavery that needed alteration, not the individual personalities who could not escape from under it. Perhaps it will take us a century to look back upon the narcotics problem to understand that its essence does not lie within the structure of the individual's psyche, but in the prevailing social interpretation and social meaning of narcotics use.

PART IV

General comments
and conclusions

Mental illness and criminal intent *

Chapter 9 is from the author's article of the same title appearing in *Changing Perspectives in Mental Illness*, edited by Stanley C. Plog and Robert B. Edgerton. Copyright © 1969 by Holt, Rinehart and Winston, Inc. Reprinted by permission of Holt, Rinehart and Winston, Inc.

MENTAL ILLNESS AND CRIMINAL INTENT ARE incompatible in Western civilization. If a life has been taken, or if someone has been sexually assaulted, a criminal act has not been committed unless the perpetrator of the act is mentally responsible.[1] This incompatibility has been the source of a critical problem of explanation and treatment: It must both be explained and acted upon how a mentally healthy member of society could healthily decide to commit a criminal act. Once pathology of the mind is excluded as a possible explanation of crime, men are left searching for reasons that contain the fewest possible residues of the idea of sickness.

The difficulty, of course, is that it is problematic in any culture to

217

conceive of criminality as healthy, reasonable, and decided upon as a normal, rational course. It seems that there must be a large element of sickness imputed to the criminal act. In its most simply stated form, this is Western man's central dilemma in the treatment of law violators: to explain crime without imputing illness.

The attempt to discern the intent of action has become the most important theoretical element in the courtroom practice of law.[2] Although this has been popularized by the mass media's saturation with courtroom procedure in criminal law, ramifications of the idea of criminal intent escape ordinary attention and reach far beyond the official administration of justice. Some of the important consequences of this absorption with establishing *mens rea* vs. mental illness are seen in the way social workers, probation officers, judges, and police see and treat people. This absorption is also a critical base to an understanding of how the typical, normal member of the society, and therefore, behavioral scientists, make sense of crime. To say that an objectionable act is provoked by mental disturbance is to give not only an explanation, but to charter as well the possible avenues to treatment, correction, and change. To say that certain criminal acts are provoked by mental illness is therefore to channel the way in which men can conceive of the correction and rehabilitation of criminals. This is only one example of a subtle consequence of how men deal with the dilemma in the interpretation of criminal behavior.

It is important to state at the outset that the whole class of persons who may be called criminals (violators of the criminal law) is such a conglomeration of heterogeneous elements as to make simple, inclusive statements about the whole class impossible. There are professional criminals who treat crime as an occupation and a way of life. There are one-time violators who otherwise regard criminal activity as abhorrent. There are serious violators who commit felonies, petty thieves and shoplifters who commit misdemeanors, and of course, those who get caught and those who do not. This is only a very partial list of important variations among criminals. It would be impossible to deal with all of the significant variations as separate categories, and equally impossible to try to discuss them all under one banner. Instead this chapter will address itself in a general way to serious crimes that are usually called felonies, and to those perpetrators who get caught.

As has been indicated, if a man is a criminal, he is mentally healthy in the eyes of the law. However much the layman may agree with this when he is impaneled for jury duty, he is hard-pressed to go along with it in his explanations of everyday life. Nonetheless, legal interpretation has its own impact, and Western men do try to live with the idea of a mentally healthy criminal. The attempts to explain how this could come about are varied, and each is of significance for how the criminal is perceived and treated.

A. *The Criminal as Immoral*

The first significant resolution of the problem is to regard the criminal as mentally capable and responsible, but antagonistic to the contemporary moral order. Thus, the murderer "knows" what he is doing. He "knows" that his actions violate the moral code of others, but he feels that he can and should commit the act anyway. He may reach this conclusion by asserting a contrary morality, but the essential point is that he refuses to subscribe to moral dictates that hold others in check. The classic statement of this would be Raskolnikov's transcendent morality in *Crime and Punishment*. He decided that he could commit murder. The rational thought processes that produced this conclusion document the mentally healthy and responsible character of his act, and for that he was held accountable.

Raskolnikov's reasoning, or some facsimile of it, is imputed to the criminal who is thought to be mentally healthy, but immoral. It is not so much that criminals are said to explicitly engage in the abstract philosophical meditation about the ethical issues, but that they do come to a position of a contrary morality that is rationally acted upon. The moral interpretation of criminality carries with it the stigma of any activity cast in moral terms. Between the state of physical fitness and the state of physical illness, men believe that passage can occur both ways. One who has been ill can become well, and vice-versa. However, as Harold Garfinkel has noted, between the state of being moral and the state of being immoral, a barrier to passage has been erected that precludes the movement of the individual back and forth.[3] Once the murderer has committed the act, he is permanently stigmatized as a kind of person who must be held suspect. The ex-convict faces the insurmountable problem of a continual confrontation with a hostile society that firmly believes that he is "morally capable" of that act again and again. The ex-convict is therefore treated in such a way as to prevent his movement back into moral normalcy by the very devices which have been used to explain his behavior. For example, at that point in time when the drug addict was transformed into a moral deviant in the eyes of the public, around 1920, he was for the first time excluded from the possibility of movement back into nonaddicted society.[4] The intensity of moral conviction and the force of moral reaction guarantee this.

The moral interpretation of criminality has long historical roots, and successfully infuses all other views of crime to some degree. To the extent that it is explicit, it undermines the concept of rehabilitation. In prisons, it can make little sense to try to rehabilitate a man who is regarded in the larger society as immoral, because even if *he* changes, his return cannot be accepted by "normals". The rejection of the ex-convict is documented by every ex-convict who goes into the world unannounced and tries to secure employment, irrespective of his moral conversion. This problem emerges again and again in every other view of the criminal.

B. *The Criminal as Psychically Inadequate*

To regard the criminal primarily as one with a personality disorder is to risk getting too close to the area of mental illness. It takes a great deal of skill and agility to impute psychic disturbance and yet not taint the individual with the imputation of mental illness. Yet, this is exactly the present situation in American courts and prisons. Treatment programs in prisons focus around the attempt to reorganize the psychic make-up of the inmate. Therapy sessions center upon the inadequacies of the inmate's personality, inadequacies which in the eyes of the therapist produced the criminal behavior in the first place.

In order to be able to live with the idea that the criminal is mentally responsible, though psychologically inadequate, it is usually necessary to impute to him the rational cognitive process. Thus, he must also be thought of as a bit immoral, if not evil, as will be illustrated below. He may have a "morbid and unhealthy need for antisocial behavior," but it is not a compulsive thing. He can control these impulses. The fact that he can but does not control them means that the inadequate personality suddenly becomes adequate in making a judgment about right and wrong, or good and evil. It is inevitable that this particular route of interpretation carries with it an imputation of immorality. Prison inmates are poignantly aware of this, and report that while they may be told repeatedly of their personality problems, what they really hear is a statement about their moral inferiority. Irrespective of whether the criminal is regarded as immoral or inadequate, rehabilitation problems are identical when the society at large refuses to allow the normal return of the ex-convict. However, which one is more important at a given time is dependent upon that point in the sequence of the administration of justice that is uppermost. Whereas the morality issue is more important in the judicial process leading up to imprisonment, the psychological issue assumes primacy in the rhetoric of rehabilitation. For the police, the prosecuting attorney, the judge, and the jury, the guilty defendant is first of all guilty of a moral breach. Each in his turn may acknowledge that the accused has personality problems, but the focus of the accusation is in moral territory. (Otherwise, he may be too close to mental irresponsibility.) However, once he is convicted and imprisoned, the focus shifts to the personality dimension. Treatment and rehabilitation programs begin with the assumption that the inmate can be helped to restructure and rebuild his inadequate psyche. As has been suggested, when access routes to normal life are cut off for the ex-convict, no amount of sophisticated and successful therapeutic treatment can rehabilitate him.

In sum, the interpretation of the criminal as personally inadequate (deficient personality, psychic disturbance) tends almost always to carry with it a large measure of the imputation of immorality. As such, each of those consequences discussed in the preceding section apply to some extent here. The difference is primarily one of the way in which selected persons can treat the criminal if they choose to do so. They may respond to him as curable and subject him to therapeutic measures designed to effect a change. The residue of moral judgment makes failure in this area the documentation of the moralists' charges, and the therapists must continually confront this issue in themselves as well as in others. If the lawbreaker is simply and completely immoral, then there is a tendency to regard his rehabilitation as hopeless. If, on the other hand, he is suffering from disturbance of personality, there may be access to change, health, and thus, correction.

C. *The Criminal as a Victim of External Forces*

There is an almost opposite interpretation, which focuses upon the conditions in which the criminal exists. This is the more sociological view, still a minority position, but held by an increasing number of laymen. The particular orientation or bias leads these observers to see forces outside the control of the individual as more determinant factors in explaining criminal behavior. Laymen of this persuasion explore and emphasize the broken home, poverty and the attendant lack of recreational facilities, pernicious influences in the community, etc. Sociologists have emphasized the social systems which surround the individual. Thus, the condition of poverty provides the context for the development of the culture of poverty. The peer group emerges as a dominant theme in the explanation of criminal behavior.[5] The individual is seen as a malleable substance, formed and directed by these external forces. It is important to recognize that individual will and responsibility make few appearances in this conceptualization. The adequacy of the personality or the moral character of behavior come into question only with regard to the relevant social system. In the culture of poverty, theft from the owner of a small, struggling store may be regarded as very immoral behavior, while theft from a large chain department store is treated as a matter of course. It is common enough knowledge that there is honor among thieves, but men often neglect to make the next logical conclusion. As for adequacy of personality, that too is determined within the limits of the relevant system in which the individual acts. One performs adequately in the role of a bureaucrat in organized crime or as a professional thief, and the issue of a basically anti-social, rebellious personality, hostile to authority, need never be raised from this orientation.

Accordingly, the analysis of organized crime in sociology begins with very traditional assumptions about how any normal bureaucracy works. In place of a pathology or an abnormality, the concepts that are used to characterize and explain a syndicated crime operation are precisely those that describe the Pentagon, a legitimate business corporation, or the line of command in an army regiment. Indeed, what is remarkable to those who have studied organized crime from this perspective is the degree to which these concepts fit.[6] The individual occupying an organizational role in the Mafia discharges his obligations with the same dedication to procedural rules as any other bureaucrat. His mobility in the organization reads like a chapter from Whyte's *Organization Man*; his view of why he ought to discharge his duties could come from Blau's *Dynamics of Bureaucracy*; and Barnard's *Functions of the Executive* just as easily apply to Capone as to Charles Wilson. At this level of analysis, say sociologists, it adds little to an understanding of the behavior in question to impute mental abnormality.

In the heyday of organized crime in Chicago in the 1920s, judges, senators, newspapermen, and city clerks were all on the payroll of the Capone organization.[7] Bootlegging was a serious and dangerous business, as evidenced by more than two hundred gangland killings in Chicago over a four-month period.[8] (The only thing sensational about the St. Valentine's Day Massacre was that seven men were killed at one standing, and the way the world press played to it.) Torrio and Capone carried out the production and distribution of alcohol with efficiency that is not characteristic of the mentally deficient or disturbed. In values, motives, and ideology one can speculate just how far Capone was from the typical successful American businessman. Gang murders were only a small part of his total operation, and it is too easy to make the mistake of concluding from these other activities that there is a difference that shades into all areas. More will be said about his subject later, but there is an interesting parallel here with the layman's tendency to regard the serious attempt at suicide as an indicator of mental illness. He also tends to regard the attempt at (or completion of) murder in the same light, despite the fact that the attempt itself may be the only behavior that can be characterized as distinctive. The obvious cautionary note is that mental disturbance is probably a generic or diffuse thing, which is reflected in more than a single act or even a single set of acts.

Organized crime is only one area of criminal activity which lends itself to traditional sociological techniques of explaining and interpreting behavior. For example, the social-systems approach is equally usable in interpreting behavior within an occupational or career setting. The professional criminal who makes crime a way of life or perhaps who makes crime his occupation, is engaged in the occupational role in a remarkably normal, patterned way. As Sutherland pointed out in his discussion of the professional thief, such occupations come complete with a code of ethics, specialized language, pecking order, and ideology.[9] Once again, there is a literature in sociology on the occupation as a career, and the parallels are more striking than are the differences between criminal occupational careers and noncriminal ones.

The major point of this orientation to crime, it seems, is that the participants are very, very normal in their ways of coping with the world. They can hardly be called hostile to authority in a generic sense, in that they respond to the bureaucratic superior in the same way as any noncriminal bureaucrat. As long as the observer is capable of seeing the criminal in terms of a social-system parameter, he sees normality and not pathology. Clearly if the behavior is compared to the activity of the middle class, the differences are striking. But if we address the forms of interaction, the man in organized crime or the independent professional criminal is identical with the normal citizen of everyday life. There is nothing in the manner or style of the criminal that sets him off from his fellow-man. It is debatable as to whether the substance of behavior is sufficient to set off qualitative distinctions. In the Eichmann Trial, the defense argued strongly that Eichmann's instrumentality in the slaughter of hundreds of thousands of Jews was purely bureaucratic. As such, the manner and style of his activity was to be viewed in these terms—and the substantive issue of *what* he did was to be treated as secondary, if not tangential or totally irrelevant.

His ultimate guilt was established for the court by the argument that he was responsible for the substantive moral decisions.

The sociologist's suggestions for the way in which the society achieves rehabilitation of this kind of criminality is accordingly quite different. Instead of focusing upon the individual and the problem of reconstructing him, he focuses either upon (1) modifying or changing the social conditions that have ordinarily enveloped him, or (2) changing the way in which the society regards that setting.

In the first instance, the change of the ex-convict's environment can be partially effected by making sure that he does not return to his old neighborhood, his old community, and the culture of his criminal past. Prisons in this country now emphasize this strategy for parolees. However, for reasons which were discussed earlier, the ex-convict is often channeled by the society in such a way that he normally and naturally gravitates back to his old environment. That is, the societal reaction is so strong and so moral, and the stigma of being an ex-convict so great, that the individual has little choice in selecting alternative environments for his acceptance. He can expect rejection in all environs but one, that from which he developed as a person.

Another tactic would be the attempt to change the old environment itself. This is clearly the more difficult task. Law enforcement authorities say that they pursue this policy to some extent when they make raids on bookie joints, sin areas, marijuana parties, and the like. A wave of public indignation may follow a newspaper's exposé of a Calumet City, in which case the Sheriffs' police are designated to go and clean up the area. These sin areas are usually in big cities, and those familiar with metropolitics know that the clean-up is more rhetorical than real in its consequences. The residents are not really committed to these reforms and this tactic is conceived in and rooted to failure.

If this first alternative is a difficult, if not impossible chore, then the other major alternative which the sociologist envisions seems unthinkable. How does one go about the task of effecting an attitudinal change in the typical member of society? Yet the rehabilitation of the criminal is inextricably intertwined with his reception in the society. It is imperative that the prospective employer, prospective mate, prospective insurance man, prospective anyman receive the ex-criminal as though rehabilitation were possible, if not a fact; and as though no stigma were attached to past associations, if the ex-criminal is to have any chance for rehabilitation.

The theoretical issues involved for sociology and social anthropology are certainly significant. There exists a category of strong moral judgment, with full moral rejection of a segment of the stigmatized population. During the last century, the history of the conception and treatment of mental illness underwent remarkable changes. In 1860, mental illness was burdened by the imputation of immorality through the idea of the individual's free will to choose among alternatives. Even today, many families are ashamed of a case of mental illness among them, whereas they will announce physical illnesses publicly as a matter of course. (Many physical illnesses, by the way, were conceived in moralistic terms in the eighteenth century and before; and men were then ashamed of such sickness or of any association with it.) With the passage of time and with the coming of the enlightenment, the West began to disassociate morality from mental illness, just as it had done previously with physical illness.

It seems legitimate to consider the possibility, then, that conceptions of crime and criminality will follow the same path. To be sure, crime is regarded as activity hostile to the society; but so too is the behavior of the mentally ill. If the behavior of the latter were thought of as constructive and beneficial, men would find a new label for it, reward it, and abandon an orientation of sickness. It is suggested therefore, that the objective antisocial character of behavior is no guarantee of its moral rejection. It is conceivable that crime could go the way of physical and mental illness in an enlightened society, where the solution is cast in remedial terms, but where the society's members themselves recognize the need to change their moral conception of the problem so that remedy is possible.

Societal Ambivalence, Inconsistency, and the Problem of Treatment

At the beginning of this chapter, it was suggested that we are pulled back and forth between two incompatible poles with regard to the criminal population: "One must be mentally healthy in order to commit a crime, but the commission of a crime reflects an unhealthy mental state." On the one hand, the criminal is said to be mentally balanced, and therefore capable of and responsible for his actions. On the other hand, his criminal behavior is popularly and professionally conceived as a reflection of a disorder of personality. This is a dilemma that is partially resolved by compartmentalizing one area of it for a period of time. For example, it is typical to regard the criminal as mentally healthy and responsible during the period of apprehension, prosecution, and conviction. The police, the prosecuting attorney, the judge, and the jury all have a tendency to view the criminal as mentally normal, sane, and responsible. However, after conviction, and beginning with incarceration, the imputation shifts and the criminal is suddenly regarded as psychologically disturbed. The warden, the prison psychiatrist, and to some extent the custodial staff tend to view the inmate as one possessed with some kind of mental problem. Upon release from the prison, the ex-convict meets a combination of these imputations. The parole officer, the half-way house administrator and staff, and the receiving community and family are likely to exhibit a large measure of ambivalence and ambiguity toward the ex-convict.

During the entire first stage of his contact with the agents of law enforcement, the accused rarely finds his psychological normality questioned. The police handle him in such a way as to reinforce the idea of his reasonability and rationality. The whole notion of a *modus operandi* in police work illustrates very clearly how the police investigators impute sanity and reason to the culprit. Once apprehended, the accused person is treated by his captors as responsive to reason. The prosecuting attorney, for example, offers a "reasonable" deal to the accused. He is presented with the alternative of pleading guilty to a lesser charge, or he risks facing prosecution and conviction for the full charge if he upsets the judicial normality and pleads not guilty. It is not only the prosecuting attorney who treats the accused as a reasonable man, but the public defender, as well, who offers a deal based on the most rational and calculated factors.[10] In Sudnow's study of one public defender's office, this procedure is well illustrated.[11] The typical pattern is for the public defender to explain why the accused ought to be rational and agreeable, accept the deal offered, and plead guilty to the agreed-upon charge. If there is any question about the imputation of psychic disturbance, it occurs only when the accused refuses to accept the defender's advice and plead not guilty. Otherwise, that possibility is never seriously entertained by the administrators of justice, at least insofar as it is reflected in behavior directed toward the accused.

Once he is placed behind prison bars, however, the convict finds that his psychic make-up is problematic. It is the focus of continual interpretation and reinterpretation. It is, as well, the primary basis upon which his behavior is explained. This is the case for both past behavior and present activity in the institution. When the treatment staff of the prison frames a question as to why the criminal act was committed, the tendency is to reconstruct the inmate's motivation in such a way that it reflects psychic disturbance. For example, what the police and judge were willing to regard as a normal, legitimate, rational thought process in the decision to steal, the prison treatment staff may reinterpret as the rebelliousness of a basically antisocial person. The same behavior which the police choose to slap down as the rational, understandable, but objectionable machinations of a "wise ass," the treatment staff chooses to regard as pathological in its hostility to authority, a quality of an aberrant personality. Therapy sessions, both group and individual, are thereby directed toward an attempt to better understand the inmate's psychic problem. This is a relatively recent development. It is an unmistakable trend however, with the more self-consciously progressive prisons in the more self-consciously progressive states placing greater emphasis upon a therapeutic community.

It must be remarkable to the inmate, when at the point when he is to be considered for parole, the sociological interpretation of criminal activity emerges as the dominant theme. The parole board suddenly wants to know what kind of social system setting awaits the parolee. Concern is expressed that the prospective parolee sever all associations with the criminal community, and proceed to a new environment. The assurance that he can obtain gainful employment is the single most important thing among factors in the receiving community. This reflects more than the fear that idle hands are the devil's plaything; it also reflects great concern for the meaning and consequences of practical problems of financial stability. This is to begin to treat the individual criminal as once again a normal, rational member of society, motivated by the same goals as typical others. As Merton suggested thirty years ago, the normal and rational response to frustration in the achievement of goals by legitimate means may well be the pursuit of illegal means.[12] That parole boards place such a premium upon the availability of an occupation is strong evidence that they have suspended the explanatory model of psychic disturbance as the central problem. If this were not the case, the parole board would need only address itself to the mended or unmended character of the inmate's personality. (If it is mended, then he should be able to go out into the world and cope with reality, and so on.) There would be no need to treat the nature of the situation in the receiving community as critical to the decision to parole.

Once back into the community, the ex-convict finds many supervisory authorities imbued with a sociological determinism: What kinds of friends does he see? What kinds of places does he frequent? In selected communities, parolees do meet for a counseling or therapy session, but the focus may be upon the exchanges that occur in the community. The parole officer's training is more likely to be in sociology than in psychology, and the review board which considers parole violations is likely to look at the conditions in which the violator lives, rather than the way in which he manages the world. That is not only easier to observe, it can also be used as an indicator of personal stability. However, the ex-convict is continually confronted by an extremely hostile society. As far as the typical member of society is concerned, the quality of having been imprisoned for a crime is never irrelevant. The prospective employer, prospective mate, prospective lender or creditor all treat the history of criminality as a quality possessed by the person, not simply as a product of varying social conditions. Therefore, even when the ex-convict changes all of his social conditions, he remains suspect *as a person*. There is a large residue of sentiment about this even among those marginally committed to an environmental or sociological determinism.

The Social Context of the Problem of Criminal Intent

In the courtroom practice of criminal law, the ability to establish or undermine the existence of criminal intent in the action is critical. The basis upon which the plausibility of intent rests is the common social reality of "reasonable," "normal," and "typical" men.[13] As an example, we can look at how the social milieu of the act determines whether it will be regarded as crime or illness.

In police precinct X, a woman is booked for her third offense within a year's time. The prosecuting attorney decides to take the case to court and secure a conviction. The woman is accused of stealing a piece of jewelry worth approximately $650. She has three children, no husband, and obtains sporadic employment from week to week as a menial household service worker, with extended periods of layoff. The judge listens to the prosecuting attorney present his case, especially the evidence which bears directly upon the commission of the act. All are satisfied that the act was committed. The next problem is to establish whether the act was committed with criminal intent. The important point here is that the judge will listen with great interest and attentiveness to the prosecution's case about the family and occupational condition of the accused. The woman was in need. The motive is set for a reasonable man (or woman) to act in such a way as to gratify that need. The judge can, in a sense, enter the world of the accused, empathize with her decision as a rational one, and pronouce her guilty of the intention to commit the crime. It is important to recognize the judge's ability to impute reason! The woman is either fined $500 or sentenced to thirty days.

In police precinct Y, a woman is booked for her third offense within a year's time. The prosecuting attorney decides to take the case to court and secure a conviction. The woman is accused of stealing a piece of jewelry worth approximately $1,400. She has two children, and a husband who is a corporation executive with an income of $175,000 per year. The judge listens to the prosecuting attorney present his case, especially the evidence which bears directly upon the commission of the act. All are satisfied that the act was committed. The defense attorney acknowledges that the act was committed. The next problem is to establish whether the act was committed with criminal intent. In this instance too, the judge listens with great interest to the familial and occupational condition of the accused. She was not in need. Any reasonable man can see that she was not stealing for the money, which is the only "reasonable need" residing in the minds of normal people. The need to possess a stolen artifact for its own sake is something entirely different. The social reality is that this desire is thought to be a reflection of an aberrant state of the mind. Whereas the judge could empathize with the reasonable need of the reasonable woman with no husband and no money, he finds it impossible to understand any criminal intent in the desire to possess an object that could easily be purchased across the counter by the husband. Upon further inquiry, he discovers that the husband has indeed purchased many such items of jewelry for the woman. This is "clearly" a case of illness, kleptomania, and not criminal intent, theft. The woman is committed to outpatient status with a psychiatrist whom she is to see once a week for a year.

The interpretation does not always go in favor of the upper middle class and against the lower classes. A twelve-year-old, lower-class urban Black is caught by the police smoking a marijuana cigarette in a raid upon a party. The juvenile authorities investigate, and after determining the age of the boy and the nature of his family and home life, decide to drop the case. They do not even bother to file a petition. The boy's father is employed by the railroad, and is seldom home. His mother is a service worker who is also periodically out of the home. The mother is contacted, informed, and warned verbally. Nothing more is done, and the authorities resignedly contemplate the inevitable pathway to trouble that they feel the boy will follow.

A twelve-year-old, middle-class, suburban white boy is caught by the police smoking a marijuana cigarette in a raid on a party. The police are shocked. The juvenile authorities investigate, and after determining the age of the boy and the nature of his family and home life, decide to pursue the case.

They find a typical, middle-class, suburban home life, family intact, stable income. The juvenile authorities cannot understand how a boy from such a home could find himself in such a situation. The parents are drawn into the case and informed of its gravity. (It is explainable if not normal and reasonable that the other boy should be in that situation, but *not this boy*.) Very few interpretations are open to the authorities, and the one which they choose is psychic disturbance. Because they can not comprehend another social reality where it would be normal for this kind of youth to do what he did, sickness is the only explanation possible. The boy is remanded to a psychiatrist's care for a period of weeks. A petition is filed, and remains with him until he becomes an adult.

Despite every attempt in democratic societies to minimize extraneous considerations, the law does not, nor can it exist in a vacuum. It may be a nation of laws and not of men, but the law is always interpreted in terms of the meanings that "reasonable men can bring to it." Judges and juries bring to the court a certain view of what is reasonable behavior. Behavior that is unreasonable and incomprehensible (e.g., kleptomania) is treated in law as an indicator of psychic imbalance. As has been suggested, the problem of the social context of law is crucial, since the same behavior may be regarded as theft when social conditions encompassing the behavior can be given a more "reasonable" meaning. For the social scientist, the problem is to uncover and explain the distribution of social meanings as they vary from one social system to another. From this perspective, the administration of justice is simply one more system, and has no greater legitimacy in defining the ultimate quality of reasonable behavior than has any other system.

So far, the problem of the criminal's mental health has been treated from the point of view of contrasting social systems. Those in the larger society surrounding the criminal population may have a view of what constitutes mental illness which has little to do with the conception of mental illness among criminals. It is instructive to return to the analogy of the layman's interpretation of the serious attempt at suicide. Since most men must pursue the daily task of living, they find it difficult to empathize with the decision to end one's own life. "Anyone who tries to commit suicide must be crazy." However, among those who recover from or are rescued from a suicide attempt, most that we know about return to routine everyday life as though nothing occurred. Except for the specific behavior connected with the would-be suicide, the individual's actions do not permit an interpretation of mental abnormality. Occasionally, individuals who attempt suicide are placed in the mental patient's ward of a hospital for several days surveillance, but they usually do not stay for more than a week. This is true despite the fact that the general population is quick to impute mental illness to anyone who seriously attempts suicide.

For the criminal, the situation is very similar except that he is incarcerated for long periods. His specific criminal activity may be interpreted as an indicator of mental disturbance by others, but not only is this untrue not only within the criminal community, a member of the general population is also incapable of making any such assessment by looking merely at the criminal's other behavior. It is acknowledged and documented by the continual questions that ex-convicts must answer on applications for employment, driver's license, passports, and so on. If their mental disturbance could be detected simply from observing behavior, there would be no need for continually calling attention to the stigma.

Mental Illness and Social Theory in Crime

We have come a long way since the days of Lombrosa's criminology. Few of us regard the shape of the head as the most important determinant of whether a man will pursue a life of crime. There are theories, however, which begin with the assumption that criminal behavior is to be explained by addressing a property of the individual. There are other theories which trace the explanation to the assumption that forces external to the individual account for crime. Indeed, it is possible to arrange theories of crime along a continuum of this sort: at one end is the individual as the complete agent of his action, possessed of either free will or compulsion, but at the very least, the motivated center of action: at the other end is the individual as nothing more than a grossly malleable substance wafting back and forth in the social currents of the time and the space most immediately pressing.

I think it is reasonable to present the proposition that the closer a theory comes to the individual-autonomy end of the continuum, the more likely is that theory to contain the imputation of mental abnormality. The obverse is also true. Theories on the other end of the continuum that deal, for example, with a qualified economic or social determinism, will rarely entertain the possibility of mental illness as an important ingredient in criminal behavior. Forces and conditions like poverty or the peer culture impel the adaptive and "mentally normal" response of crime.

The question to be raised about these theories is twofold. First, of what significance is each to the discipline of which it is a part? Second, what are some of the consequences for a society which adopts one over another for the explanation of crime?

In sociology, recent theories of crime which have emphasized the response of social systems developed primarily from an increasing concern for theory in the sociology of deviance. At the turn of the century, research in deviance centered primarily around individuals who constituted social problems. Sociology during this period sponsored longitudinal and case studies of prostitutes, alcoholics, tramps, and the like. Because such studies focused upon the individual deviant, they tended to emphasize the unique and idiosyncratic qualities of the deviant, an analytic technique that blocked a broader understanding of deviance in its other forms. Mental illness is a kind of deviance that should prove to be the most fruitful subject matter for social theories of order and disorder. The reason is that it is a form least tied *a priori* to substantive problems. Drug addiction, for example, is always associated with the empirical issue of drug use, irrespective of the social group that is using or interpreting. The same is true for prostitution and alcoholism. While it is true that the meanings of these activities vary from group to group, one can still determine whether or not drug addiction is a deviance problem in a particular group. Mental illness, on the other hand, will always be an issue to be dealt with by a community. The same thing can be said for crime, or for a more universal concept, deviance. The community must handle deviance as a generic problem of social control. It seems both natural and inevitable then, that the trend in social-science theories will be a broader incorporation of theories of mental illness (lay and professional) into the newly emphasized concern for social reaction to deviance.

CHAPTER 10

Law and morality: some summary considerations

G IVEN THE LARGE HISTORICAL TREND IN WESTERN Civilization in the direction of increasingly humane treatment for physical and mental illnesses, it is an anomaly and an anachronism that drug addiction should today be treated with such passionate moral outrage, while in the nineteenth century the addicted were regarded with both sympathy and compassion. As noted earlier, we now would consider it barbaric to deny medical treatment to one suffering from a disease because of objection to the moral situation in which it was contracted. It is both humane and sensible to treat the physiological problem first, saving the moral question for later. Yet, because the psychological-physiological problem of addiction-habituation has been intertwined with the moralistic problem of willful sensual pleasure and flight from responsibility, the view and response to addiction has taken a moralistic form. The psychological interpretation of opiate addiction has led to a brutal conservatism in the conception and treatment of the problem. Current professional and common-sense theories of the "disorder" have come to rest on explanations of the psyche and what is seen as its retreat, its immaturity, and ultimately, its pleasure-seeking immorality. The addict is denied physical treatment for his suffering because of the moral judgment of the social meaning of addiction and drug use.

It is the moral condemnation of addiction *per se* that allows the Federal Narcotics Bureau to report with a sense of accomplishment that the number and proportion of addicts has decreased greatly since 1914. What gain is there in this when the present smaller number of addicts do far more damage to society and to themselves than all those addicted in 1914? What gain is there when the society has created a smaller population that is far more destructive than the larger population of an earlier more civil and humane period?

Americans have tied themselves into a circular knot on the drug problem because they have come to believe that the physical treatment of the addict with drugs is itself immoral.

To explain how this came about, several themes have been developed in this book. The analysis has consistently focused upon the various conceptions of moral behavior. Both individual moral action and claims for morality which transcend the community have been avoided in the task of explaining the emergence of communal moral judgment.

This has not been a diatribe against the use of a moral stance on the problem of the distribution and use of narcotics. (It is neither desirable nor possible to rid a society of moral judgment, for social structure is also moral order.) Rather, the position has been that the moral posture towards drugs should be assumed only after there is firm, adequate knowledge of the physical effects. If a drug destroys body tissues (e.g., alcohol), then a moral stand on the destruction of body tissue, not on the independent and isolated social meaning of taking a drink, should be forthcoming. If a drug dulls the senses and relieves anxiety, then a moral stand on whether that should be done under certain circumstances should be taken. Instead, in ignorance we have categorically defined heroin use as morally different from barbiturate use due to its social-legal base, not its physiological base. Grossly inconsistent, we listen with silent approval to radio advertisements for drugs that relieve anxiety and produce calm women's club presidents out of the previously distraught. We then revert to moral fervor to condemn for its social meaning what we define as the same quality act among addicts. For those who would bring the "deviant" back within the boundaries of "normal" society so that he can have some kind of relationship to it, it is self-defeating to stigmatize the deviant as though he were a totally different kind of person. In so doing, we guarantee that his deviance will simply take the form of the response that in some degree either (a) accepts that judgment of the self or (b) rejects that judgment, and in so doing, rejects other normal standards of the society that placed him there. The United States has taken the lead in treatment of the addict as a social deviant. Among all Western nations, it has had the largest problem with the illegal use of narcotics. It is now very alarming to note that the United States may be serving as a model for other industrial nations. The "drug problem" is becoming more evident in Western Europe, England, and Japan. In England and Sweden, increasingly restrictive measures *and the way of thinking about the problem* have been inherited from America. A Swedish newspaper recently advised that Swedish physicians come to America to see first-hand how the Americans, "who have had a long experience with the problem," are handling it. Given certain indications that some of the rest of the world is moving in the direction of the total moralistic interpretation of the drug user, a public reassessment might prove fruitful.

The Proposal and the Argument

At some point, in some part of the body, all suffer some physical or organic illness. Most of these ailments do not get in the way of the daily management of affairs. When they do, organic treatment is now generally accepted by almost all but a few very religious sect members. To be dependent upon organic treatment is no shame. We have come to the point where such dependence is not regarded as immoral. The successful professional who cannot sleep at night and who needs a strong dose of barbiturates may develop a "dependency." Here is a problem with a psychic base that is handled physiologically, and no imputation of immorality is made. Also, at some point, on some issue, all men probably suffer from some neurotically based inability to handle a problem. For most, it does not get in the way of the daily management of affairs. When it does, therapy is an alternative, either psychotherapy, some organic treatment, or the invoking of gods. No one argues that such treatment is itself morally wrong. The imputation is made when the psychic and the physical are intertwined, in the case of heroin use. As we have seen in this book, the answer lies partly in the fact that the kind of people who are known to use heroin are those in social categories most vulnerable to the charge of immorality. So long as an activity is engaged in predominantly by those in the "center" social categories, the likelihood of moral condemnation for the activity is miniscule, for it is the "center" of society which establishes the criteria for moral condemnation.[1]

Even when the stage is set and the conditions are ripe for the labeling of men and their behavior as immoral, the effectiveness of the law in bringing about changes in the behavior presents a basically different problem. It is the latter question which brings about lay assertions on the relationship between legislation and morality. Many believe that in certain areas (notably civil rights), the law cannot and should not precede and shape the moral order.

Americans invoke the cliché, "You can't legislate morality," but they are extremely inconsistent and apply the idea selectively to different kinds of behavior. They are typically very much in favor of legal sanctions to enforce strong moralistic feelings about the use of marijuana, and they have typically supported legislation that reinforces the current moral conception of appropriate sexual behavior. Prostitution in all forms and homosexuality in most forms are outlawed across the country. Moreover, almost everyone favors laws to protect the sexual exploitation of the very young. These are clearly areas where the law is used to buttress strong moralistic conceptions. This inconsistency is not faced directly and honestly. Instead of making reasoned and rational solutions to emotional commitments (as psychologists have long noted) we erect rational justification for our emotional proclivities. Thus, fear of "aliens" living in the same neighborhood is rationalized into the "inalienable right to property" (which, if not challenged by the prospective tenant, means his right to property is undermined) and the belief that you can't legislate morality. At the same time, fear of the drug addict is rationalized into more and more repressive legal measures against the addict with the unconscious commitment to the idea that we can, indeed, legislate the morality of young marijuana users.

However, the purpose of this work has not been to show that men are inconsistent—a commonplace and well-documented finding—but to demonstrate that a set of moral beliefs about the deviant (and the consequent behavior) creates, sustains, perpetuates, and exacerbates the deviance. It is time to reconsider the mindless assertions about heroin as "our real concern being for the wasted manpower" and "the unthinkably immoral act of the community supporting an addict's habit." That is not the real concern. If it were, concern for the barbiturates would be much greater. If it were, we would ban certain commercials from the television and radio which peddle anxiety-reduction pills as a viable solution to problems. The moral beliefs upon which we have based our public policy are themselves founded on myths about both the physical effects of drugs and errors about the total quality of persons addicted.

We have seen the argument made that the apprehension and rehabilitation approach to addiction is bound to fail so long as the addict is viewed as morally different from others. However, *there is a solution that is suggested by the very mechanisms which created the problem*—namely, a legal change that alters the conditions of the addicted. Things began to move this way in 1914, when the law forced the most vulnerable social categories into the limelight as the publicly known users of the opium derivatives. It is by this means as well that a resolution can be effected.

It has been pointed out time and again that the moral posture toward a drug and subsequent legal implementation should be based upon the effect that the drug has upon the body. The depressant qualities of the opiates are known. These drugs do not evoke any hostile, aggressive, or destructive tendencies toward the self or toward the society. The morphine or heroin addict operating a daily life at a productive equilibrium is not a myth, but as the history of the late nineteenth century reveals, is very real. That is not to encourage heroin use, which is a separate moral problem worthy of more discussion. We might want to take up at some future time the question of to what extent a society ought to permit the depression of psychic and physical pain. My own view is that while many, if not most, psychic problems are best worked out without the use of drugs (e.g., social and personal solutions), *some psychic and physical problems benefit most from the administration of drugs*. This is not a question which a physician or psychiatrist is better equipped to answer than say, an attorney or a schoolteacher or a bricklayer. It relates to the moral order of the society and no profession can lay claim to being the most legitimate "moral entrepreneur."[2] Experts in dealing with the mind and body are most capable of providing information that is to be used in the development of those stances. Solutions to the massive drug problems must begin with a reassessment of the social meaning of heroin and morphine use. The key to our correct handling of other problems such as marijuana, LSD, pep pills, and the barbiturates lies first with our reassessment of the opiates, for the opiates are the hard stuff that people fear most, and about which we are most irrational and self-defeating. The link between this reassessment and marijuana is clear, for the fiercest charge against marijuana is that it supposedly leads to the opiates. Marijuana cannot be discussed or explained calmly until basic questions about the opium derivatives are resolved. The link between this problem and LSD and other drugs is more subtle, but I would argue that just as cocaine colored all conceptions of the wild, aggressive "dope fiend" in the thirties, so the model of the willful, sensual, retreatest heroin addict of the sixties dominates public thought about the meaning of drug use. To undermine the basic myth is to allow reasonable pursuit of discussions about the actual physical effects of other drugs, and perhaps to provide a new climate for research upon those effects. In short, so long as the social and moral meaning of drug use is tied up with the dominance of heroin, other drugs are colored by common-sense notions of heroin use. The layman usually lacks even a sufficient knowledge of the various drugs to distinguish between amphetamines, marijuana, and LSD. In such a situation, it is only natural that "drugs" or "narcotics" are lumped together in his mind as a similar class of objects. The dominant theme in that class of objects revolves around the heroin addict, and the first breakthrough must come there. That is one of the reasons why most of the theoretical case presented here has rested on the heroin problem as strategic in this analysis of deviance. Reassessment and change must start here, but it would be utopian dreaming to leave the argument with a simple admonition neglecting guidelines to remedial action. A solution is suggested by the turn of events that brought about the problem.

Almost overnight, in 1914, thousands of addicts were driven by legal circumstances into underground and criminal activity. Just as quickly and dramatically, the law could create conditions which would point towards a possible viable relationship between the addict and the society. I refer to the dispensation of the opiate derivatives from clinics and from private physicians. Once the society made its first move, the choice would be that of the addict, not the society. It would be the *addict's choice*, and it should be welcomed in that form. Able to decide whether to live a life with a physical-psychic dependency or without it, some will undoubtedly opt for the dependency, and we must be willing to face that as a possibility and even to see its positive side. Opium addicts are incapacitated neither physically nor mentally. Artists from Coleridge to Cocteau have been addicted, and they have made significant contributions of lasting merit far exceeding that of many "who just wouldn't dare." That argument is only specious insofar as one interprets it to coincide with a general advocacy of opium or a eulogy of its positive effects. It is neither. It simply points out that a society can expect return of inestimable worth from addicts allowed to live their lives without the stigma of moral deviance.

The Clinical System

Any clinical system for the dispensation of narcotics should be a supplement to the ability of private physicians to prescribe. Further, in keeping with the central theme of this work, the clinics should not be separate physical structures, but should be incorporated into existing community hospitals. We would go far to remove the stigma of the addict if we allowed him similar "moral" treatment to that accorded to others who have a physical-psychological dependency upon medicine. So long as the present attitudes toward drug addiction remain, it would be unwise to erect separate buildings as dispensing clinics. Those who became patients there would be identified in the community, only making their adjustment impossible.

As was pointed out in the first chapter, the clinics of 1918-1921 were not the failures that the propaganda of the Federal Narcotics Bureau leads one to believe. Rather, sensational newspaper accounts of abuses in only two of the scores of cities brought about strong public reaction and the demise of the clinics. It should be recalled that the clinics were set up after the authorities had recognized that many addicts had been cut off from a legal source, as they were unable to pay a private physician for individualized treatment. Thus the addict had already been stigmatized by 1919, and much of the public outrage was to be explained on these grounds. The early clinics then, did not "fail to solve the drug problem," they failed to operate long enough for that to be true.

In a present-day clinical system, addicts would be supplied on some periodic basis. There would be abuses in the first few years, and these must be expected due to the nature of the problem we have created. Some registered addicts would undoubtedly supply others not register-ed, or incapacitated, or even some novices, but this number would be far less than those youth who now by the scores of thousands can expect to enter a life of drugs. A major argument against such a program is that "the state should not give sanction to drug use," as a moral example. The fallacy of this position is that the state would no more be sanction-ing such use than it would in any other sphere, where it simply regulates the supply and distribution of a drug, as in the case of the barbiturates. Does the state sanction barbiturates? Further, as a moral issue, why is the need for sleep a higher moral achievement than the physiological equilibrium? Those who would offer the glib response that the addict ought always to handle his problem psychologically must be prepared to say the same about other classes and forms of psycho-somatic problems that men develop.

The advantages of a clinical system for the ambulatory treatment and supply of the addict are numerous. It is a system where most parties would gain, with the loss minimized. For the society, the gain would be in the drastic reduction of individuals who prey upon it daily for millions of dollars in theft to supply the addiction. The gain would also involve the undermining of the system of black-market controls that feed into the increased power of organized crime. These gains have been pointed out before by many other commentators on the drug question, but there is one gain that clinical dispensation would provide that is unique. This would be the slow but definite erosion of the moral stigma of being addicted, a gain of incalculable magnitude—for it would free a literal army of hundreds of thousands of abnormally intelligent and sensitive men to relate again to their society in a way that is not pathological.

Who can guess how many writers or artists or political thinkers there are among those denied a means for expression by the present situation around narcotics?

Some simple changes in the laws would accomplish a great deal. The present drug laws should be changed with respect to the opium derivatives so as to allow clinical dispensation. Based upon the best knowledge we have available about the effects of the drug, present marijuana statutes are ludicrously out of proportion. Marijuana is in a class with alcohol as a mind-transforming drug, and should get the same moral and legal treatment. As for LSD and the class of psychedelics, the paucity of research and the misinformation make recommendations impossible, except that we need to legally free the drug for more research. The amphetamines and the barbiturates are not now "morality-evoking" drugs, as the terms have been used. That is not necessarily a good thing. Based upon their physical effects, perhaps it should be reexamined whether or not these kinds of drugs deserve special treatment for distribution and control. Addiction to either class of drugs is a serious physiological problem, more serious, as noted earlier, than addiction to morphine or heroin.

There are not only positive gains from a legal change that would sanction clinical dispensation of the opiates, there are negative gains as well. Drug use is engaged in privately, not publicly, and there is no party to the act who has an interest in being the plaintiff. For these reasons, the law will not be effective in bringing about a change in the behavior or morality of the law violators. Thus, millions of dollars are spent in a fruitless attempt to stamp out the problem that could better be used upon some constructive program. At the very least, the negative gain would involve the elimination of the pursuit of an impossible task.

There will be objections to this suggestion, and they will predictably take two forms. First, the change touches upon a moral area where people are invested with strong feelings. Thus, even though the physical and psychic consequences of sustained heroin use are detailed in a dispassionate manner, Americans may still object to the legal dispensation to the addicted because it is "wrong." But there is already precedent for considering drug addiction as a sickness or disease. A joint report of the American Medical Association and the American Bar Association came to this conclusion in the early 1960s.[3] It is the right direction, though I am opposed to that conceptualization of the problem because in this instance it borders too closely to the charge of immorality. In any case, this precedent for viewing the problem in terms of illness means that a legal shift that permitted medical supervision of the addicted would not meet with such strong resistance. The legal and medical professions could provide a moral cloak for the addicts for a period long enough for an enlightened attitude to emerge, as was the case with epilepsy and certain forms of mental illness. There is no simple and direct move from a change in the law to a change in the moral order, but *the law would change the social conditions and thereby the climate for a reinterpretation of the moral issues.*

There is a second objection to this proposal that is predictable; and that has to do with the implementation upsetting and undermining strongly vested interests in the present way of handling the problem. Organizations, agencies, bureaus, and centers established to handle a problem employ men, and place some in high positions. These men develop what Veblen termed a "vested" interest in the maintenance of the organization or agency. The longer such organizations persist and the more permanent the funding of their operation, the more entrenched become the interests of those in higher echelon occupational roles. One reason for this is that careers develop around a special competence or a particular bit of expertise. Either a massive reorganization or a scuttling of the whole venture of the organization poses a serious threat to those whose careers have been narrowly defined by the pursuit laid down by the original interest. Lindesmith has voiced his concern as it relates to the establishment of more and more centers and organizations for the handling of the drug problem.[4] He cites this as an important force of conservatism and resistance to reforms in the laws relating to the punishment of drug offenders. One can expect strong opposition from these quarters, but the merit of the arguments should be examined critically, beyond earshot of entrenched fortresses.

In the beginning of this work, I touched upon some relationships between legal change and moral order that deserve exploration. During the course of the development of the problems around the deviance of drug use, some of these relationships have been clarified. A summary statement of some of the relationships that have been thrown into sharper focus is in order. We know that people who materially benefit most from the status quo tend to see their societies as basically just and legitimate. However, even those who stand to gain from a redistribution of the wealth and power often justify the perpetuation of that order. Without that belief on the part of the subordinate, there could be no "right" of the privileged to exist the way they do. The prevailing conditions in a society are not simply things to be dealt with, they have moral force in the community.

For example, since everyone goes to elementary school, it soon becomes a part of the moral order that everyone ought to go. As "everyone" goes off to form his own nuclear family, people begin to think that so ought everyone. As "everyone" marries for a romantic conception of love, so ought everyone, and so forth. It is equally true that matters of social deviance obtain their moral imperatives from a reading of the existing conditions: As males do not express affection toward each other, so ought they not. As females do, so should it be. A change in the morals of men does not come about from a "a change of heart," but from some alteration of the conditions in which they live.

Men did not suddenly decide to give women the right to vote because of a change in their morality—the conditions changed before men changed. So it is with deviance. Drug addiction became immoral because the social conditions revolving around it changed and, as I have tried to demonstrate, peculiarly lent itself to such a moralistic interpretation.

Many factors operate to alter the conditions, and they are so numerous and complex that it would be fruitless to begin to name them —though technological change is clearly the most dramatic and far-reaching element that could be identified. A second element that is prime among these factors is the law.

It is difficult to regulate such things as the rate of technological change and development, for it is dependent upon such matters as the distribution of skills and the economic base. The law, however, is relatively within control of a designated group at a given time. Because legal changes can alter the way in which police and other authorities behave towards a deviant group, they can alter the conditions of their existence and thus, as I have argued, the moral interpretation of that existence. The essential features of the drug addict's life, which make others impute to him unconscionable morality, are his associations with criminal activity, the belief that he leads an "unproductive and wasteful life," and the imputations of psychic weakness. Each of these could be dealt a death blow by legal changes that destroyed their basis. It has been pointed out by dozens of writers who have commented on the drug problem that the black market and the criminal tieups with drugs would be undermined by legal clinical dispensation of narcotics. The other advantages of the kind of legalization advocated here are more long range and less dramatic, but are no less important. The view that drug users are not productive can be dispelled better by eradicating the invidious distinctions between addicts and nonaddicts than by demonstrating that some addicts, like morphine-using physicians, can be and are productive. In the latter case, the disbelievers simply have recourse to the idea that those are the exceptional cases, and addicts aren't really like that. Thus, no claim is made that in changing the law we would demonstrate that individuals can be productive while addicted. We know that already. Rather, legal dispensation would go far in eliminating the socially arbitrary immorality attributed to selected kinds of drug use. It would do this by freeing the addict to participate in what others could clearly see as life as usual. It must be clearly pointed out that this is not a proposal to designate the addict and then let him reveal how he can be "normal." (This would be the equivalent of confronting a bigot with a member of an ethnic minority who would be acceptable in the bigot's terms. This would merely be treated as the exceptional case once again, while generic bigotry remained.) The point to be made is that the addict, supplied a drug without stigmatization, would make the case that has been presented: that he cannot be identified among "normal" men without a chemical test, and could therefore lead that kind of social life which would negate the charge of psychic weakness. It was not an issue in 1895 when there were proportionately so many more opiate addicts in the population, and it would not be an issue today if the circumstances were conducive.

A major thesis of this work has been that certain classes of persons in any society are more susceptible to being charged with moral inferiority than other classes of persons. The behavior in which persons indulge is often less important than the social category from which they come. In order to understand how certain acts get labeled deviant over time, and how other acts get the deviance label lifted from them, it is necessary to take into account the conditions under which persons in the "moral center" of society are publicly associated with a given behavior. Indeed, the thesis can be stated more categorically: When it is part of the public view that the predominant perpetrators of the act come from the moral center, that act cannot long remain "immoral" or deviant; it can become deviant again only under circumstances where the public conception is that the "morally susceptible" classes are those who are the primary indulgers.

I have tried to show how certain behavior (morphine and heroin use) was tolerated or ignored so long as it was more associated with "decent and respectable" elements of society than with any other part. Later, as the conditions changed so that the public viewed the unrespectable elements as the primary indulgers, the behavior came to be treated as deviant and immoral. The same point is made when we review what has happened to the moral status of alcoholic consumption in this last century. The point is the same, though the direction of the change was in reverse of the heroin problem. In the case of alcohol, it was an instance in which behavior once condemned by the moral center and associated in the public view as a vice of the vulnerable social categories later became acceptable, normal, and moral behavior due to conditional changes. These changes were of such a nature as to make it appear that respectable elements were associated with the behavior, thereby giving it a new, acceptable moral status.

From Gusfield's work on the temperance movement, we learn that its leaders were drawn from the professional and white-collar class from 1870 through Prohibition.[5] As Gusfield argues, this was the primary source of its strength, for these proponents of abstinence spoke from within the society. The Pennsylvania Amish also favored abstinence from alcohol, but were an alien group who railed from without. The Women's Christian Temperance Union (WCTU) was a middle-class movement that took a benign posture toward the lower classes and the problems of poverty and failure. Abstinence was a panacea that would cure all ills; economic, social, political, psychological, and moral. In a word, temperance advocates could and did argue that abstinence was a virtue of the successful in the "moral center." (What then developed was just the opposite of what was to occur with morphine-heroin use.) In increasing numbers and proportions the middle-class began to indulge in the public arena. The Eighteenth Amendment, for alcohol, like the Harrison Act for heroin, made production and distribution illegal. There was one dramatic difference. The narcotics laws, as we have seen, made available to the middle classes a channel for a supply and made it seem as if only the lower classes were indulgers. The new alcohol law cut off the legal supply completely to all classes, and made violation the only alternative to those middle-class persons who insisted on imbibing. Such flagrant violations did occur, producing the conditions for a public reappraisal of the moral status of alcoholic consumption.

The historical development of a new morality around narcotics usage followed a different route to make the same point. Namely, a public reappraisal of the moral meaning of heroin use occurred when

public identification of users shifted from the least vulnerable to the most vulnerable class.

One of the major purposes of this book was to develop some ideas that might serve to contribute to the sociology of deviance. We have already seen studies that have dealt with the cohesive consequences of deviance, the labeling and identification of deviance, and the life-styles of the deviant. The present work is an attempt to relate these themes with an additional explication of forces that produce and sustain select social categories of men for deviant careers. At the same time, it is insufficient to merely describe and analyze a phenomenon or problem of the magnitude of narcotics use without pointing to where that analysis might lead in the way of resolution. The first step to an empirical test of the theoretical propositions offered is to point where that analysis leads one to seek practical solutions. The opportunity now exists for a simultaneous contribution (1) to our understanding of some broader issues in the development and change of laws and morals, and (2) to a mundane solution to an important problem. A clinical system of dispensation with ambulatory treatment has the potential of accomplishing both. It is time we ended an anachronism that degrades men and refuses them assistance unless they comply with the prevailing middle-class moral interpretation of psychic health.

Notes

1. The legislation of morality

1. Philip Selznick, "Sociology of Law" (mimeographed, Center for the Study of Law and Society, University of California, Berkeley) April, 1965. Prepared for the *International Encyclopedia of the Social Sciences*.
2. *Ibid.*
3. *Ibid.*, p. 23.
4. Charles E. Terry and Mildred Pellens, *The Opium Problem* (New York: Bureau of Social Hygiene, 1928), p. 66.
5. *Ibid.*, p. 69.
6. *Ibid.*, p. 75.
7. Marie Nyswander, *The Drug Addict as a Patient* (New York: Grune & Stratton, 1956), 1–13.
8. B. H. Hartwell, "The Sale and Use of Opium in Massachusetts," *Annual Report Massachusetts State Board of Health*, 1889.
9. Terry and Pellens, *op. cit.*, p. 17.
10. C. W. Earle, "The Opium Habit," *Chicago Medical Review*, 2 (1880), 442–90.
11. A. P. Grinnell, "A Review of Drug Consumption and Alcohol as Found in Proprietary Medicine," *Medical Legal Journal*, 1905, pp. 426–589.
12. A much longer list of references is cited by Terry and Pellens, *op. cit.*, and the following are only a small but representative portion: H. Dreser, the man credited with the discovery of heroin, writing of his own findings in an Abstract to the *Journal of the American Medical Association*, 1898; two reports by M. Manges in the *New York Medical Journal*, November 26, 1898 and January 20, 1900.
13. G. E. Pettey, "The Heroin Habit, Another Curse," *Alabama Medical Journal*, 15 (1902–1903), 174–180.
14. Terry and Pellens, *op. cit.*
15. E. G. Eberle, "Report of Committee on Acquirement of Drug Habits," *American Journal of Pharmacology*, October, 1903, p. 481.

16. Terry and Pellens, *op. cit.*, p. 468.
17. C. S. Pearson, "A Study of Degeneracy as Seen Among Addicts," *New York Medical Journal*, November 15, 1919, pp. 805–808.
18. For example, cf. T. S. Blair, "Narcotic Drug Addiction as Regulated by a State Department of Health," *Journal of the American Medical Association*, 72 (May 17, 1919), 1442–44.
19. G. D. Swaine, "Regarding the Luminal Treatment of Morphine Addiction," *American Journal of Clinical Medicine*, 25 (August, 1918), 611.
20. Terry and Pellens, *op. cit.*, p. 499.
21. *Ibid.*, p. 475.
22. S. D. Hubbard, "The New York City Narcotic Clinic and Differing Points of View on Narcotic Addiction," *Monthly Bulletin of the Department of Health, City of New York*, February, 1920.
23. Terry and Pellens, *op. cit.*, p. 11.
24. Earle, *op. cit.*
25. Terry and Pellens, *op. cit.*, pp. 470–471.
26. J. McIver and G. E. Price, "Drug Addiction," *Journal of the American Medical Association*, 66 (February 12, 1916), 477.
27. Hubbard, *op. cit.*
28. Nyswander, *op. cit.*
29. Alfred R. Lindesmith, *The Addict and the Law* (Bloomington: Indiana University Press, 1965), p. 6.
30. *Annual Report* of the Commissioner of Internal Revenue for the Fiscal Year ended June 30, 1920, Washington, D.C.: U.S. Government Printing Office, pp. 33–34.
31. Lindesmith, *op. cit.*, pp. 139–61.
32. *Ibid.*
33. *Ibid.*, p. 143.
34. "What to Know About Drug Addiction," Washington, D.C.: Public Health Service Publication No. 94, 1951.
35. Lindesmith, *op. cit.*, p. 37.
36. *Ibid.*
37. Raymond W. Mack, "Do We Really Believe in the Bill of Rights," *Social Problems*, 3 (April, 1956), 264–69.
38. Edwin Schur, *Crimes Without Victims* (Englewood Cliffs, N.J.: Prentice-Hall, 1965).
39. Lindesmith, *op. cit.*, 1965.

40. "Public" is here used to mean both (a) an *area* where strangers congregate and (b) a *situation* where strangers may be involved in an exchange.

2. The effects and uses of narcotics and moral judgment

1. Louis S. Goodman and Alfred Gilman, *The Pharmacological Basis of Therapeutics* (2d Ed.; New York: The Macmillan Co., 1960), p. 222.
2. A. Wikler, M. J., Pescor, E. P. Kalbaugh, and R. J. Angelucci, "Effects of Prefrontal Lobotomy on the Morphine-Abstinence Syndrome in Man; an Experimental Study," *A.M.A. Arch. Neurol. and Psychiat.* 67 (1952), 510–21.
3. Goodman and Gilman, *op. cit.*, pp. 216–274.
4. See Chapters 6 and 7 of this book for reports of research on apprehended morphine and heroin addicts.
5. See Chapters 6 and 7.
6. William B. Eldridge, *Narcotics and the Law* (New York: University Press, for the American Bar Foundation, 1962), pp. 6–7.
7. Charles Winick, "Narcotics Addiction and Its Treatment," *Law and Contemporary Problems*, 22 (Winter, 1957), 9–33.
8. See especially the excellent discussion of this in Marie Nyswander, *The Drug Addict as Patient* (New York and London: Grune and Stratton, 1956).
9. The data upon which this section is based were gathered upon the population of drug addicts incarcerated at the California Rehabilitation Center in 1964; the methodology and the study itself are reported in Chapters 6 and 7.
10. Goodman and Gilman, *op. cit.*, p. 10.
11. *Ibid.*
12. Aaron Cicourel, *The Social Organization of Juvenile Justice* (New York: John Wiley, 1968).
13. Joseph Gusfield, "Social Structure and Moral Reform: A Study of the WCTU," *American Journal of Sociology*, 61 (November, 1955), pp. 221–232.
14. Eldridge, *op. cit.*, pp. 1–34.
15. Howard S. Becker, *Outsiders: Studies in the Sociology of Deviance* (New York: The Free Press, 1963), pp. 41–78.
16. Goodman and Gilman, *op. cit.*, pp. 171–72.

17. S. Allentuck, "Medical Aspects" in *The Marijuana Problem in the City of New York*, Mayor's Committee on Marijuana, New York (Lancaster, Pa.: The Jacques Cattell Press., 1944).
18. Becker, *op. cit.*
19. Alfred R. Lindesmith, *The Addict and the Law*, Bloomington: Indiana University Press, 1965), pp. 228–31.
20. *Ibid.*, pp. 222–42.
21. Goodman and Gilman, *op. cit.*, p. 174.
22. Lindesmith, *op. cit.*
23. Actually, total abstainers would also have to be the subjects of an intensive study in order to make reliable statements about a probable relationship.
24. Isador Chein and others, *The Road to H* (New York: Basic Books, 1964).
25. *San Francisco Chronicle*, March 31, 1966, p. 1.
26. A. Wikler, "Sites and Mechanisms of Action of Morphine and Related Drugs in the Central Nervous System," *Pharmacological Review*, 2 (1950), 435–506.
27. Aldous Huxley, *The Doors of Perception* (New York: Harper and Row, 1954).
28. Egon Brunswick, *Perception and the Representative Design of Psychological Experiments* (2d Ed., Berkeley: Univ. of California Press, 1956).
29. *Ibid.*
30. Sidney Cohen, *The Beyond Within* (New York: Atheneum, 1965).
31. Lindesmith, *op. cit.* pp. vii–xiii and pp. 222–42.
32. Richard Harris, *The Real Voice* (New York: The Macmillan Co., 1964), pp. 99–112.
33. Lindesmith, *op. cit.*, pp. 222–42.
34. Alfred Schutz, *Collected Papers I, The Problem of Social Reality* (The Hague, Netherlands: Martinus Nijhoff, 1962).

3. *Who* is *a drug addict?*

1. Robert S. DeRopp, "Torture by the Drug," in Dan Wakefield, ed., *The Addict* (Greenwich, Conn.: Fawcett, 1963), pp. 43–46.
2. *Ibid.*, pp. 43–44.
3. *Ibid.*, pp. 44–45.
4. Alfred R. Lindesmith, *Opiate Addiction* (Bloomington: Principia, 1947).

5. Suppose, for example, such an individual decided to take symptomatic treatments, or some synthetic substitutes in smaller and smaller quantities until he achieved equilibrium again; or suppose he decided to abstain with no symptomatic treatment? In either of these instances, was the individual not addicted?

6. Charles E. Terry and Mildred Pellens, *The Opium Problem* (New York: Bureau of Social Hygiene, 1928), Chapters 1–3.

7. James Weeks, "Experimental Narcotic Addiction," *Scientific American*, 210:3 (March, 1964), pp. 46–52.

8. *Ibid.*, p. 46.

9. *Ibid.*, pp. 46–52.

10. *Ibid.*, p. 47.

11. *Ibid.*

12. *Ibid.*

13. *Ibid.*, p. 52.

14. Aaron Cicourel, *The Social Organization of Juvenile Justice* (New York: John Wiley, 1968) Chapter 5.

15. See Chapters 7 and 8.

16. Terry and Pellens, *op. cit.*

17. A fuller discussion appears in the next two chapters.

18. A fuller discussion of "total" and "partial" identities appears in the fourth chapter. The discussion of total identity in particular is indebted to Harold Garfinkel's "Conditions of Successful Degradation Ceremonies," *American Journal of Sociology*, 61 (1956), 420–24.

19. Herbert Bloch and Gilbert Geis *Man, Crime, and Society* (New York: Random House, 1962), pp. 161–86.

4. *Analytic and empirical approaches to the study of morality*

1. Talcott Parsons, E. A. Shils, et al. *Towards a General Theory of Action* (New York: Harper and Row, 1962).

2. The term "own" here is a bit evasive, and is tapped at one level in common-sense terms. However, to be more precise, it should be said that by "own beliefs" it is meant here those sets of beliefs that the individual subscribes to which are invariant to his movement back and forth from different social groups and systems and which are often contrary to the social system of immediate context. It seems that the

surest empirical way for the sociologists to deal with "own" in this sense is by treating the negative case. There are some problems here that can shift over into the ontological realm with the slightest push, but this distinction can suffice for the present usage.

3. See Note 2, above, for explanation of this usage.

4. Statement by David McReynolds, issued by War Resisters League, 5 Beekman Street, New York, New York, November 6, 1965.

5. Emile Durkheim, *The Division of Labor in Society*, Trans. G. Simpson (New York: The Free Press, 1947).

6. Alexis de Tocqueville, *The Old Regime and the French Revolution* (Garden City, New York: Doubleday-Anchor, 1955).

7. P. McHugh and G. Platt, "On the Failure of Epistemological Truth," paper read at the *61st Annual Meeting of the American Sociological Association*, Miami Beach, Florida, August 31, 1966.

8. R. Bendix, *Work and Authority in Industry* (New York: John Wiley & Sons, 1956), Part I.

9. E. C. Hughes, "Dilemmas and Contradictions of Status," *American Journal of Sociology*, 50 (March, 1945), 353-59.

10. Howard S. Becker, *Outsiders: Studies in the Sociology of Deviance* (New York, The Free Press 1964), p. 33.

11. *Ibid.* pp. 32-34.

12. *cf.* Max Weber, *The Protestant Ethic and the Spirit of Capitalism*, trans. Talcott Parsons (London: Allen and Unwin, 1930); and Svend Ranulf, *Moral Indignation and Middle Class Psychology* (Copenhagen: Levin and Munksgaard, Ejnar Munksgaard, 1938), pp. 1-95.

13. Weber, *op. cit.* and Ranulf, *op. cit.*

14. Becker, *op. cit.*, p. 34.

15. Harold Garfinkel, "Some Sociological Concepts and Methods for Psychiatrists," *Psychiatric Research Reports*, 6 (1956), 181-95.

16. R. H. Blum and M. L. Funkhouser, "Legislators on Social Scientists and a Social Issue: A Report and Commenatry on Some Discussions with Lawmakers about Drug Abuse," *The Journal of Applied Behavioral Science*, 1 (1965), pp. 84-112.

17. *Ibid.*, pp. 99-100.

18. Richard A. Smith, "The Incredible Electrical Conspiracy," in M. E. Wolfgang, L. Savitz, and N. Johnston, eds., *The Sociology of Crime and Delinquency* (New York: John Wiley & Sons, 1962), pp. 357-72.

19. Anselm Strauss, ed., *George Herbert Mead on Social Psychology, Selected Papers* (Rev. ed., Chicago and London, 1964).

5. *Deviance and the reaction of society*

1. C. Wright Mills, *The Sociological Imagination* (New York: Oxford University Press, 1959). Also see Alvin W. Gouldner, "Anti-Minotaur: The Myth of a Value Free Sociology," in I. L. Horowitz, ed., *The New Sociology* (New York: Oxford University Press, 1964), pp. 196–217.

2. The early section borrows directly from an earlier paper on this problem, Cf. Troy Duster, "Patterns of Deviant Reaction: Some Theoretical Issues," *Social Psychiatry*, 3, 1 (Jan., 1968), 1–7.

3. See Alfred Schutz, *Collected Papers I, The Problem of Social Reality* (The Hague, Netherlands: Martinus Nijhoff, 1962); Harold Garfinkel, "Some Conceptions of and Experiments with 'Trust' as a Condition of Stable Concerted Action," in O. J. Harvey, ed., *Motivation and Social Interaction* (New York: The Ronald Press, 1963), pp. 187–238. See also his "Studies of the Routine Grounds of Everyday Activities," *Social Problems*, 11 (Winter, 1964), 225–50. Another exception is Howard S. Becker's *Outsiders: Studies in the Sociology of Deviance* (New York: The Free Press, 1964), pp. 189–224.

4. Sociology asks the same question in reverse requesting an explanation of deviance in the terms of psychological determinism: Why are the lower classes and ethnic groups so disproportionately represented in deviance and crime? Is it that 'those kinds of psychological problems' don't exist among other groups—or that something quite social is operating as a powerful force to screen them?

5. R. A. Cloward and L. E. Ohlin, *Delinquency and Opportunity: A Theory of Delinquent Gangs* (New York: The Free Press, 1960).

6. R. K. Merton, *Social Theory and Social Structure* (Rev. ed., New York: The Free Press, 1957), pp. 121–94.

7. A. K. Cohen, *Delinquent Boys, the Culture of the Gang* (New York: The Free Press, 1955).

8. Cloward and Ohlin, *op. cit.*

9. E. H. Sutherland and D. R. Cressey, *Principles of Criminology* (6th Ed.; Chicago: J. B. Lippincott, 1960).

10. E. Lemert, *Social Pathology* (New York: McGraw-Hill, 1951).

11. Garfinkel, *op. cit.*, 1963 and 1964.

12. Becker, *op. cit.*

13. J. I. Kitsuse, "Societal Reaction to Deviance: Problems of Theory and Method," *Social Problems*, 9 (Winter, 1962), 247–56.

14. Emile Durkeim, *Suicide* (New York: The Free Press, 1951).
15. No reference is here intended to Lindesmith's quite empirically observable proposition about prior knowledge and addiction, discussed in Chapter 3.
16. The data from the California Rehabilitation Centre reveal a case of an apprehended addict who claimed only to be in attendance at his first marijuana party. See Chapters 6 and 7.
17. This is not simply to say that if society ignores a certain kind of deviance, there will be no more of that deviance. That is simply tautological truth, which says nothing of consequence about the nature and process of the relationship between the normals and the deviants. I am concerned here with the positive activities in which a society engages that exacerbate deviance and block a return to normality. Cf. Kai T. Erikson, "Notes on the Sociology of Deviance," in Howard S. Becker, ed., *The Other Side: Perspectives on Deviance* (New York: The Free Press, 1964), pp. 9–20.
18. See the discussion of this subject in Chapters 1 and 2.
19. Synanon is discussed in Chapters 7 and 8.
20. H. Garfinkel, "Conditions of Successful Degradation Ceremonies," *Americal Journal of Sociology*, 61 (1956), 420–24.
21. Students enrolled in the first semester, "Introduction to Sociology," University of California, Riverside, Fall, 1964.
22. See Chapter 9.
23. This discussion also elaborated in Chapter 9.
24. Kitsuse, *op. cit.*
25. *Ibid.*
26. *Ibid.*

6. *The California Rehabilitation Center*

1. R. Volkman and D. R. Cressey, "Differential Association and the Rehabilitation of Drug Addicts," *American Journal of Sociology*, 69 (September, 1963), 129–42.
2. G. Sykes, *The Society of Captives: A Study of a Maximum Security Prison* (Princeton: Princeton University Press, 1958). Also see D. Clemmer, *The Prison Community* (New York: Rinehart, 1958).

3. *Ibid.*
4. Erving Goffman, *Asylums: Essays on the Social Situation of Mental Patients and Other Inmates* (New York: Doubleday, 1961).
5. *Ibid.*, pp. 3–124.
6. *Ibid.*, p. 4.
7. Harold Garfinkel, "Conditions of Successful Degradation Ceremonies," *American Journal of Sociology*, 61 (1956), 420–24.
8. August B. Hollingshead and Frederick C. Redlich, *Social Class and Mental Illness* (New York: John Wiley & Sons, 1958), pp. 66–168.
9. *Ibid.*
10. *Ibid.*, pp. 194–250.
11. For the details on sample selection and method, see Chapter 7.
12. See Chapter 7.
13. Richard Harris, *The Real Voice* (New York: The Macmillan Company, 1964), pp. 99–112.

7. *The moral implications of psychic maladjustment in the deviant*

1. O. Temkin, *The Falling Sickness* (Baltimore: The Johns Hopkins Press, 1945).
2. This is not to say that such an assessment of the addict's psychic disorder is necessarily accurate. That can be determined only empirically by looking at specific individual addicts, and not by lumping a diverse category together and asserting psychic imbalance by the definition of narcotic use.
3. J. K. Galbraith, *The Affluent Society* (Harmondsworth, Middlesex, England: Penguin Books, Ltd., 1962). The second chapter of Galbraith's book deals with the concept of the "conventional wisdom." My usage of the term here can be read both for its common-sense terms and in the more precise way Galbraith uses it.
4. T. W. Adorno, *et al.*, *The Authoritarian Personality* (New York: Harper and Row, 1950).
5. D. Ausubel, *Drug Addiction, Physiological Psychological, and Sociological Aspects* (New York: Random House, 1958, pp. 41–42).

6. *Ibid.*, p. 42.
7. Natalie Rogoff, "Recent Trends in Urban Occupational Mobility," in R. Bendix and S. M. Lipset, eds., *Class, Status, and Power* (New York: The Free Press, 1953), pp. 442–54.
8. See Chapter 1.
9. Ausubel, *op. cit.*, p. 34.
10. A. R. Lindesmith, *The Addict and the Law* (Bloomington: Indiana University Press, 1965), pp. 111–22. Lindesmith skillfully takes official figures from official sources and shows how the conflict between them indicates dramatic underestimation of the number of unapprehended addicts.
11. K. H. Houck, "A Brief Outline of the CRC. Program," pamphlet issued by the Chief Psychiatrist of the California Rehabilitation Center, July 17, 1963, Corona, California.
12. "A Legislator looks at the California Rehabilitation Center," *Correctional Review*, Department of Corrections, State of California, Sacramento, California, 1965.
13. *Ibid.*
14. Eight individuals selected into the sample for the purpose of being respondents for the interview received their parole notices and departed before they could be contacted. In these cases, others were chosen by the same method.
15. Aaron V. Cicourel, *Method and Measurement in Sociology* (New York: The Free Press, 1964).
16. I. Chein, et al., *The Road to H* (New York: Basic Books, 1964).
17. Findings from the smaller interview sample.
18. W. Miller, "Lower Class Culture as a Generating Milieu of Gang Delinquency," *The Journal of Social Issues*, 14 (1958), pp. 5–19.
19. See Chapter 3.
20. The discussion in Chapter 2 points to the difficulty in this position.
21. M. V. Miller and S. Gilmore, eds., *Revolution at Berkeley* (New York: Dell Publishing Co., 1965), pp. xxiv–xxix.
22. *Ibid.*, sections II, III, and IV.
23. See Chapter I.
24. Andrew Billingsley and Amy T. Billingsley, "Illegitimacy and Patterns of Negro Family Life," in Robert W. Roberts, ed., *The Unwed Mother* (New York: Harper and Row, 1966), pp. 133–57. Also see E. Franklin Frazier, *The Negro Family in the United States* (Chicago: University of Chicago Press, 1939).

8. *Perspectives on the addicts' world view*

1. See Chapter 3.
2. It is only "occasionally" that the addict regards himself as superior to the alcoholic. The former is continually reminded of the legal and illegal aspects of their respective behavior.
3. The CRC addicts strongly believed that they were not so dramatically affected by the drug that they could not perform these tasks quite well.
4. The working ideology of the rehabilitation center is referred to here, namely, that the way out is through revealed self-knowledge that the fault lies within the individual.
5. In Chapter 1, see pp. 21–22.
6. See Chapter 2.
7. Less than 20 per cent of the inmates of CRC retained a private attorney during the legal proceedings that led to their commitment.
8. David Sudnow, "Normal Crimes: Sociological Features of the Penal Code in a Public Defender Office," *Social Problems*, 12: 3 (1965), 255–76.
9. Raymond Mack's lectures in Race Relations, Northwestern University, 1955.
10. Walter B. Miller, "Lower Class Culture as a Generating Milieu of Gang Delinquency," *Journal of Social Issues*, 14: 3 (1958), 5–19.
11. David Matza, *Delinquency and Drift* (New York: John Wiley & Sons, 1964).
12. Thomas Szasz, *The Myth of Mental Illness* (New York: Harper & Row, 1961).
13. Unpublished manuscript by Aaron V. Cicourel on Argentina family.
14. *Ibid.*
15. Isador Chein, *et al.*, *The Road to H* (New York: Basic Books, 1964).
16. Marie Nyswander, *The Drug Addict as a Patient* (New York: Grune & Stratton, 1956).
17. See Chapters 3 and 7.
18. Howard S. Becker, *Outsiders: Studies in the Sociology of Deviance* (New York: The Free Press, 1964).
19. Harold Finestone, "Cats, Kicks, and Color," in Howard S. Becker, ed., *The Other Side: Perspectives on Deviance* (New York: The Free Press, 1964), pp. 281–97.
20. Miller, *op. cit.*

21. Finestone., *op. cit.*, and Miller, *op. cit.*

22. Marsh B. Ray, "The Cycle of Abstinence and Relapse Among Heroin Addicts," *Social Problems*, 9 (Fall, 1961), pp. 132–40.

23. One can anticipate the objection that the analog is inappropriate because the slaves were slaves against their will, while addicts voluntarily become addicted. However, this analogy concerns the *condition* of the slave and the addict, and the escape from that condition, not the circumstances leading to the condition. (In any case, the reasoning that the addict is mentally different because he began using narcotics is tautological.)

9. Mental illness and criminal intent

1. The M'Naghten Rule of 1843 established the basis for the plea of insanity as a legitimate defense for the accused. Cf. Daniel M'Naghten's Case, in N. Johnston, L. Savitz, and M. Wolfgang Eds., *The Sociology of Punishment and Correction* (New York: John Wiley & Sons, 1962), pp. 42–46.

2. J. Hall, *General Principles of Criminal Law* (2nd Ed.; Indianapolis: Bobbs-Merrill, 1960).

3. H. Garfinkel, "Conditions of Successful Degradation Ceremonies," *Amer. J. of Sociol.* 61 (1956), 420–24.

4. C. E. Terry, and M. Pellens, *The Opium Problem* (New York: Bureau of Social Hygiene, 1928).

5. A. K. Cohen, *Delinquent Boys, the Culture of the Gang* (New York: The Free Press, 1955). Also, Cf. R. Cloward, and L. Ohlin, *Delinquency and Opportunity: A Theory of Delinquent Gangs* (New York: The Free Press, 1960).

6. G. Tyler, Ed., *Organized Crime in America* (Ann Arbor: Univ. of Michigan Press, 1962), pp. 227–336.

7. *Ibid.*, pp. 138–39.

8. *Ibid.*

9. E. H. Sutherland, Ed., *The Professional Thief* (Chicago: Univ. of Chicago Press, 1937).

10. D. Sudnow, "Normal Crimes: Sociological Features of the Penal Code in a Public Defender Office," *Social Problems*, 12:3 1965, 255–76.

11. *Ibid.*

12. R. K. Merton, *Social Theory and Social Structure* (Rev. Ed.; New York: The Free Press, 1957), pp. 131–60.

13. A. Schutz, *Collected Papers I, the Problem of Social Reality* (The Hague, Netherlands: Martinus Nijhoff, 1962).

10. Law and morality: some summary considerations

1. Svend Ranulf, *Moral Indignation and Middle Class Psychology* (Copenhagen: Levin and Munksgaard, Ejnar Munksgaard, 1938), pp. 1–95; and Joseph Gusfield, *Symbolic Crusade* (Urbana: University of Illinois Press, 1963).

2. Howard S. Becker, *Outsiders: Studies in the Sociology of Deviance* (New York: The Free Press, 1964), pp. 147–63.

3. American Bar Association and American Medical Association Joint Committee on Narcotic Drugs, *Drug Addiction: Crime or Disease?* (Bloomington, Indiana: Indiana University Press, 1961).

4. Alfred R. Lindesmith, *The Addict and the Law*, Bloomington: Indiana University Press, 1965.

5. Gusfield, *op. cit.*, p. 129.

Index

Ausubel, D., 155-6, 259, 260
authoritarian personality, 154-5

barbital, 38
barbiturate addiction,
  dangers of, 38-41
barbiturates,
  as addicting, 38-41
  effects of, 31, 38-41
  in combination with
    alcohol, 38
  in combination with
    opiates, 40
Barnard, C. I., 223
Becker, H. S., 43, 44, 89, 91, 201,
  253, 254, 256, 257, 258,
  261, 263
Bendix, R., 256, 260
benzedrine, 37
Billingsley, A., 260
black market,
  and its origins with
    heroin, 16-23
Blacks,
  and heroin use, 184-7
  and marijuana use, 184-7
  changing rates of addiction
    of, 21
Blair, T., 252
Blau, P., 223
Bloch, H., 255
Blum, R. H., 96, 256
Boggs Amendment, 20
Boylan Act of 1904, 13
Brando, J., 93
Brunswik, E., 50, 254
Buckley, William F., Jr., 84

California Rehabilitation
  Center, 69, 133-52
  characteristics of total
    population, 165-78
  enthusiasm of staff, 144
  residents,
    age at admission, 165-6
    as opiate salesmen, 173
    class membership, 167-70
    commitments prior to
      CRC, 175
    ethnic group
      membership, 167
    home residence, 168-9
    I.Q.'s of, 171-2
    jail history, 170
    juvenile history, 171
    marijuana use, 173-4
    marital status, 172
    offenses by, 176-8
    prior drug use, 176
    use of "hard" drugs, 174-5
Calvinist-Lutheran doctrine,
  on evil, sin, and total
    identity, 90-1
Cannabis, 43
Capone, A., 223
case descriptions,
  of contact with addicts, 117-29
Catholic Church,
  and views of morality, 90-1
character transformation,
  and relapse, 211
Chein, I., 46, 254, 201, 260, 261
chimpanzees,
  addiction of, 61-2
chloromycetin, 51

nalline tests,
for addicts, 109, 209
Narcotic Drug Control Act,
of 1956, provisions of, 20
narcotics,
varied use of term, 30-1
narcotics clinics,
opposed by Federal Narcotics
Bureau, 17-19
origins and decline, 17-20
narcotics and drugs,
attempts at international
control of, 13, 14
National Socialists, German, 81
Never on Sunday, 67
"normalizing,"
described, 50
Nyswander, M., 201, 251, 252,
253, 261

Ohlin, L. E., 105, 257
On the Waterfront, 93
opiates,
description of, 31
opium,
international conference
on, 13, 14
opium dens, 8, 23
opium smoking, 8, 13
Organization Man, 223
organized crime, 222-6

parole,
eligibility, 137
night visits, 209-10
parole officer,
and middle class morals, 206-9

Parsons, T., 80, 255, 256
partial identity,
defined and described, 88-95
partial identity, 150-1
Pearson, C., 252
Pellens, Mildred, 8, 9, 11, 251,
252, 255, 262
pentobarbital, 31, 40
personality inadequacy, 155-7
and addiction, 139-45, 149,
213, 220-2
and social class, 156-7
Pescor, M., 253
Pettey, G., 251
pharmaceutical dispensaries,
studies of, 7
phase movement,
and theories of criminality,
221, 227-9
phenobarbital, 31, 38
Philadelphia General Hospital,
study of, 12
physical dependence,
on opiates, 56-63
Platt, Gerald, 87, 256
political conversion,
and moral acceptability, 93-4
political deviance,
and immorality, 93-5
possession of drugs,
and felony conviction, 97
Price, G. E., 12, 252
price-fixing, 98
prison riots,
explanations of, 183-4
Prohibition,
and law-morality arguments,
4, 101-2